The Best of

The Whiteboard Blog

By

Danny Nicholson

www.whiteboardblog.co.uk

ISBN : 978-1-4467-9158-5

Cover photo credit: Dan Zen
http://www.flickr.com/photos/danzen/105653250/

Contents

About the Whiteboard Blog

The Whiteboard Blog was set up in December 2007 as a way of sharing ideas to support teachers using their interactive whiteboards in the classroom. As well as interactive whiteboards it also covers other educational technologies that would be of interest to teachers such as digital storytelling and other "web 2.0" tools.

This book contains the best articles from over three years of the blog. For the most recent articles, and to access all the links in these pages, visit www.whiteboardblog.co.uk

About the author

Danny Nicholson is an independent trainer and consultant. He is a former science teacher and now delivers ICT and science training to teachers all over the UK and overseas. He is an accredited interactive whiteboard trainer on both Smart and Promethean whiteboards and has delivered many successful courses on their use in the classroom. He has also delivered IWB training in corporate environments as well as the military. In addition he is also a science PGCE lecturer working with student teachers at both primary and secondary level.

Danny has written teaching and training materials for many different publishers, including Heinemann, Serif and Learn Premium.

Authors Note

I have tried where possible to copy across all the links from the original blog posts. As you can imagine, the nature of the internet is that links change and vanish, so I have tried to fix these where possible. In some cases URL shorteners have been used to make it easier to copy them into a web browser from a book format. It's recommended that you visit the original blog page where possible – then you can just click on the links.

There are also other articles that have not been reproduced here for a number of reasons – usually because they contain video, presentations or other media. Again, please do visit the blog for the full media-rich experience.

Thanks to my wife, for putting up with my geekery, and to all the great people I've worked with over the years that have helped generate a lot of these ideas. Plus to my twitter network who have provided most of the others!

Thanks for reading!

Danny Nicholson
danny@think-bank.com

Southend on Sea, January 2010
www.whiteboardblog.co.uk

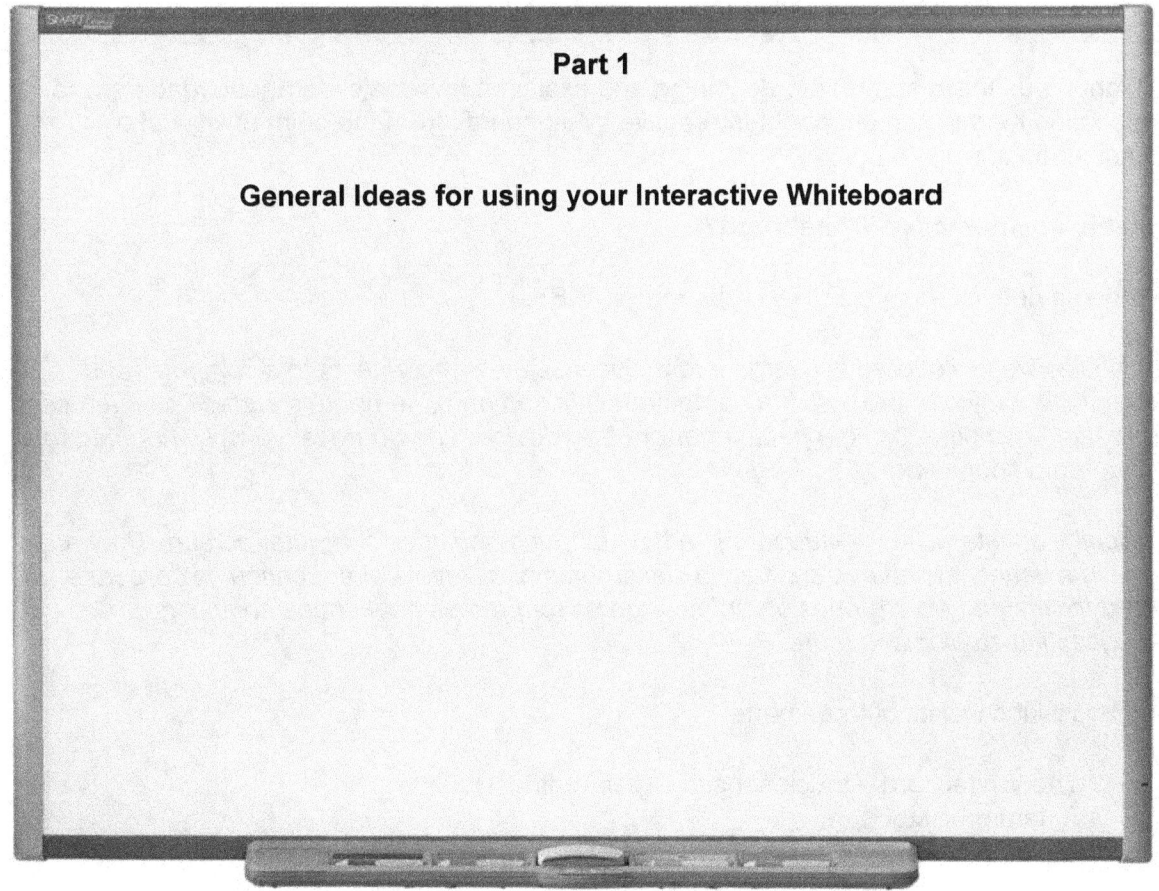

Part 1

General Ideas for using your Interactive Whiteboard

Whiteboards – A Beginners Guide #1

Originally posted March 27 2008

http://www.whiteboardblog.co.uk/2008/03/whiteboards-a-beginners-guide-1/

It might be useful to start at the beginning and explain a few basics for those readers who are coming here to find out about Interactive Whiteboards from the point of view of a complete beginner.

What is an interactive Whiteboard?

Wikipedia defines an Interactive Whiteboard (IWB) as

An interactive whiteboard is a large interactive display that connects to a computer and projector. A projector projects the computer's desktop onto the board's surface, where users control the computer using a pen, finger or other device. The board is typically mounted to a wall or on a floor stand.

Basically, an interactive whiteboard is a type of touch-sensitive computer screen. They are used in a variety of settings such as in classrooms of all levels of education, in corporate board rooms and work groups, in training rooms for professional sports coaching, broadcasting studios and more.

The basic kit consists of three parts

- The Whiteboard – touch sensitive (pen or finger)
- A data projector
- A laptop or PC

The computer projects an image of the computer screen onto the Whiteboard. The user can then interact with the whiteboard screen and move the mouse pointer from the board, rather than having to use a mouse.

Some newer versions involve adding touch capabilities onto a very large LCD monitor. As the price comes down I can see this eventually replacing the need for the data-projector.

Most whiteboards do not have built-in speakers. But often they are bought as part of a kit that includes a speaker and amplifier to enhance the multimedia experience. A decent set of speakers is highly recommended when installing a whiteboard system in your classroom.

There are three main types of board:

1. Membrane / Resistive Boards

This uses several thin layers of material that are stretched across the front of the board. When the surface layer is touched it makes contact with other layers and causes the board to respond. The main type of board that uses this technology is the Smart Board.

Advantages: anything can be used to write on the board, different coloured pens and an eraser can be picked up without having to click on floating tool bars, generally cheaper than solid-state boards of a comparable size. Many children like the fact that they can move things on the board just using their finger. Very nice with SEN pupils.

Disadvantages: board is activated if touched by mistake (you can't lean on it), the surface could be more easily damaged than solid-state boards. If two children are working at the board they need to take turns to touch it as touching it at the same time will confuse the system.

2. Electromagnetic Boards

These boards have a durable hard surface that covers the mesh of electrical wires buried in the board. A special pen containing a magnet is used to interact with these sensors and activate the board. Some of these pens work on their own, others need batteries or to be recharged. Some boards come with a small writing tablet that can be passed round the class, and is used to enter information onto the main board. The main example of this type of board is the Promethean ActivBoard. Cambridge / Hitachi boards also work in this way.

Advantages: Durable surface, higher resolution, faster tracking speeds. Pupils near the board cannot interact accidentally unless they have the pen. Newer boards allow two pens to work at the same time.

Disadvantages: Will only operate with supplied pen (replacement pens can be expensive), changing pen colour or to erase mode requires clicking on floating tool bars. Pens can be prone to cracking or breaking. Buttons can stick and give odd effects.

3. Infrared / Ultrasound

These devices clip on to a conventional non-interactive whiteboard and give it some of the functionality of a 'true' interactive board. They consist of a receiver unit attached to the edge or the corner of the board or flipchart and a set of large pens that transmit a signal to the receiver unit when pressure is applied to the tip. Examples of this kind of system include Mimio and EBeam.

Advantages: Very cheap (about a fifth of the cost of dedicated boards), very portable, comes with several different coloured pens and eraser.

Disadvantages: Pens are big and bulky and use batteries or need charging. The system is more fiddly to set-up and does not respond as quickly or accurately as other technologies. Often the software supplied is quite lacking in features when compared to that supplied with "proper" interactive whiteboards.

Software

The whiteboard is simply an input device that gives the user control of the computer where their finger/pen becomes the mouse. Any computer software can be used on an interactive whiteboard in exactly the same way if you were sitting at the computer.

Most boards will come bundled with their own software which allows the board to be used like a regular whiteboard – but the notes you write can be saved, stored, manipulated, and printed. They allow multiple pages, banks of clipart, different page backgrounds such as graph paper and desktop capture.

Not all software works the same way and allows the user a simple interactive experience. If you are buying a board – please test the software out first. Usually you are tied to the software provided. The cheapest boards often come with very user-unfriendly software. This can be a false economy if your teachers then do not use the board because they cannot do the things they want to do easily.

Also be aware of the TDS ActivBoard. TDS is the parent company to Promethean and they sell a board which is almost identical to a Promethean ActivBoard – and does come a lot cheaper. Unfortunately, what is not usually explained is that it does not come with ActivStudio/ActivPrimary software and that this software will not run on the boards. Again you are saving money but getting the useful software that will make using the board a much better experience. I have been in so many schools that have bought these boards thinking they are Promethean boards.

Smart and Promethean do generally have the best software, and are the two boards I would recommend. It then becomes an issue of whether you want to use your pen or your finger and this can be a personal preference.

Whiteboards – A Beginners Guide #2

Originally posted March 27 2008

http://www.whiteboardblog.co.uk/2008/03/whiteboards-a-beginners-guide-2/

There are many ways an IWB can benefits your teaching. Some of them are summarised here:

Motivation: Pupils say that they find it motivating because it is big, bright, and colourful and they can get more involved with the lesson. Teachers find it motivating because it opens up a wealth of resources from which they can select their teaching materials.

Use of images and colour: The IWB/Projector provides a much better quality of image over a traditional overhead projector acetate. This can make diagrams easier to understand. Photographs have more impact. Colour can be used on concept charts/brainstorms to link related ideas.

Use of multimedia: Watching a video has been possible in lessons using a video/dvd player and television but now including short bursts of multimedia is much easier with an interactive whiteboard. These can provide excellent lesson starters or form part of a plenary.

Items can be moved on screen: Text and pictures can be 'dragged and dropped' on screen. This can help with a variety of tasks (see below). Using traditional methods, this could only have been achieved through using cut-out pictures or words and blu-tac which was time-consuming for the teacher and may not have been as visually clear for the pupils.

Saving and retrieving materials: All teachers have banks of resources which they use from year to year. However, having them stored as computer files on a laptop or USB stick means that a teacher has all their resources with them all the time. Recapping at the beginning of lessons is proving to be very useful (reload last week's notes) and saving completed lessons provides a record of work done. The sheer volume of material that can be accessed from a networked computer leaves a well-prepared teacher with a huge bank of resources to draw on. This would be almost impossible in a classroom with no computer.

Hard Copy: It is possible to print a copy of the notes that have been written onto the screen. This means that the teacher can have evidence of work carried out or a group could each be given the results of some collaborative work such as a brain storm task. The screens can be printed for revision purposes too.

Why not just use a Data Projector?

One question often raised is "Why have an interactive whiteboard?" Many teachers have already experienced the benefits of linking a computer to a projector but why not just work at the computer – what difference does it make working at the board?"

Research has provided two answers here:

1) being able to write on the board, either on a blank screen OR over the top of other software is very useful- you couldn't write with a mouse – you would have to type and this isn't as spontaneous.

2) working at the board: many pupils enjoy being able to come and work at the board. They perceive the position at the front of the class as being important and enjoy having the opportunity to make their point before their peers.

There is something almost theatrical about working at the board. The fact that a teacher can pick something up and move it in front of an audience and the fact that other events can be triggered by pressing on certain buttons. This could be done on a computer at the side of the board, but the visual impact is not as great and this creates a certain effect on the observer.

Anecdotally, teachers who have taught firstly with a data projector and then with the addition of a whiteboard all say that they would feel very awkward having to return to their computer each time they want to do something on screen. One remarked that he didn't feel part of the class when working on his computer. The students are looking at the screen while the teacher is talking somewhere else in the class. With an IWB the focal point is both the teacher and the screen.

(source – The Review Project)

Whiteboards – A Beginners Guide #2

Originally posted March 27 2008

http://www.whiteboardblog.co.uk/2008/03/whiteboards-a-beginners-guide-3/

There are many different ways of interacting with the IWB to support teaching and provide learning opportunities.

Introduction: – Lesson starters, giving the lesson aims and objectives, "Awe and Wonder" introductions

Main body: Explaining practical work/tasks or illustrating main concepts. Using software/ simulations or other software.

Plenary: collecting in results, analysing data as a group, summarising the lesson aims (can easily call them back up from the screen used at the start of the lesson)

The following techniques can all play a role in each of these sections of the lesson.

1. Drag and Drop: This allows the user to move items – either text or pictures around the screen. This is ideal for matching activities, ordering items or labelling diagrams.

There are a range of uses for this simple technique:

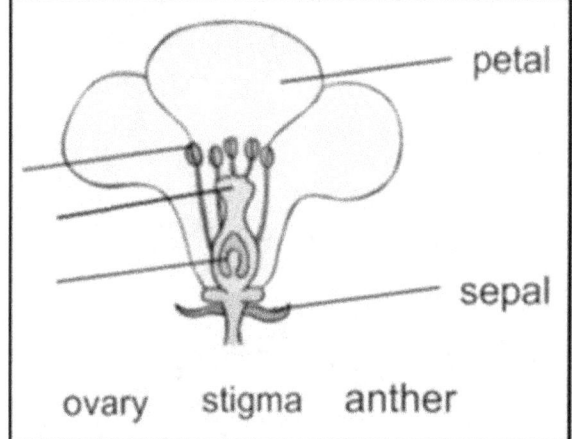

- **Sequencing** – putting events into the correct order, e.g. steps in an experiment, phases of the moon, stages of digestion, timelines,
- **Ranking** – putting things in order of importance or magnitude e.g. electromagnetic spectrum in order of wavelength
- **Matching** – matching words to their definitions, putting matching halves of sentences together, characters and moods, sums and answers
- **Sorting** – e.g. renewable and non-renewable energy sources, healthy and unhealthy foods
- **Labelling** – e.g. Putting labels onto diagrams
- **Word Walls** – drag words to fill in the gaps in cloze procedures.

2. **Rub out to Reveal**: this involves placing a layer of colour over the top of a word or picture in order to hide it. Use the eraser to reveal the hidden item. If you want to, you can cover the item in the same colour as the background – this makes the item invisible but you do need to remember what you have hidden underneath. Use this for hiding labels on diagrams, or words in sentences.

3. **Annotating over Windows**: Being able to write over the top of any other software (for example a CD ROM, an internet page or a Microsoft Office document) is very useful. Adding comments, highlighting items, writing additional notes, drawing arrows – all things that can be done by the teacher or by the pupils to discuss and analyse what's on the board. For example adding annotations over a graph in Excel show how to read data from the graph or

pausing a video of different levers and adding arrows to show the direction of different forces.

4. Screenshots: Bringing in resources from other software and the internet can be done easily by using a screenshot. This can be a whole screen, but it is often more useful to take an area screen shot. Google images can be a very useful source of pictures for all subjects. Please note that there are copyright implications and the pictures should only be used in teaching and not sold or widely distributed without the consent of the website owner.

5. Spotlight and reveal: Some whiteboard software allows you to place a spotlight over the area of the board where you want to focus the pupils' attention. You can also use a reveal technique to show a bit of the board at a time.

6. Using simulation software: Using a combination of data projector and interactive whiteboard it is possible to interact with simulation software such as Crocodile Physics or Focus Science Investigations. The whole class can observe the experiment and suggest changes etc.

Nearly all the features discussed above are available whichever interactive board software you are using. What you need to do is take time to think about the interactivity of each page you create or each task you set.

Lesson Starter Ideas for Your Whiteboard

Originally posted July 2nd 2010

http://www.whiteboardblog.co.uk/2010/07/lesson-starter-ideas-for-your-whiteboard/

Here are a few ideas taken from some of the talks I have given this academic year for ideas on using your Interactive Whiteboard during lesson starters. They could also be used as plenary tasks. Some of the ideas you may have seen before in various places (such as the Canada, Germany talks), but I'm bundling them up into one file for you to download.

Here are some of the activities that are in the file:

Organ Reveal: A student comes to the board and pulls out an organ. They then have one minute to talk about the organ and its role in the body without repetition or pauses…. I've also included the fishing rod and balloon activities from previous presentations.

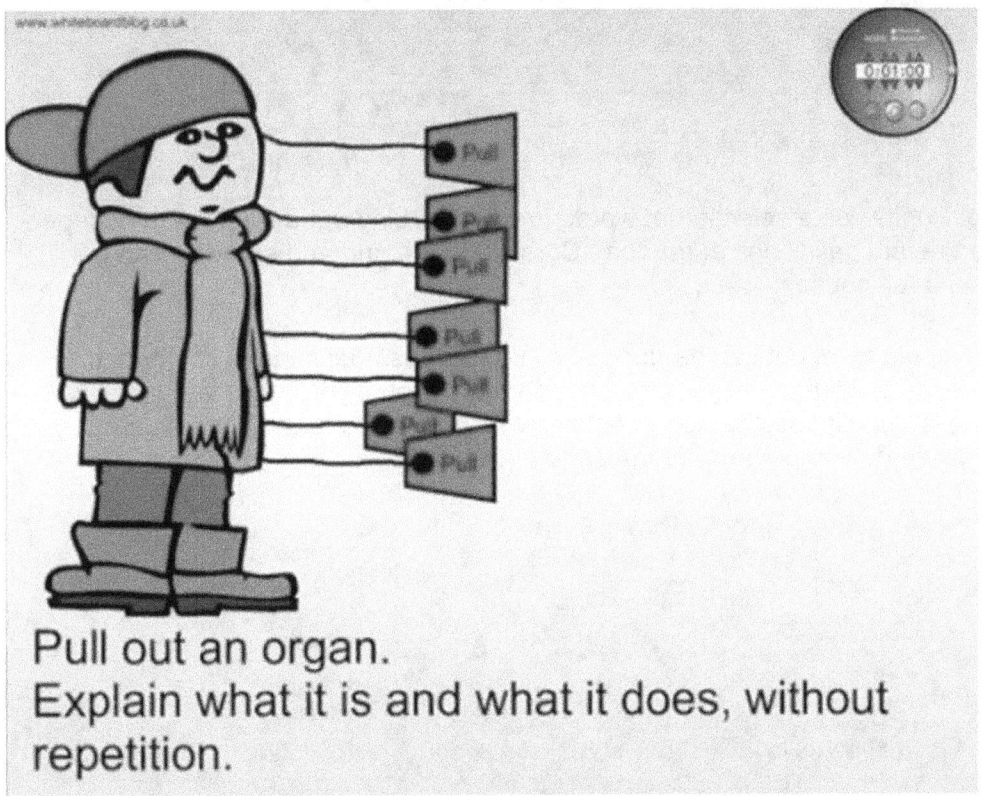

Pull out an organ.
Explain what it is and what it does, without repetition.

Put it in the box: This activity makes use of the layer feature. One group of objects will go into the box, the other group will not go into the box. In this example drag the insects into the box…. Easily adaptable for any two groups of objects.

To customise. Add all the items to the page. Unlock the front of the box and "send to front". Relock. Then select all the objects that do not go into the box and "send to front". They will stay outside, while the other objects will now go inside the box again.

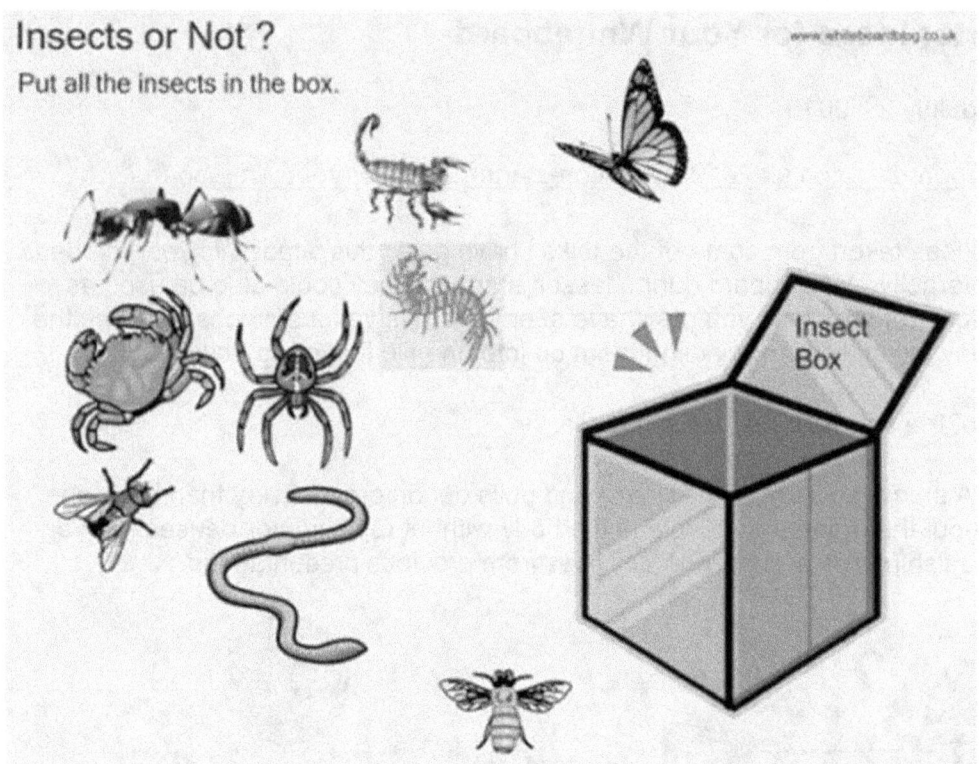

Keyword Bingo: Pupils use a selection of words to create a bingo grid on a piece of paper. Teacher can then reveal definitions at random. Cross it off the grid and see who can get three in a row and a full house.

Plenary Circle: Simple idea, but can be used at all key stages. Pull in pairs of words to make "I know that…. " sentences. If you have a more able group, you could leave one word in for the next pupil to use in their sentence – this means you have to think more carefully about the range of words you put around the edge of the circle.

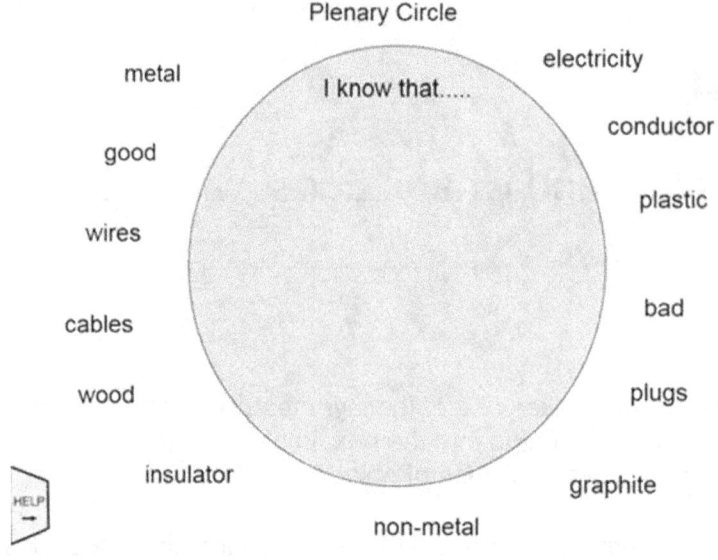

www.whiteboardblog.co.uk

Word Builder: How many words can you make that relate to science? Give everyone time to make as many words as they can. Students can come to the board to show examples of the words they have made.

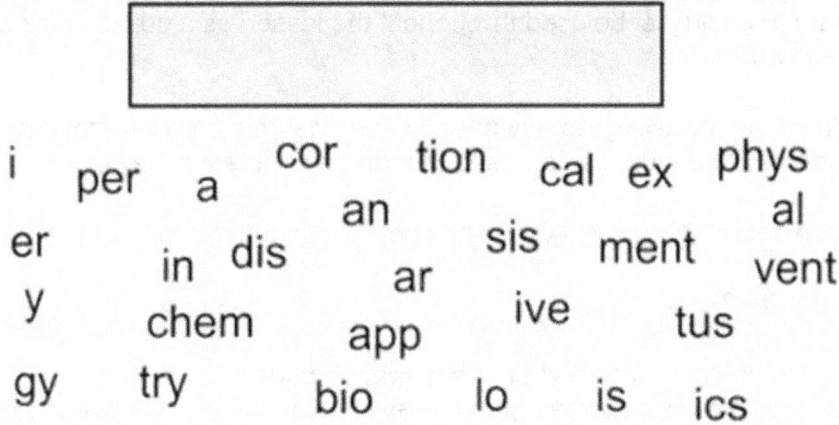

How many words can you make that relate to science?

i per a cor tion cal ex phys
an al
er in dis sis ment vent
ar
y chem app ive tus
gy try bio lo is ics

Use the links below to download a version of the file for your whiteboard:

Promethean ActivInspireVersion : http://bit.ly/fRJz5j

Smart Notebook 10 Version : http://bit.ly/gjIzKF

Easiteach : http://bit.ly/hL9NDK

Common IWB Format : http://bit.ly/ggeybD

If you use the files, I'd love to hear how they went. If you do adapt them for your own subject, please let me know what you did – I'd be interested in having a copy. It's always good to get ideas from other subjects. All my resources are covered by a Creative Commons Share-Alike license. I am more than happy for you to pass on, rework and modify any of the files that I produce. BUT.... share alike. You got it for free, please pass it on for free ☺

And a subtle plug – if you ever want training sessions on how to make these kind of resources – please get in touch. I'm happy to travel around the UK and can go further afield if dates allow. Email me for more information. info@think-bank.com

Rub and Reveal

Originally posted January 16 2008

http://www.whiteboardblog.co.uk/2008/01/rub-and-reveal/

Here's a quick idea for using an interactive whiteboard. It could be a lesson starter, or form part of a plenary or could just be used throughout the lesson as a quick check on what the students have learnt so far.

This is something that always goes down well when I demonstrate it in training sessions as it is so quick and easy to do, but can be used in a range of different ways.

Watch the video here: http://www.think-bank.com/iwb/video/rubandreveal.html

How do you do this?

1. Use the text tool to type some text on the notebook page
2. Use the pen tool to draw over the top of the text to hide it (you may want to make the pen thick and match the colour to the background)
3. When you are ready to reveal the writing, click on the Eraser tool and rub out the pen to reveal the text hiding behind it.

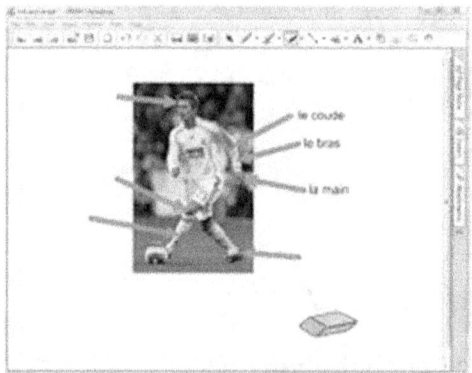

Another way of hiding the text could be using shapes to hide the text which can then be moved away or deleted when you want to reveal the word.

How might you use this?

This could be used as the example in the video for hiding labels on a diagram, getting the students to label it, and then revealing the correct answer.

It could also be used to hide the answers to questions given to the students on the screen.

A photograph could be completely covered in black pen, and then the eraser used to gradually reveal parts of the photograph, asking the students at different stages what they can see and what they can infer from what they see.

This is also a quick way of producing missing words activities – type or copy/paste in a block of text and instead of having to go through and delete the missing words and add spaces, just cover each word you want to take out with white pen. It's also easier to reveal the correct answer too.

If you want the Smart Notebook file with the above example of labelling David Beckham in French, then you can download it here :
http://www.whiteboardblog.co.uk/files/rubandreveal.notebook

(Footnote: apologies to any readers from across the sea if I keep calling it the rubber tool on the video. I try to call it the eraser, but over here we call it the rubber. I do know that word has different connotations over in North America, but just put it down to English eccentricity and go with it!)

Creative Use of Colour in IWB Files

Originally posted January 24 2011

http://www.whiteboardblog.co.uk/2011/01/creative-use-of-colour-in-iwb-files/

Here are a couple of ideas that are very simple to produce, but make use of colours to create interesting lesson activities for any IWB. None of these use anything too complicated apart from shapes, text and the ability to change the background colour 😃

Hidden Words

In this example we're looking at what happens when you add a "y" to the end of each word. Each word is written in yellow and red, with the background set to red at the end to hide all the red words. A shape (in this example a magnifying glass, but it could just be a light coloured rectangle) is put on the back layer ("send to back") so that as you move it about it reveals the letters.

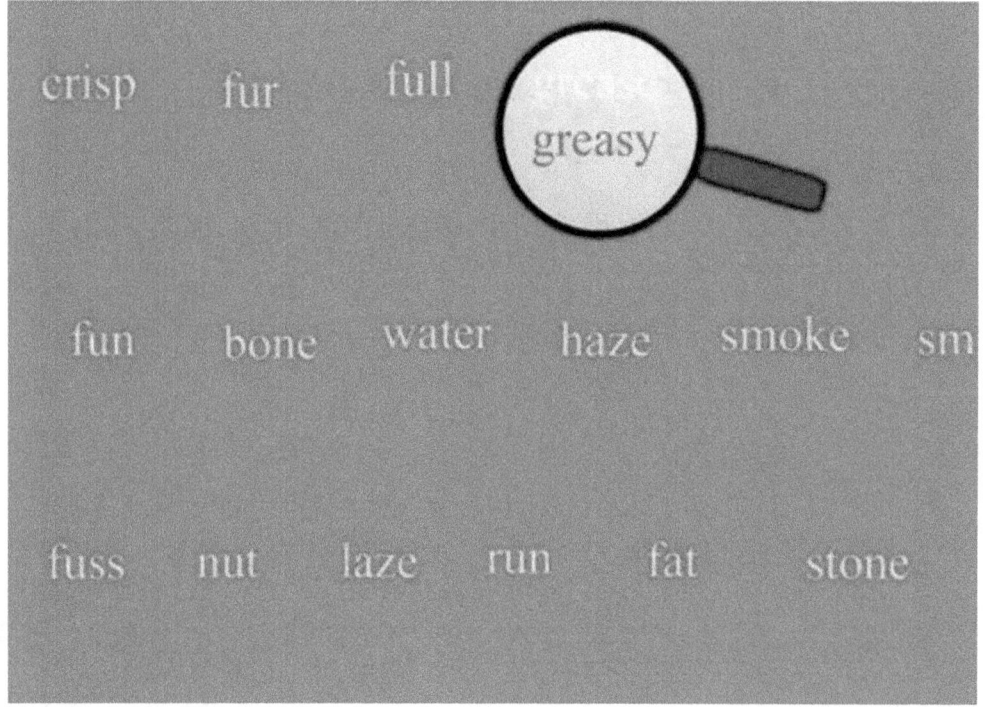

Shapes

Several shapes have been drawn, and their lines and fills set to be the same colour as the background (again make this with a white background first to make things easier). A white shape has been "sent to back" which can be used to investigate.

Ask the pupils what they think the shape is from just the small piece of information they can see – look at the angle – what do they think it could be.. is it a square? etc. etc.

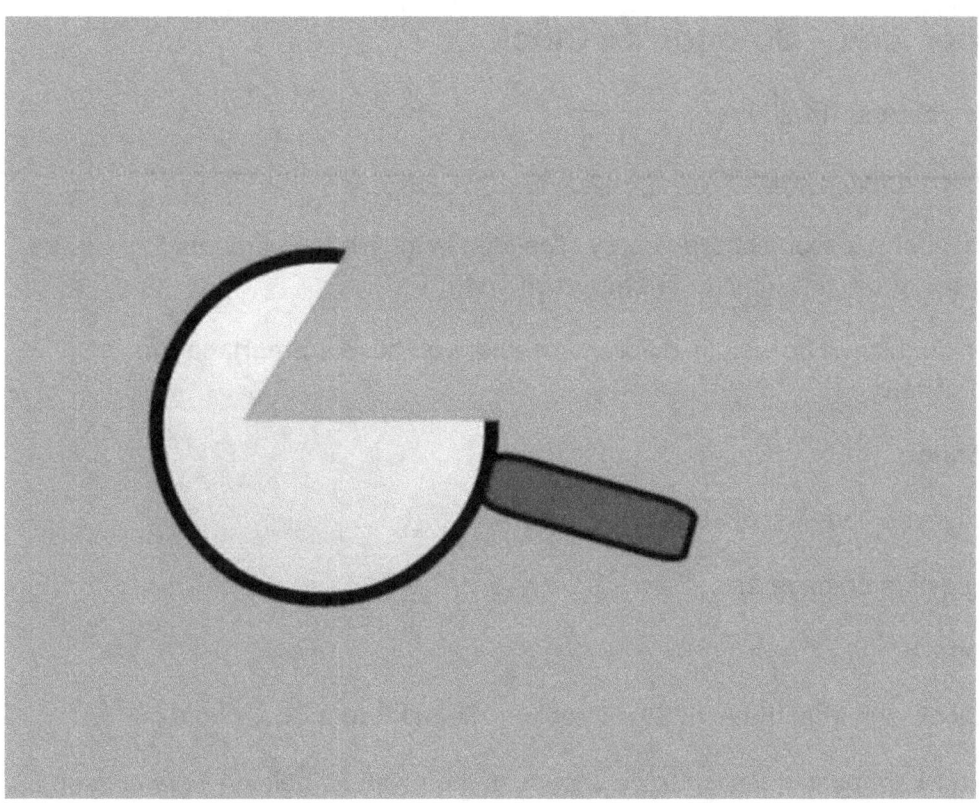

Magic Paper

The sums on the left have their answers written in yellow so you cannot see them. Drag them over to the right and the answers are revealed. All students have "thinking time" to solve them, then can drag over to the other side to see if they are correct.

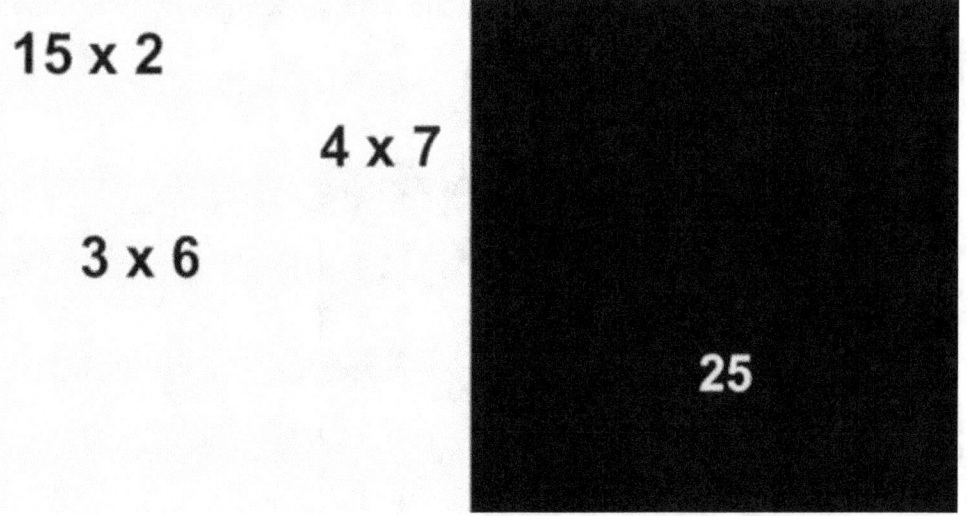

If you want to investigate these ideas, you can download these three pages and take a look at how you could adapt these ideas for your own subject.

Download links via original article:
http://www.whiteboardblog.co.uk/2011/01/creative-use-of-colour-in-iwb-files/

A quick starter idea – Countdown Clock

Originally posted February 14 2008

http://www.whiteboardblog.co.uk/2008/02/a-quick-starter-idea-countdown-clock/

Here's a quick idea for a lesson starter/plenary. The idea is to give the students 5 quick-fire questions and a set, short, time limit to answer each one.

The way you can do this will be slightly different whether you have a Smartboard or an Promethean ActivBoard

Promethean Version

1. On page 1 write/type your first question.

2. Put another question on page 2, 3, 4 etc.

3. Go back to page 1

4. Click on the Clock icon from the ActivStudio toolbar. Select Count Down from the list.

5. Set the time you want each question to be shown. In the example below I have chosen 30 seconds.

6. You can set a sound to play at the end of each time limit. Click on the drop down arrow to choose a different sound.

7. In the second drop down, choose "Turn to next page".

8. Make sure the Repeat box is checked. This will make the clock work on every slide rather than just the first one.

9. Then click OK

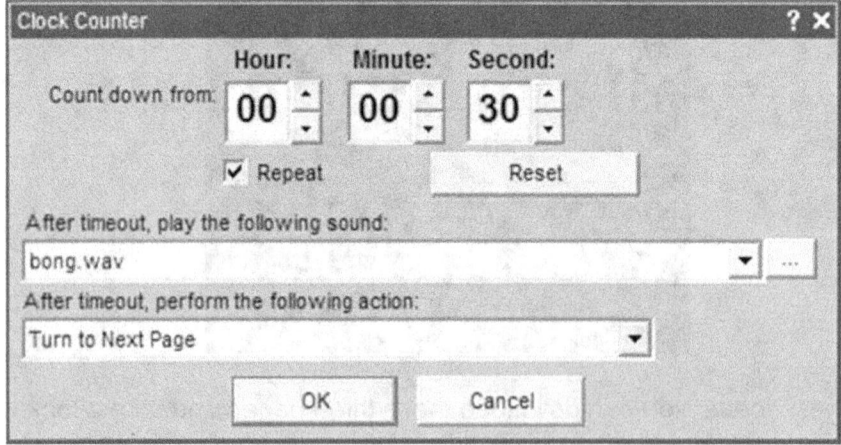

What will happen is that the first question will be displayed and the clock will start counting down. When it reaches zero, the sound will play and ActivStudio will immediately turn to the second question. This will repeat for all the questions you have written.

SmartBoard version

Smart Notebook does have a countdown timer, but it does not turn the pages automatically.

You can find the timer in the gallery in several places. Check under – Essentials for Educators – Mathematics – General Resources – Tools. Drag the timer from the gallery onto your 5 question pages.

Set each clock to Count Down and set the time to 30 seconds.

Once the clock has counted down, move to the next page. You will have to do this manually.

Quick Tips

Smart Quick Tip #1 – If you use the Timer a lot, it is well worth dragging it into your My Content area of the gallery so you can find it quicker.

Smart Quick Tip #2 – You can search the gallery by keyword. So a quick way to find the timer would be to type the word Timer into the search box at the top of the gallery. All the items that have a keyword of Timer will be returned in the search.

General Tip #1 – If you want to set up the questions during a lesson and you do not want the students to see them before you are ready, You can use the Blank or the Freeze button on the remote control to hide what you are doing until you are ready.

Go Fish

Originally posted May 5 2009

http://www.whiteboardblog.co.uk/2009/05/go-fish/

Here's a quick idea for a lesson starter or a plenary. Hidden in the bucket, on the ends of the fishing rods are different keywords. When you pull the fishing rod out of the bucket it reveals the keyword. Students then have to explain what that word means, or explain what it does etc.

You can put anything you want on the end of the fishing rod. You could adapt it to include maths problems, chemical symbols, times tables, words in French/Spanish, or even images and shapes.

The rods were created using the line tool and grouped together. The words can then be added as text boxes and then grouped with the rod to stick it on the end of the line.

One thing you may have to do if you adapt your own is change the ordering of the bucket to send it to the front. You might also want to lock the bucket in place to stop it being dragged accidentally.

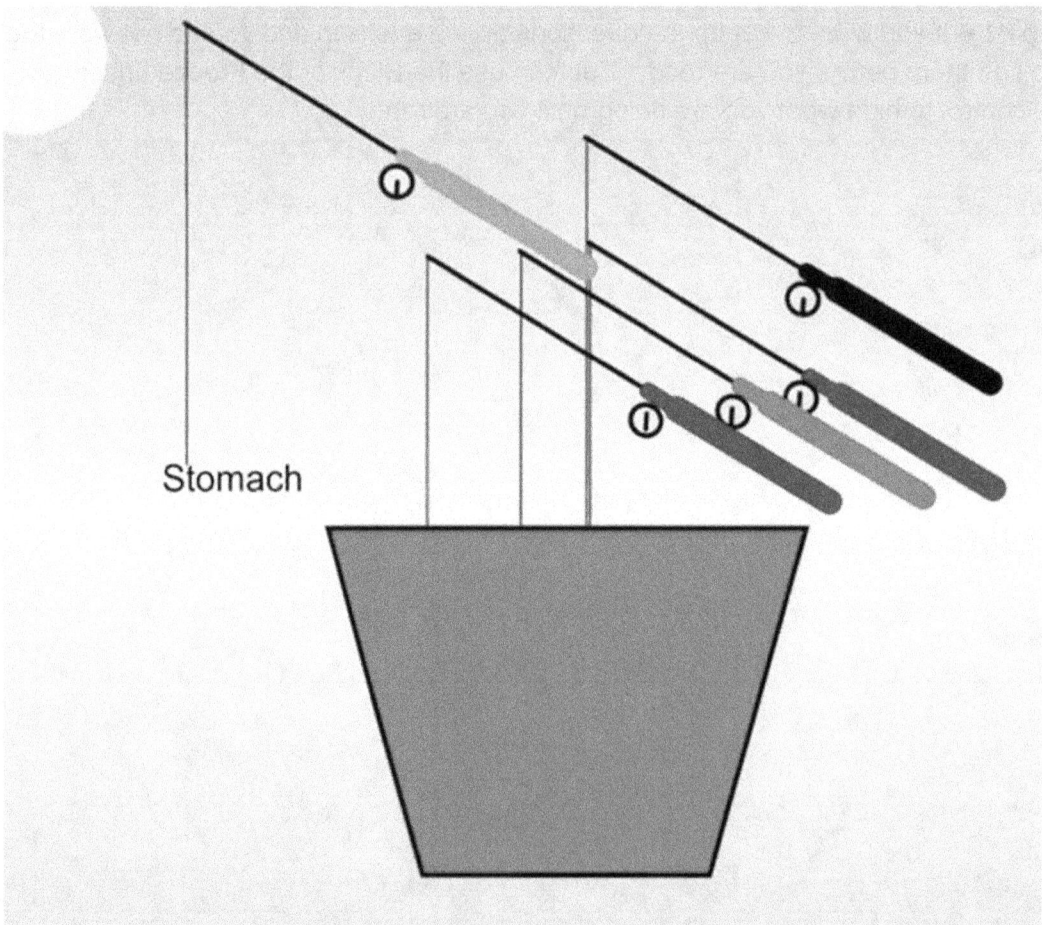

You can download the ActivInspire and Smart Notebook versions of this file from the Think Bank website here: http://think-bank.com/iwb/science.html

I've included one quick version for organs of the body, and a blank page which you can adapt to include your own keywords.

Update – Lynne Horne (@lynnehorne) has already produced a nice variation to use in Numeracy. Get the file here: http://lmhtob.wikispaces.com/SmartNotebook+Files

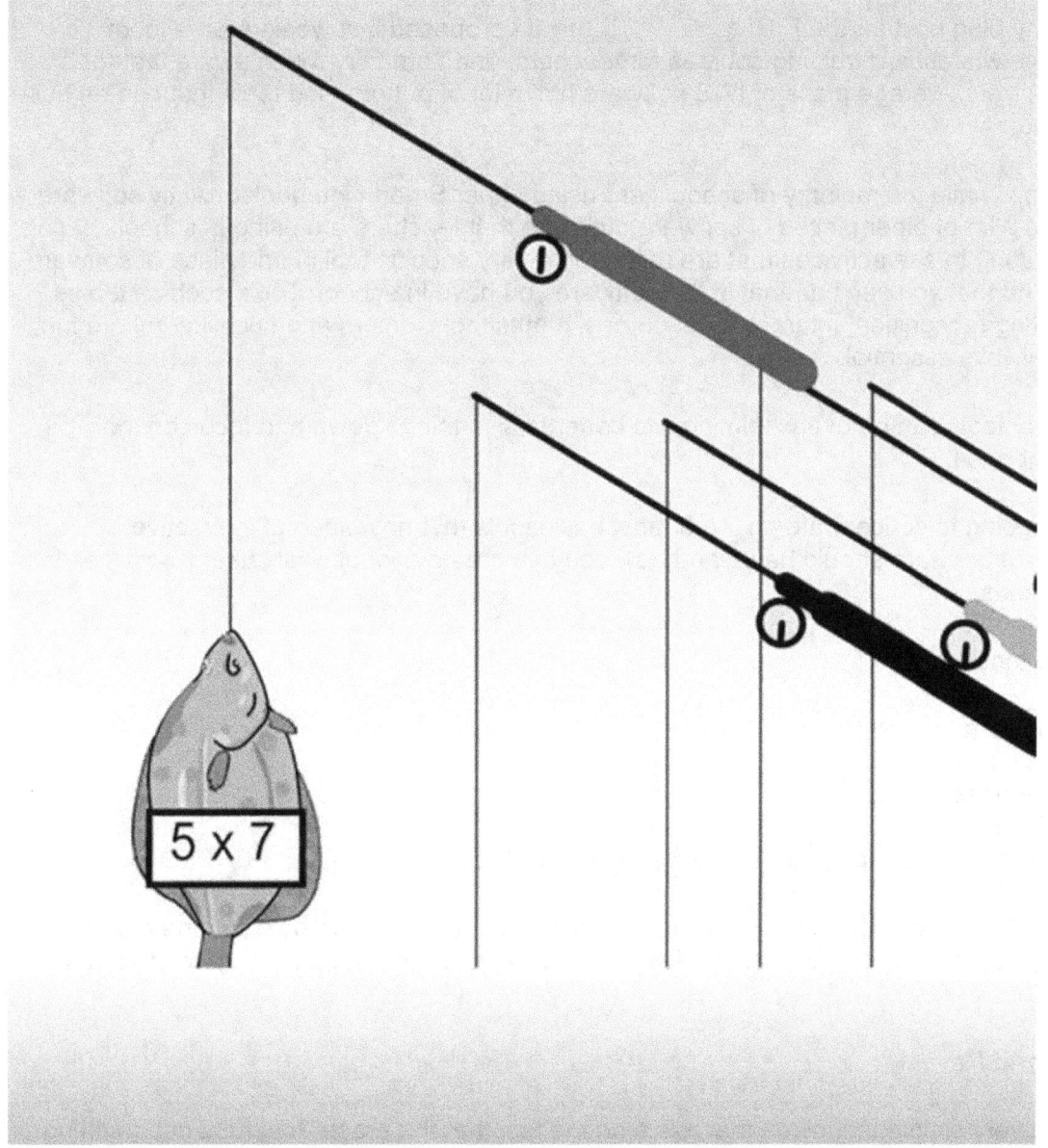

Update – you could also lose the bucket and use a large blue rectangle across the bottom third of the screen (as shown above). With this rectangle moved to the front (top layer) you can hide the words / objects behind it. This will give the impression of pulling things from the sea!

IWB's 8 Ideas to Keep it Simple

Originally posted January 25 2011

http://www.whiteboardblog.co.uk/2011/01/iwbs-8-ideas-to-keep-it-simple/

Here's my blog post for the Ed Tech Blog Carnival I proposed last week. I run a lot of interactive whiteboard training courses for teachers, and I am very much aware that for a new user your average piece of IWB software has a lot of buttons and tools that can be quite confusing.

In addition, while the majority of schools are using either Smart Notebook or Activ software there are a lot of other pieces of software out there that teachers are using in schools. It can be frustrating to see activities that are reliant on a very specific tool in one piece of software, only to find that you can't do that in the software you have in school. Tools such as tables, handwriting recognition, interactive resources, maths tools, timers and suchlike. All are fun, but not always essential.

Too many tools can be overwhelming, it's better to slim things down and focus on the important ones.

So I am going to concentrate on the 5 most basic tools that any piece of interactive whiteboard software should have, and how you can create a lot of really useful activities for your lessons.

Those 5 tools are:

- Freehand Pen
- Text
- Shapes
- Eraser
- Images (via copy/paste or a screen capture tool)

With just these tools, there are so many things you can do. Also handy would be to know how to group shapes together and to lock some objects on the page so they can't be moved by accident.

1. Rub and Reveal

This is a very simple technique that relies on the fact that the eraser tool rubs out anything drawn with the pen tool, but does not rub out typed text. If you change the pen tool to have a thick line, and change the colour so that it matches the background of the page, then you can quickly make text disappear by simply drawing over it. This is a very quick way to make cloze activities (fill in the gaps) or to hide labels to a diagram such as in the example below.

To make the text appear, switch to the eraser tool and then rub out the pen. The words will appear as if by magic. It's a simple technique, but very effective.

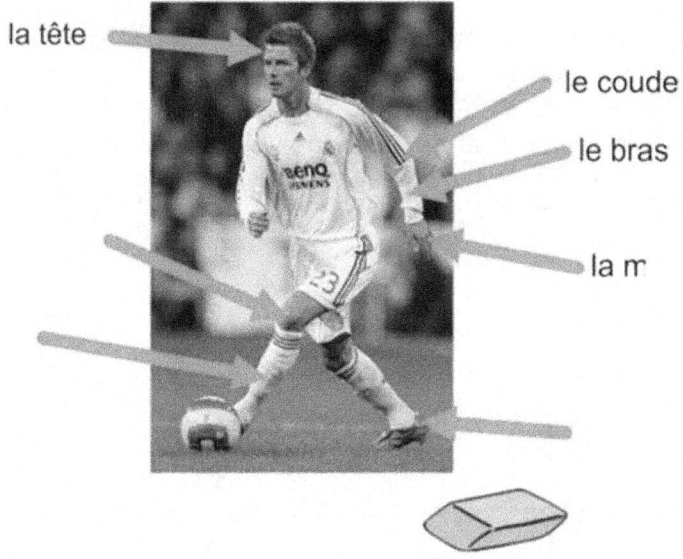

la tête

le coude

le bras

la m

2. Anagram Keyword Games

At its most simple level, all this activity is made from are two blocks of text – one is an anagram of a keyword, and one is the correct answer. I have then drawn two rectangles and filled them in. These are then used to cover the two words.

In this example I have added text to the two boxes so I can remember which is the anagram and which is the answer.

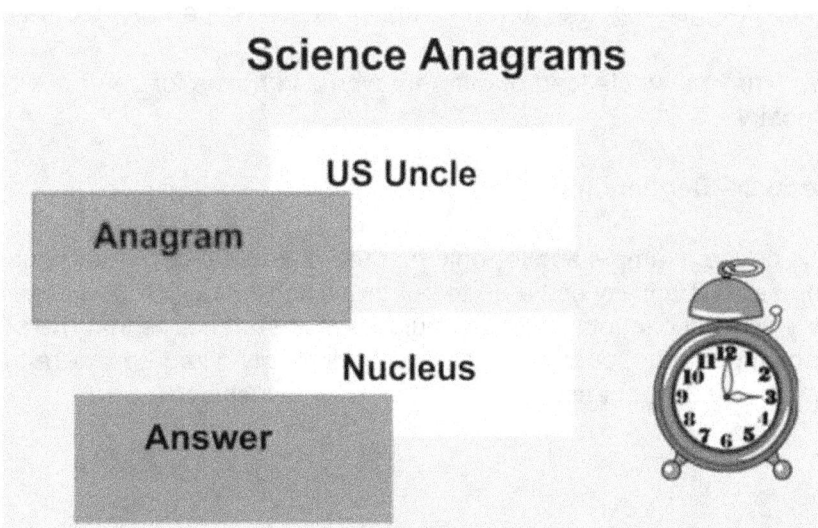

Science Anagrams

US Uncle

Anagram

Nucleus

Answer

You can make it more interesting if you want with the optional step of adding a clock with a "countdown" piece of music that I downloaded from the internet. Or if your whiteboard software has on-screen timers you could use them. But this is not really necessary.

By way of speeding up the generation of anagrams from your keywords – just go to the Wordsmith Anagram Generator (http://wordsmith.org/anagram) and type your keyword in. It will make anagrams for you.

3. Drag and Drop 1 – matching

A very simple activity to use at different times in a lesson to check on understanding, these are simply text boxes which then need to be matched.

To speed things up, I created one blue box and one yellow box using the shapes tool and then added text. I then cloned these boxes several times (or copy/paste) to get many identical boxes. Then change the text in each one.

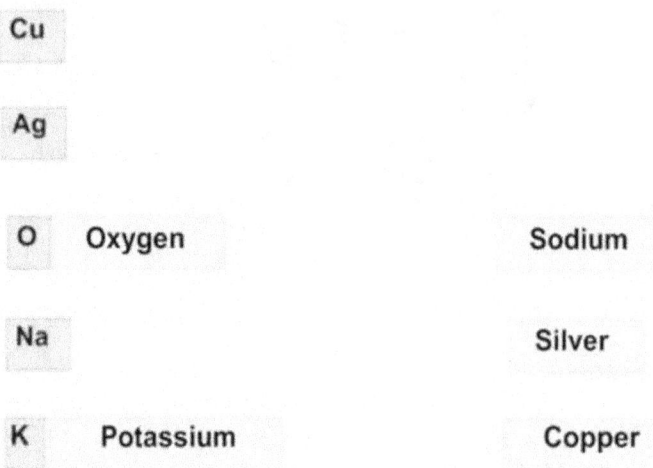

The boxes could contain words and their definitions, beginnings and ends of sentences, dates and events, words in one language and their corresponding word in english.

The boxes can be dragged together to match up. Or lines can be drawn to pair them up.

As an extension – have a whole load of different words in boxes for sentence rearranging or fridge magnet poetry...

4. Drag and Drop 2 – Sequencing

This is the same as the example above, only that the boxes are larger and contain a sentence or phrase. The activity could be to put these sentences into the correct order either based on a story or a set of events. These could also be statements that the pupils need to rank into order of importance, or strongly agree and strongly disagree where there may not be correct answer as such, but acts as a stimulus for discussion.

The Story of Much Ado about Nothing

Don John plots to trick Claudio into believing Hero is a loose woman. Hero is totally unaware of this as she prepares for her wedding day.

At the tomb the repentant Claudio discovers Hero is not dead and the two couples (Claudio & Hero/Benedick & Beatrice) end up together.

The priest devises a secret plan to pretend Hero has died of grief. Meanwhile Benedick & Beatrice declare their love for one another.

Benedick is tricked by his friends in to believing Beatrice loves him. Beatrice is tricked by her friends into believing Benedick loves her.

At the wedding, Claudio shocks everyone by publically rejecting Hero, who he believes is having an affair.

The lies against the virtuous Hero are discovered and Claudio, feeling bad, decides to visit her mock grave.

Beatrice & Benedick quarrel, while Claudio notices and falls in love with 'the short and pretty Hero': they become engaged.

Everyone is excited to see the men arrive back at Leonato's house after a battle.

5. Drag and Drop 3- sorting

This activity relies on the screen being split into two (or three) columns with text boxes placed at the bottom. The words can be dragged into the correct columns. The example in the image is more complicated that it needs to be as I have made a table out of several boxes. But you could just put a line down the middle of the screen.

The obvious alternative is to use circles to create a Venn diagram.

Metals	Non-Metals
Shiny	Not shiny
Can be flattened into sheets	Poor conductor of electricity
Normally solid at room temperature	Brittle. Breaks when hit or pulled
Good conductor of electricity	Poor conductor of heat

Its oxides are acidic.
Good conductor of heat

Its oxides are alkaline (bases)
Can be pulled into wires
Solids, liquids and gases at room temperature

6. Drag and Drop 4 – matching words and pictures

If you can get pictures onto your IWB page then you could adapt the earlier matching example to include images. In the example below images were copied and pasted from the internet, or found in the clipart gallery, and then text boxes were made with words in.

7. Drag and Drop 5 – Plenary Circles

A simple idea for summarising what pupils have learnt at the end of a lesson. It consists simply of a large circle, with text arranged around the outside. All pupils get thinking time to come up with several sentences that start "I know that...." and then use two of the words to finish the sentence. So "I know that Metal is a Conductor" for example. Some pupils can then come to the board to pull the two words in and make their sentence to share with the rest of the class.

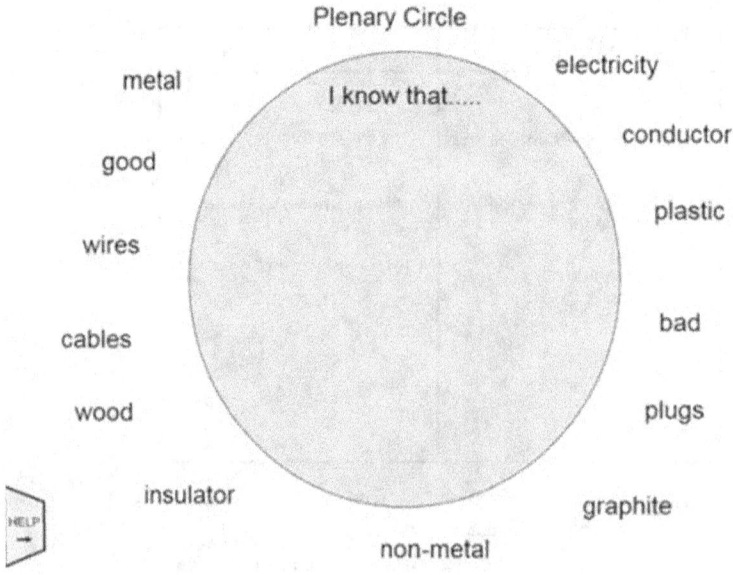

8. Fishing Rods / Balloons

I'll combine these two ideas as they're basically the same. Attach questions, words or phrases to other objects so that you can reveal them at random by pulling them out from behind an object or pulling them from off-screen.

The fishing rod is just made from several lines using the line tool, and then grouped together. The "sea" is just a big blue rectangle that's been put in front to hide the objects on the end of the rod.

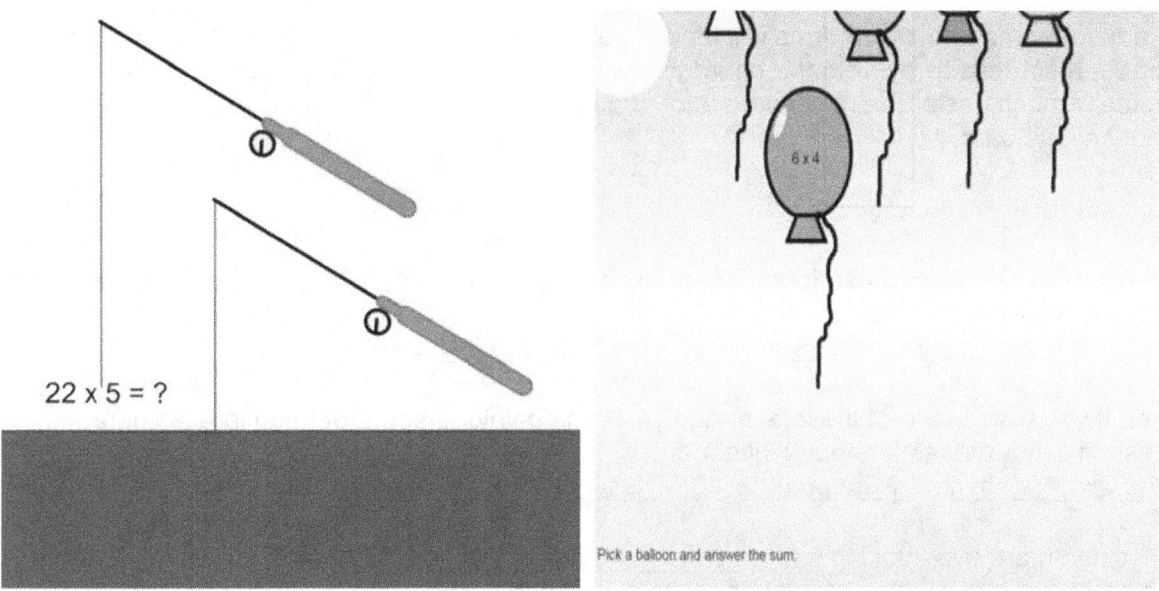

The balloons are simply made from a few shapes and a line grouped together. The sky and ground art simply made from two rectangles that have been filled with a gradient fill, sent to the back and then locked in place.

Pupils would come to the board, grab a string and pull down the balloon. They then have to answer the sum that's been grouped to the balloon.

The balloons and fishing rods are making things more complicated than they need to be, but they look fun. At the most basic level I have done this by typing a word or phrase, drawing a squiggly line and grouping the two together. The word can then be pushed off the screen leaving the line visible so it can be pulled back on when needed. The balloons look nicer, but again it's just extra fluff 😊

In Summary

All of the ideas given above make use of the most basic tools that any interactive whiteboard software worth owning should have. As long as you can write with the pen, type text, make simple shapes and insert images then you can make these. As an added plus, being able to group boxes and text, or add text quickly to a box will also help.

With all these activities, remember that you don't need to use all the whistles and bells of your IWB software to make engaging activities. It doesn't need a degree in computer science to move away from using your IWB as just a screen to show videos or PowerPoint.

Remember that most IWB firms will let you install their software at home so that you can create resources away from the board to then bring into the class on a USB stick etc. It's actually much easier to pre-prepare a lot of this stuff away from the board with a mouse/keyboard.

Learn more

You can see some of these ideas in action here, with the demonstration I did for TeachMeet Essex last year:
http://www.whiteboardblog.co.uk/2010/11/lesson-starter-ideas-for-your-iwb-talk/

And if you want some of these activities you can download some of them in a file here: Lesson Starter Ideas for your Whiteboard:
http://www.whiteboardblog.co.uk/2010/07/lesson-starter-ideas-for-your-whiteboard/

Plus if you are ever looking for interactive whiteboard training, do bear me in mind. I can come in and show your staff how to make all these things.

If you like these ideas, and you make anything great – I'd love to see what you've made. Please get in touch!

The Plenary Circle

Originally posted January 15 208

http://www.whiteboardblog.co.uk/2008/01/the-plenary-circle/

Here's a simple idea for using an Interactive Whiteboard for an end-of-lesson plenary activity. It's a very simple slide to produce;

1. Draw a circle and fill it in.
2. Lock the circle to the background.
3. Add text boxes with keywords from the lesson around the outside of the circle.

And that's it. At the end of the lesson, get different pupils to come to the board and pull in two words to complete the sentence "I have learned that...." For example "I have learned that body cells contain 46 chromosomes."

Every pupil should have some thinking time first to think of several combinations they could use before calling pupils to the board.

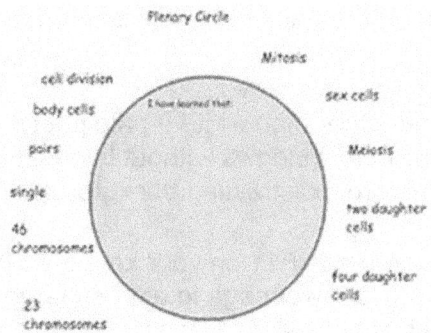

This could be made more involved by "chaining" the words so that one word is left behind for the next pupil to use... but this means more thought has to be put into the words provided by the teacher in the first place.

If the room layout makes it difficult to get the pupils up to the board easily, then it may be worth investing in a wireless mouse that can be quickly passed around and allow them to move the words themselves.

I have produced a quick video about this activity. You can view it here:
http://www.think-bank.com/iwb/video/plenarycircle.html

The Smart Notebook and Promethean file that includes this activity can be found on this page. http://www.think-bank.com/iwb/science.html Scroll down to the Biology section and download the Mitosis and Meiosis lesson.

Tips for Using Your Interactive Whiteboard

Originally posted January 21 2008

http://www.whiteboardblog.co.uk/2008/01/tips-for-using-your-whiteboard/

This list is based on the one originally produced by the Review Project a few years back. Sadly their website is no longer active so I will repost it here since it's a handy list of things to consider.

1. Make sure there is plenty of space both in front and to either side of your whiteboard so that you can move around it and access all parts of the screen easily. It helps to be able to stand to the sides of the board to minimise shadow and to be able to face the class without being dazzled by the projector.

2. If you can, install wall mounted speakers. This means that sound is of better quality and carries better across the classroom.

3. Use a font type and size that can be easily seen at the back of your classroom – Arial, Comic Sans and Sassoon Primary are recommended fonts for schools. Check your presentations are legible: stand at the back of your classroom and see if you can comfortably read it.

4. Try to use background colours other than white – pale pastel colours improve legibility and if you have a problem with glare from windows without blinds, try using black/dark blue and using white or yellow for writing. Avoid distracting backgrounds.

5. When viewing a website, if you press F11 on your keyboard it will remove all the toolbars at the top of the page, displaying your webpage in a much larger screen, making the site more visible. To bring toolbars back, press F11 again.

6. Look into using a wireless keyboard which can be placed near your whiteboard for times when you want to add text. This saves dashing back to your computer each time you need to enter text. A wireless mouse may also be useful when you want pupils to interact with the materials on the board without the disruption of moving them around the room.

7. If you are going to use a website in a lesson, add it to your Favourites / Bookmark it and then you can access it quickly and easily without typing in complex web addresses. Or add it as a hyperlink to a page in your whiteboard presentation.

8. Try and create documents where you do not need to scroll up and down – instead of 3 paragraphs on one page, add 1 paragraph to 3 pages. Space your work well to leave room for annotations and comments, which can be retained if you do not need to scroll up and down the document.

9. Get the whiteboard software put onto your home/staffroom computer so that you can prepare pages in advance of the lesson without having to be at the whiteboard. Save the files onto USB stick to bring into school or email to your school account

Screencasting with IWB Software

Originally posted December 6 2010

http://www.whiteboardblog.co.uk/2010/12/screencasting-with-iwb-software/

If you have a Smartboard or a Promethean board then you already have the software to allow you to make screencasts. A screencast is a way of capturing everything that you do on a computer screen with audio narration, and save it as a movie file to share later.

By using this technique you could run through a presentation and capture it with your own voice over the top. It could allow teachers to record parts of a lesson, or to create revision guides. If coupled with the interactive whiteboard it would also record all your handwritten annotations as well. You'd need a longer microphone lead, or you could plug a USB microphone into the USB port on some newer smartboard models.

Even better, you could get pupils to create their own screencasts to demonstrate what they know.

I used the Smart Recorder bundled with Smart Notebook to record my lesson starters talk the other week. (http://bit.ly/98MT3b)

For examples of a screencast produced by a teacher to demonstrate mathematic principles, visit the

Mathademics YouTube Channel: http://www.youtube.com/mathademics

Smart Notebook

Look for the small blue/white Smart Notebook Icon in your system tray, or look in Start -> Programs -> Smart Technologies -> Smart Notebook -> Smart Recorder (or similar path)

The Smart Recorder tool will open and look like this:

By clicking on the narrow button next to the record button you can choose whether to record the whole desktop, a chosen area or a chosen window, depending on what you want to demonstrate.

Hitting the record button will start the recording. Hit the stop button when done and it will ask you for a filename and save the file. Still need help? Here's a guide I found: http://www.youtube.com/watch?v=Nc-aKZ9vFmw

In Promethean ActivInspire

From the Promethean Toolbar click on Desktop tools.

This will minimize the ActivInspire software and leave the small floating tools icon. Click on this to open it up and select the screen recorder tools. Again you can choose whether to record the whole screen or a chosen area.

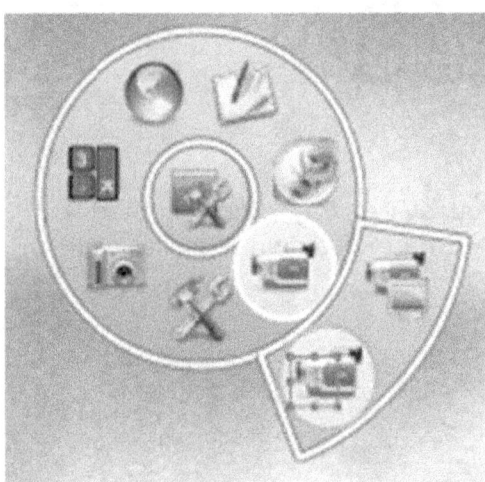

What to screencast?

Using the screen recorder tool, pupils could:

- Make audio stories – move clipart characters on the "stage" of an IWB page to tell a story.
- Explain how they carried out a particular piece of work
- Make revision guides
- Produce instructional guides
- Make a tourist guide to their area combined with Google Maps / Street View
- Role play in a foreign language

and much more.

In both cases the recorded screencast can be used as-is, or could be edited in video editing software such as Movie Maker to add other elements before being published. Upload to YouTube to share with the world, or put onto the school Learning Platform / VLE to share with a smaller audience.

There are other pieces of software out there that will do screencasting, but if you already have one of these two boards you should already have something on your computer which, for free, will do the same job!

Enjoy!

Smart Notebook 10 Toolbar

Originally posted April 23 2008

http://www.whiteboardblog.co.uk/2008/04/smart-notebook-10-toolbar/

I've always found it useful when doing IWB training to give teachers a sheet with all the icons on the toolbar and what they do. Many teachers like to print this off and stick it on the wall next to their IWB.

Here is my new guide to the Smart Notebook 10 toolbar. If you want, you can download it as a pdf file here: http://bit.ly/hS5wxV

The Smart Notebook 10 Toolbar

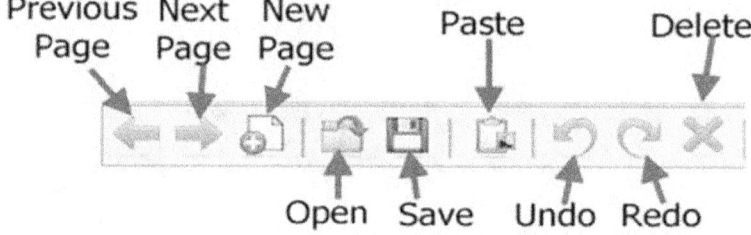

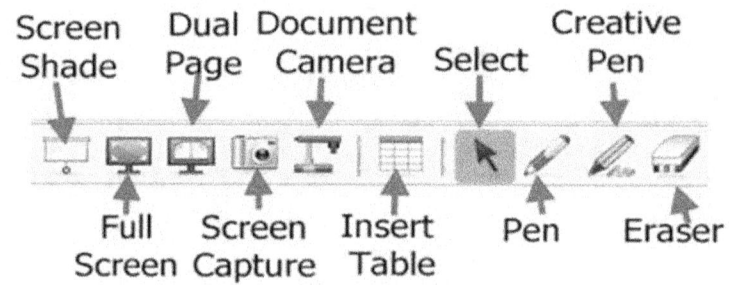

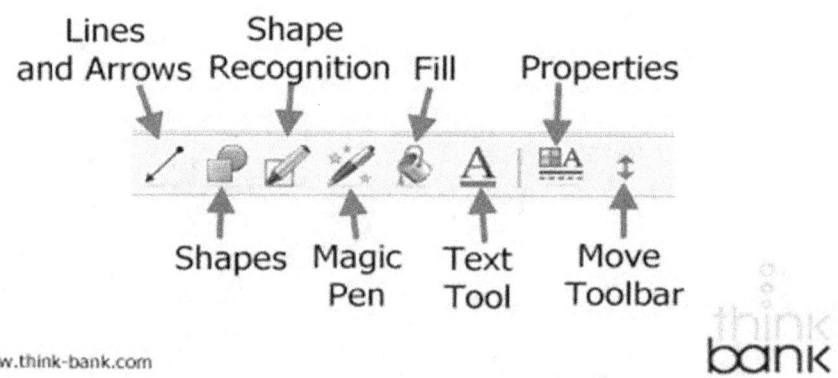

www.think-bank.com

think bank

Smart lesson toolkit

Originally posted April 16 2009

http://www.whiteboardblog.co.uk/2009/04/smart-lesson-toolkit-20/

Smart have just made available version 2.0 of their excellent Lesson Activity Toolkit for Notebook 10. The Lesson Activity Toolkit contains templates for several activities that you can use to keep your students involved and make learning fun. There are over a dozen types of customizable activities including: anagram, category sort, image match, keyword match, multiple choice, pairs, tiles and word guess.

You can read a pdf file about the new version here: http://bit.ly/fzXN55

To get hold of it, open Smart Notebook 10 and click on the gallery tab. In the top right corner you will see an icon of a spanner. Click on that and choose Check for Updates, and then Lesson Activity Toolkit 1.0

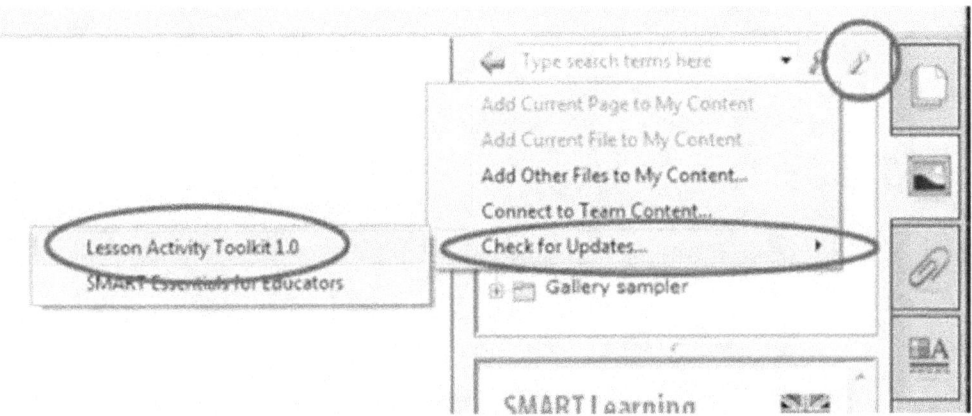

The software should connect to the internet and give you the option to update to version 2.

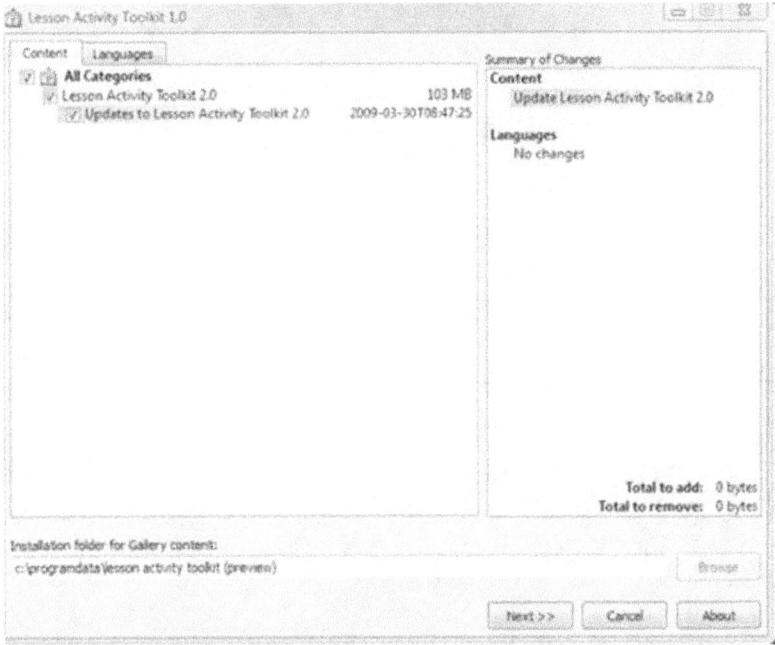

Check the box next to Lesson Activity Toolkit 2.0 and click on Next. The rest should happen automatically.

Once updated, you will be able to access the Lesson Activity Toolkit 2.0 from the gallery. For activity and game ideas, open the Examples folder in the Lesson Activity Toolkit.

If the update does not work, you can download the toolkit from the Smart website. I checked just now and I think it's still giving the 1.0 version, but keep an eye on that page and see if they put the new one on

Update – the toolkit is now on the Smart Notebook download page – scroll down here http://bit.ly/hd6pmu

The Smart Notebook Magic Pen

Originally posted April 25 2008

http://www.whiteboardblog.co.uk/2008/04/the-magic-pen/

One of the small niggles I had with Smart 9 was that there was no spotlight tool on the toolbar in Smart Notebook. I know you could get it via the floating toolbar, but it annoyed me that I couldn't get it quickly in Notebook without having to use workarounds.

So I was really happy when I was first shown a beta of Smart Notebook 10 with the tool called the Magic Pen.

The Magic Pen is brilliant.

If you write with the Magic Pen it stays on the screen for a few seconds and then fades away. This is great for adding quick annotations that you don't want to last – underlining an area on the screen, circling a key point etc.

If you draw a circle on the screen with the Magic Pen then it automatically turns into a Spotlight tool! This is my favourite!

If you draw a rectangle on the screen it will turn into a magnifier – making an area of the screen larger. Good for making text larger such as web addresses etc.

Here's a quick video that shows how to use the Magic Pen. I made this with the beta but couldn't show them due to the NDA, which is why it talks about being the second video... I can't find part 1!!

http://www.screencast.com/t/WBCypM5Pcn0

Smart Notebook Licence and Activation

Originally posted December 7 2010

http://www.whiteboardblog.co.uk/2010/12/smart-notebook-licence-and-activation/

If your school has Smartboards, then your staff are allowed to install Smart Notebook onto their home machines for preparation of lesson resources. I am amazed at how many schools I go into and staff I speak to who are not aware of this fact.

For many it can fundamentally change the way they use their whiteboard. If the only place you can make lesson resources using Notebook is at the board, many staff will not do so. Choosing instead to use PowerPoint presentations. Give a teacher the ability to make Smart Notebook resources at home, with mouse and keyboard, and it becomes a lot easier to create interactive materials to then use at the Smartboard.

Now the terms of the Smart Licence state that you can install it on a reasonable number of boards for the school site. Section 8 of the licence states that if you have one board, you can put it on the machines of all the staff.

Download link : http://bit.ly/gbGOTW

The only thing you cannot do is run Smart Notebook on another brand of Interactive Whiteboard or presentation technology. The licence covers you to prepare resources with it for a Smartboard, not use it as a way bypassing the lack of functional software with cheaper brands of IWB.

So – how do teachers get hold of Smart Notebook?

To download the software, go to the Smart Download Page. (http://bit.ly/hd6pmu)

Click on Choose a Product and select Smart Notebook for Windows (or you can get Mac/Linux versions, plus older versions of the software)

Scroll down and click on Download. Enter your school details and Smart Notebook should start downloading.

The software will install as a 30 day trial. Follow the next few steps to unlock it.

To unlock Smart Notebook

First you will need your serial number for your smartboard (or one smartboard in school). You will find this on a sticker somewhere on the side or bottom of the board. It should start with "**SB**". If you can't find your serial number, Smart have produced some guides on where to look.

Once you have your serial number, you need to go to this page:
http://vault.smarttech.com/nb10productkey/default.aspx

Follow the instructions on that page, enter the serial number and an email address. Smart will then email you a Product Key which will unlock Smart Notebook. Keep this Product Key safe in case you need to reinstall in the future. This key can be used more than once to unlock copies of the software on other staff computers.

You could bypass this step and just ask the IT technicians for the product key they used to unlock the software on the school computers. Hopefully they'll share it with you. If they say they can't refer them back to the Smart Licence, and this post.

Spread the word!

If you work in a school where the staff do not have Smart Notebook outside their classrooms, then please pass this post on, and make sure you inform your IT technicians that you are allowed to have copies.

Smart Notebook 10.6 New Tools

Originally posted January 25 2010

http://www.whiteboardblog.co.uk/2010/01/smart-notebook-10-6-new-tools/

Smart Notebook users should be aware of a new update that came out last week. Version 10.6 has a couple of very neat new features.

The most obvious feature is a new icon on your toolbar that gives you access to Measurement Tools. This is basically a ruler, protractor, compass and set square that may look familiar if you've ever used Promethean software ☺ All of these tools should prove very useful to maths teachers.

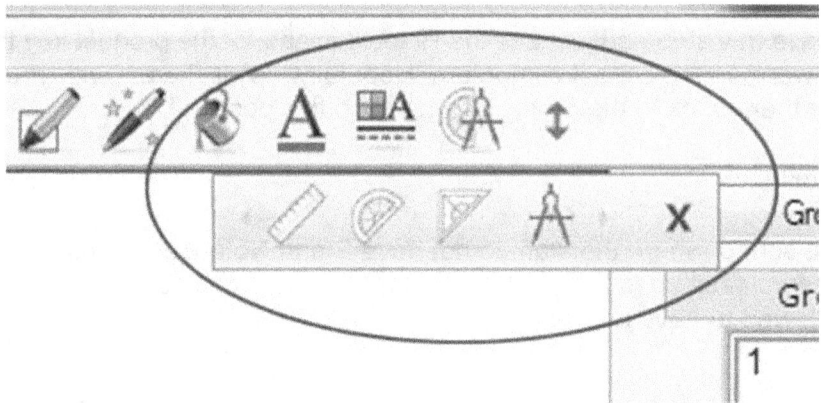

Clicking the ruler icon places an interactive ruler onto the page. You can make it bigger and smaller just like any other object. Grab it in just the right spot and you can rotate it around. A number in the corner shows the angle of rotation. If you use the pen very close to the edge of the ruler, it will let you draw a perfectly straight line, however wobbly your hand is! Useful for lines of best fit on graphs perhaps? The set square works in the same way but you can draw on all three sides.

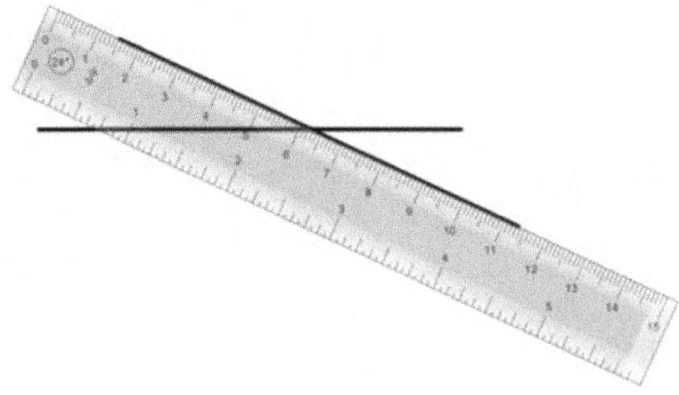

Working in a similar way is the protractor tool. Use the pen near the edge to draw a perfect arc. You can toggle between 180 and 360 degree versions by clicking the blue circle near the base of the protractor. Dragging the green circle (and the grey circle) will let you move two lines. When you click the green arrow it will inject those lines onto the page, with the angle between them clearly marked.

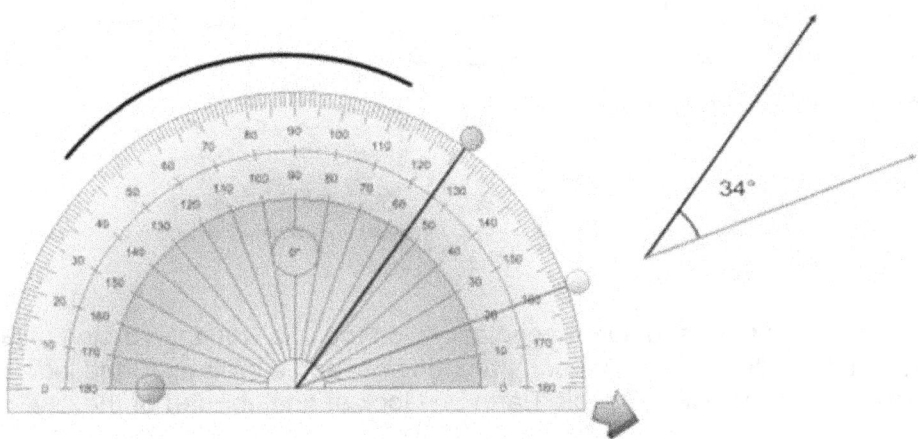

The compass tool should also be familiar to Promethean users. Click and drag at the top of the pencil to move it in and out. Drag the green circle to move the compass around without drawing – and click on the point of the pencil to draw the circle.

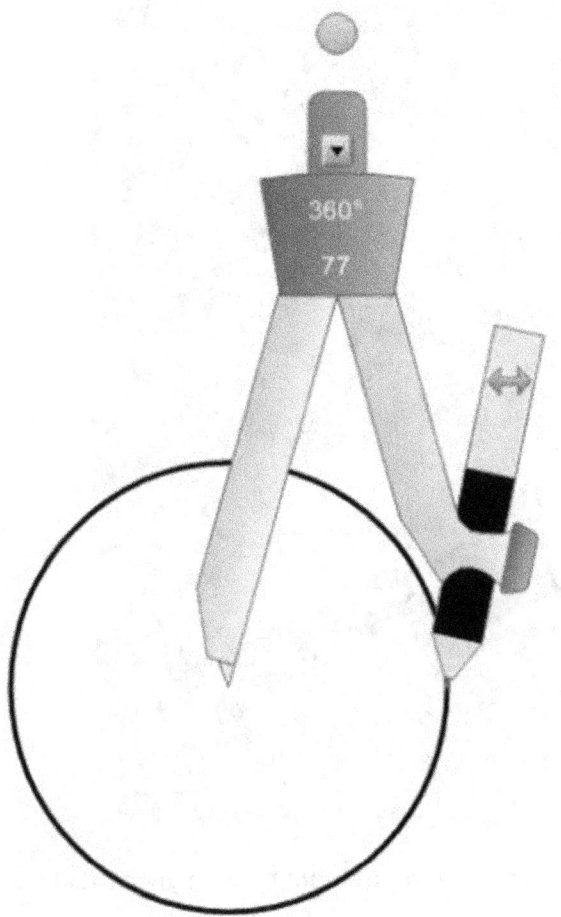

Another very innovative feature is the totally transparent notebook. In the past you've been able to use pen tools over the live desktop, but it's been a little fiddly. By clicking the Transparent Background icon your notebook page vanishes, leaving a small strip of icons that lets you annotate and use the measuring tools over any application, while at the same time still being able to click and manipulate the applications.

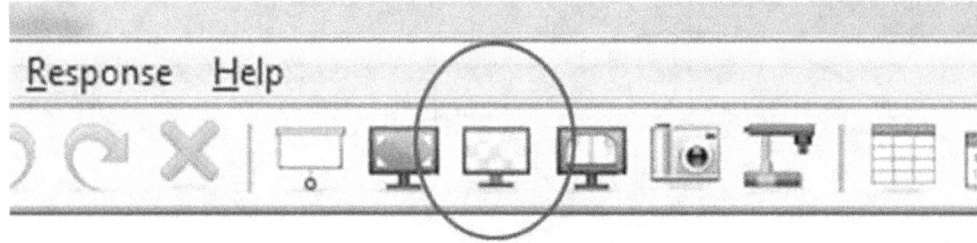

For example – here is a ruler and some annotations on top of a working version of Google Earth. I can move the ruler around and compare lengths, add a protractor and look at angles and at any time move the view in Google Earth and look at another part of the city.

Use the camera icon to take snapshots from here and put them back in your main notebook page

Both of these new features offer some very different ways that you could use Smart Notebook that you couldn't do before. The transparent background is a very simple idea that is actually very powerful.

A minor change includes adding some new shapes to the shape tool : perfect circle, perfect square, isosceles triangle, equilateral triangle, scalene triangle, regular polygons, half-circle and rounded square.

In addition there is now a link to the Smart Exchange in the Gallery. Smart Learning Marketplace is also still there.

The other change with Notebook 10.6 is support for Windows 7. But annoyingly they are still not supporting 64-bit versions.. so I still can't use my new laptop with Smart Response. Seems to work OK with the actual Smartboard though.

Smart Notebook 10.6 also comes with a 30 day trial of Smart Notebook Maths Tools, which has been in beta for a while and should hopefully be available for purchase soon.

On the whole, the new tools are a great addition to what is already a great piece of software. Nice one Smart!

Smart Notebook Express

Originally posted January 21 2011

http://www.whiteboardblog.co.uk/2011/01/smart-notebook-express-out-of-beta/

SMART have recently announced that their SMART Notebook Express web application is now available globally and is no longer in beta. SMART Notebook Express is a lightweight version of their SMART Notebook™ collaborative learning software

http://express.smarttech.com/

SMART Notebook Express enables educators to open, edit, save and share .notebook files from anywhere, at any time, regardless of whether they have access to the Internet. Depending on their needs, users can access SMART Notebook Express online by visiting express.smarttech.com or offline by downloading SMART Notebook Express to their desktops.

Both versions offer the same intuitive user interface. Educators who do not otherwise have access to SMART Notebook software will now be able to use SMART Notebook Express to open and interact with SMART Notebook lessons for use in their classrooms and to share those lessons with colleagues, students and parents.

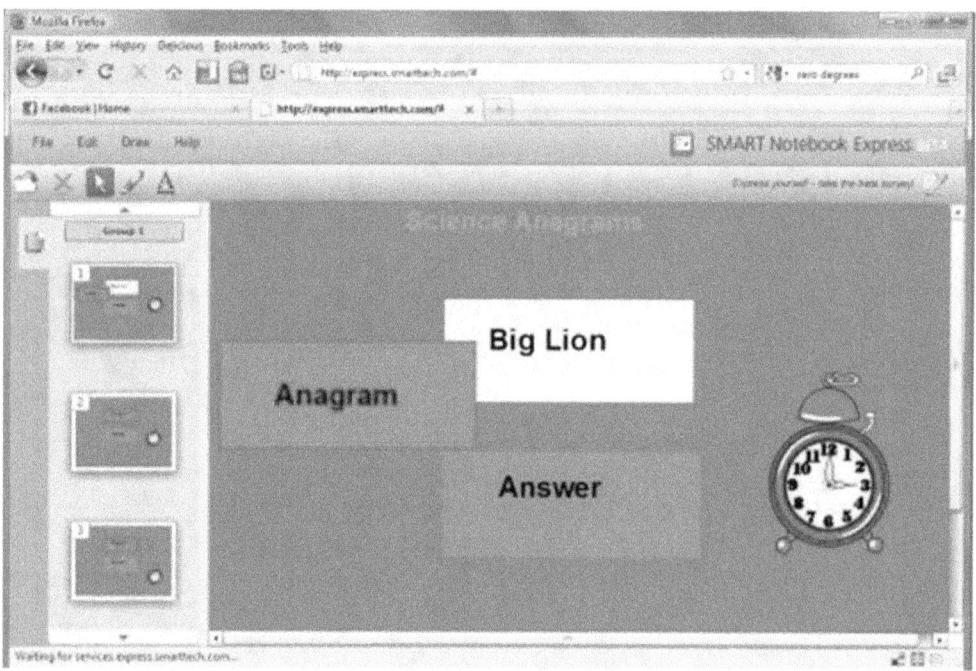

SMART Notebook Express allows for simple editing of Notebook files with the following features:

- **Online or offline** – Open, edit and save .notebook files from anywhere, at any time, whether online or via a downloaded desktop application
- **Platform agnostic** – Works with Microsoft Windows, Mac and Linux operating systems
- **Save function** – Save SMART Notebook files to your computer, including any new content you've added or changes you've made to the pages

- **Page Sorter** – View SMART Notebook software pages as thumbnails and reorder the pages of any presentation by simply dragging and dropping the thumbnails
- **Text-editing tool** – Add or edit text and change the font style, colour and size
- **Pen tool** – Highlight information or write over SMART Notebook files with digital ink using a variety of colours and line styles
- **Object manipulation** – Select and move or delete any object on a SMART Notebook software page
- **Multiple languages** – Available in U.S. and UK English, Spanish, French, German and Italian
- **Create new pages or files** – Add new pages to any SMART Notebook file, or create a new file
- **Multimedia support** – Open and view Adobe® Flash® files, video, audio and object animations

Also – with the release of SMART Notebook 10.7 (expected March) there will be support for the common whiteboard format .iwb files.

It's a very handy application to have bookmarked – especially for those teachers who want to access their Smart files from home and who haven't installed the software for whatever reason. It's also useful to point pupils there so they can open notebooks produced in a lesson for revision purposes.

http://express.smarttech.com/

Whiteboard tips presentation

Originally posted January 28 2008

http://www.whiteboardblog.co.uk/2008/01/whiteboard-tips-presentation/

Just wanted to flag up a great initiative by Tom Barrett who has produced a presentation about whiteboards using Google Docs. http://bit.ly/fC1sc6

Google docs allows a number of users to collaborate on a single document over the internet, which has a great many implications for how we work and share information. You can produce text files, spreadsheets and PowerPoint-style presentations.

The idea behind the Tom's presentation is simple – users are asked to give a tip for using their interactive whiteboard. You can read his thoughts about the presentation here. (http://bit.ly/hTHlt5)

Starting with 1 page, the resource has grown amazingly. Currently, there are 31 different tips for using your IWB. Most are general tips and a few are Smartboard specific.

You can see the presentation here. http://bit.ly/fC1sc6 And if you want to add any tips, get in touch with Tom to get access rights and get to work!

Update Jan 2010 – it's currently now at 50 tips and counting!

Quick IWB Tip – the Zip File Trick

Originally posted July 31 2008

http://www.whiteboardblog.co.uk/2008/07/quick-iwb-tip-the-zip-file-trick/

Here's a quick tip that I was reminded of after a question on Twitter today.

Let's say you have a Smart Notebook file or Promethean flipchart which has lots of images in it, and maybe even some embedded flash files. How do you get those resources out to use elsewhere?

Well, if you select the file in your regular file management window you should be able to rename it. Change the bit after the dot of the filename that says .xbk, .nbk, .notebook or .flp and change it to a .zip instead. If you can't see the extension on the end of the filename you may need to change your folder properties since Windows can hide these by default.

Once you have changed the extension to .zip, your computer now thinks it is a zip file. So now open it up inside WinZip or whatever software you use to open zip files with.

You will see a listing of all the assets inside the flipchart/notebook file listed as if this was just another zip file. You may even see an Images folder with all the picture files inside. All you need to do now is select out the images/flash files you want and copy/paste them to another folder. And that's it. You might want to make a copy of the notebook file before you do this in case you wreck it ☺ But it's pretty straightforward.

Easiteach Next Generation

Originally posted July 17 2010

http://www.whiteboardblog.co.uk/2010/07/easiteach-next-generation/

Easiteach Next Generation is the latest version of the whiteboard software from RM/Lightbox. Now I'll nail my colours to the mast early. I am a Smart and Promethean person. I have also loved their software equally above anything else I've used out there. Mimio, Ebeam and Starboard software just didn't have the features and ease-of-use that the big two have had since their very early days. One piece of software that I had mixed feeling about was RM Easiteach. In some places it was very nice, but in others it still lacked the tools of Smart & Promethean. I remember writing a (sadly defunct) training package that featured all three, and there were many things Smart and Promethean software could do that Easiteach couldn't.

I was interested then to hear of a new version of Easiteach that is on its way. And even luckier to be sent an early trial version to take a look at. It looks a little slicker than the older version I last looked at a few years ago now. The trial version I had is still under development, so didn't have every feature in place.

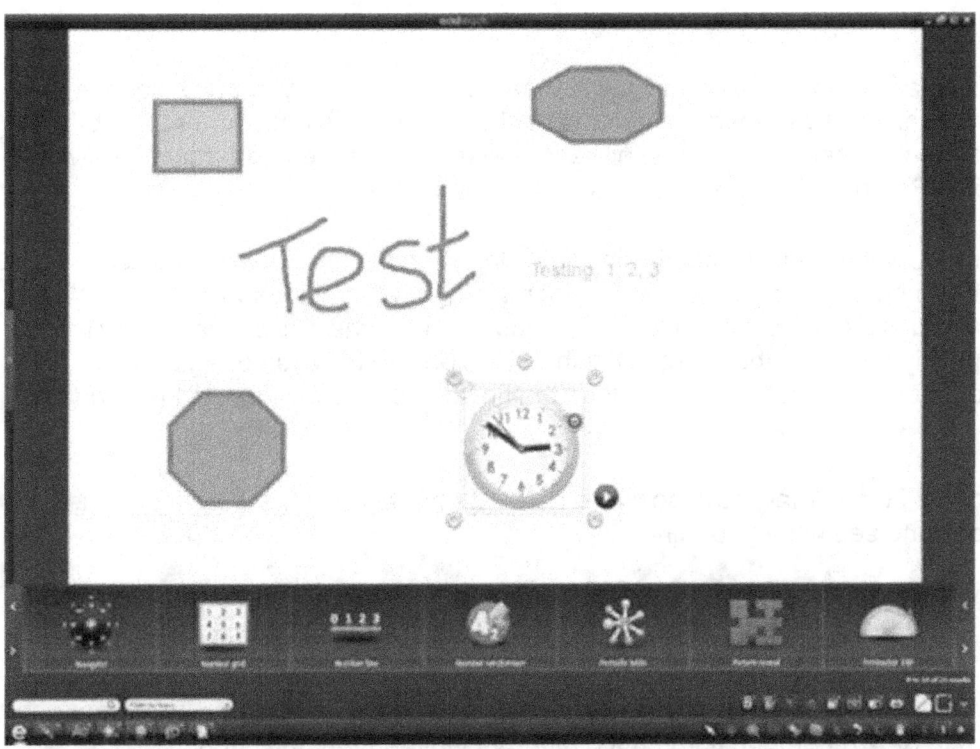

Menus are reasonably clear, with coloured icons placed at the bottom of the screen for younger students (or shorter teachers!) to reach. Object manipulation on the page is simple, with large clear anchor points around each object.

Tools such as handwriting and shape recognition are still there. A feature that the others don't do yet is Text to Speech, which is nice. Although not sure how useful most schools will find it.

A new feature is the Widget Bank. Flash items that run on the page such as calculator, clock, periodic table, protractor, picture reveal, dice, random item generator, navigator and more. There are currently 20+ widgets available in the bank with more to be added with each new release. Moving and resizing these on the page is simpler than Smart Notebook.

The localised and searchable media bank within Easiteach will comprise over 4,500 curriculum-based resources including over 70 videos.

Users are able to record sound and video directly on to a page. Using the media bank you can also capture images, record sounds and record videos using external hardware, such as microphones or digital cameras, and add them to your page and then also add them to your personal media bank.

Tools that I couldn't find include Desktop Capture – which I still think is a massive omission, as well as desktop annotation. Desktop capture should be there though. I found I couldn't even copy and paste an image from the web and paste it in, or even drag it in. There's no reason for such a fundamental omission. I could save images to a folder, then import or import from scanner or camera into my image bank then putting onto the page, but that's not the same and is a little too cumbersome.

Screenshade and Spotlight tool are also things that any self-respecting IWB software should have. No idea why these are missing. Hopefully they'll be in the final version. There's a whole "special effects" icon that as yet does nothing, but says coming soon.. so hope they're on there.

Easiteach works on all brands of interactive whiteboards – as long as you buy a licence. The ability to import and export Easiteach documents as the common IWB file format ".iwb files" should also mean that in theory you can share and use resources created on other software packages – should Smart and Promethean adopt the .iwb format too.

On the whole I like it, but for now I'll be sticking with Smart and Promethean. If I was stuck in a school with Hitachi boards, and wanted to buy something that I could legally use on the board then I'd consider Easiteach. I'm not happy about some of the basics that are still missing, but hopefully they'll be there in the finished version. It's always hard getting an opinion from a not-quite-complete version. Once the finished product is done I'll take another look.

You can download a 30 day trial of the software here: http://www.easiteach.com/eng/trial/ so go and take a look and see what you think!

Update – this was a review of a pre-release version and a lot of the things I mentioned as lacking are now in place with the full release version. Please go check it out! It's a very good alternative to Smart or Promethean if you have different whiteboards in school.

Whiteboard Health and Safety

Originally posted February 1 2008

http://www.whiteboardblog.co.uk/2008/02/health-and-safety/

When I deliver IWB training sessions I do get asked quite a bit about the health and safety implications of using a whiteboard and projector, especially after a report appeared in the Times Newspaper a few years back.

There are several guidance documents that are worth referring to. Many schools now have this guidance printed out and stuck on the wall next to the IWB.

Health and Safety Executive Guidance : http://bit.ly/enKmVR

Becta Guidance : http://bit.ly/gBa35k

Teachernet Guidance : http://bit.ly/h4YGdN

Basically, the guidance can be summarised as follows:

- Staring directly into the projector beam should be avoided at all times.
- Standing facing into the beam is minimised. Users, especially pupils and students, should try to keep their backs to the beam as much as possible. In this regard, the use of a stick or laser pointer to avoid the need for the user to enter the beam is recommended.
- Pupils and students are adequately supervised when they are asked to point out something on the screen.
- Employers should also try to ensure that projectors are located out of the sight line from the screen to the audience; this ensures that, when presenters look at the audience, they do not also have to stare at the projector lamp. The best way to achieve this is by ceiling-mounting rather than floor or table-mounting the projector.
- In order to minimise the lamp power needed to project a visible presentation, employers should use room blinds to reduce ambient light levels. The brightness on the projector can then be turned down via its internal settings.

In addition to this advice, I would like to add a few comments

1. Make sure that both sides of the board are free from clutter – so that it is possible to stand either side of the board when addressing the class. This minimises the need to stand directly in the beam.

2. Check the remote control of your projector (or a. Find your projector remote control and b. check it!) and see if it has a button that says **Blank** or No Show, Mute/Pic or Show/Hide or something like that. This button will dim the output of the projector, basically blanking the screen if you do not want to use it for a while. You can now talk to the class without being dazzled by the beam. Obviously this is only handy if you do not want to refer to the board as well. This is better for the projector bulb than turning it off and on all the time using the power button.

(On a side note – most projector remotes also have a **Freeze** button which lets you freeze the projector on the current image while you sort out the next piece of work.. maybe put up a problem for the pupils to solve while you then find the next part of the presentation or a web game etc. The other use (and one I obviously do not condone!) allows you to check your emails while the pupils are copying something off the IWB!)

3. As I mentioned before, reduce the glare of the board when giving presentations by using a pastel page background instead of a white one.

IWB's and Raising Attainment

Originally posted November 4 2009

http://www.whiteboardblog.co.uk/2009/11/iwbs-and-raising-attainment/

Robert Marzano has just published an article in Educational Leadership (http://bit.ly/gqVY0v) that is worth a look. It's based on the research project he carried out for Promethean (http://bit.ly/gL1jTS) which was published earlier this year (which I covered on the Blog)

Direct link to the research: http://bit.ly/gqVY0v

His research found that in general the use of an interactive whiteboard did produce a rise in student attainment.

He found that there were three features of the IWB that had a statistically significant relationship with student achievement. These were:

- **Student-response devices** – Voting kits such as Smart Response or ActivExpression. He found this accounted for a 26 percentile point gain in attainment.
- **Use of graphics and other visuals**. Marzano found that using images, charts and videos was also associated with a 26 percentile point gain.
- **Use of whiteboard reinforcers**. Simple "checks of knowledge" that can be played on the board such as "rub to reveal" "drag and drop" etc. to reinforce the learning in the lesson. This had a 31% gain. Which is pretty impressive.

Pitfalls

Marzano also found that in 23% of classes, using the IWB did not lead to better results. In fact in those classrooms students did better without the IWB

On examining the evidence, Marzano and his researchers discovered that there were potential pitfalls in using interactive whiteboards:

- **Using the voting devices but doing little with the findings**. In many classrooms, teachers simply noted how many students obtained the correct answer instead of probing into why one answer was more appropriate than another.
- **Not organizing or pacing the content well**. In these cases, the teachers incorporated video segments from the Internet or images intended to represent important information in their digital flipcharts. However, they ran through the flipcharts so quickly that students, although impressed with the graphics, did not have time to analyze and interact with one another about the content.
- **Using too many visuals**. Digital flipchart pages were awash with visual stimuli; it was hard to identify the important content.
- **Paying too much attention to reinforcing features**. For example, when teachers who had worse results with the technology used the virtual applause feature to signal a correct answer, the emphasis seemed to be on eliciting the applause rather than on clarifying the content.

His recommendations

It is probably true that for some learners, the use of an IWB is not going to make them learn any better. In other cases the simple fact that an IWB is being used is not going to magically make the learning experience better.

Marzano suggested a few ways to improve the use of the IWB in the classroom:

- Teachers should think about how to organise the lesson on their IWB. They should group information into small segments before creating digital resource.
- Digital flipcharts should contain visuals – but not too many as to confuse and distract. Make the focus clear. Also don't contain too much written information. I'd also add to this to be aware of clashing colours or backgrounds that make the information hard to read.
- When using voting kits, don't just say which answer is correct. Take time to discuss the correct answer (and wrong answers) and elicit opinions from students. Get them to explain **why** they thought X or Y was correct etc.
- When using reinforcing activities – again be sure to focus on the answers and explain why something is correct or incorrect. Don't let it get lost in the flashy response to an answer (such as a sound effect or animation)

My thoughts on all this

I'm sure we've all been in training sessions where the speaker uses PowerPoint and the session is deathly dull and no learning takes place. But a different speaker, with the same tools at their disposal can create a fantastic learning experience.

There is a definite need for training to show teachers how to best make use of the IWB to support learning. Just dumping one on a classroom teacher will not make the lessons better and raise achievement.

I'm still amazed at the number of schools that will spend tens of thousands of pounds on interactive whiteboards. But then will not spend the £600 or so to get a trainer in (subtle plug) to actually show the staff how to use it. The expensive equipment then doesn't get used, or doesn't get used effectively. It's a real shame.

You can also benefit from taking a look at some of the excellent IWB websites out there where teachers share their ideas. You can find a few in the sidebar of this blog.

I've just been reading an excellent blog post by Chris Betcher about IWB's (http://bit.ly/gKxdAu). His closing paragraph is this:

The REAL trick to all this is to ensure that this potential is being realised by teachers who understand the world of possibilities their IWB offers. If a teacher cannot see the potential, then of course we will struggle to see genuine "newness" in the way the IWBs are being used. As always, it is the creativity and insight of a talented teacher that brings this potential to the surface. Let's stop being so hung up about whether IWBs can add value to a classroom. They can. The real question is whether the teachers who work with them can make the most of that potential and use them to bring that "revolution" into their classrooms. http://bit.ly/gKxdAu

Which puts into words exactly how I feel about the potential for IWB's in the classroom.

Interactive Whiteboard Research

Originally posted April 20 2008

http://www.whiteboardblog.co.uk/2008/04/iwb-research/

I'm using this post as a bit of a brain-dump to collate some research articles. I haven't read all of them yet, but am linking them here to remind me to start going through them.

The ICT Impact Report: A Review of Studies of ICT Impact on Schools in Europe.
http://bit.ly/eALozo

MILLER, D. J. (2006). The magic box – enhancing interactivity, Mathematics Teaching, 197, pp. 28-31. http://bit.ly/gluuSV

MILLER, D.J., GLOVER, D., AVERIS, D., & DOOR, V. (2005). From technology to professional development: How can the use of an interactive whiteboard in initial teacher education change the nature of teaching and learning in secondary mathematics and modern languages? Training and Development agency, London. Report made to the Teacher Training Agency. http://bit.ly/dWbIFT

MILLER, D.J., GLOVER, D., & AVERIS D. (2005). Developing Pedagogic Skills for the Use of the Interactive Whiteboard in Mathematics, British Educational Research Association, Glamorgan. http://bit.ly/e8348k

MILLER, D.J., GLOVER, D., & AVERIS D. (2005). Presentation and pedagogy: the effective use of interactive whiteboards in mathematics lessons. In Hewitt, D. & Noyes, A., Proceedings of the sixth British Congress of Mathematics Education, BSRLM proceedings, vol. 25 (1), pp. 105-112. London: British Society for Research into Learning Mathematics. http://bit.ly/dOsR3s

GLOVER, D., MILLER, D.J & AVERIS D. (2004) Panacea or prop: the role of the interactive whiteboard in improving teaching effectiveness, the Tenth International Congress of Mathematics Education, Copenhagen
http://bit.ly/fKMeAE

Interactive Whiteboards and Learning: A Review of Classroom Case Studies and Research Literature. (SMART Technologies Inc, Apr 2004) http://bit.ly/gsgcys

MILLER, D.J & GLOVER, D. (2001) Missioners, Tentatives and Luddites: leadership challenges for school and classroom posed by the introduction of interactive whiteboards into schools in the United Kingdom, part of the Symposium: New Technologies and Educational Leadership at the British Educational Management and Administration Society Conference, Newport Pagnell, UK. http://bit.ly/fwu4Tz

Delivering E-Learning Using Interactive Whiteboards
http://bit.ly/eWO7ai
(E-Learning Centre, United Kingdom, 2004)

What the Research Says About Interactive Whiteboards.
http://bit.ly/gewZjW
(British Educational Communications and Technology Agency (BECTA)ICT Research, Coventry, U.K., 2003)

How is the Interactive Whiteboard Being Used in the Primary School and How Does This Affect Teachers and Teaching
http://bit.ly/gXlAao
Cogill, Julie. (Virtual Learning, 2002)

Interactive Whiteboards.
http://bit.ly/ef1Uvg
Kollie, Ellen
Explains features of interactive whiteboards, illustrated with cases where they have helped students who are mildly learning disabled, autistic, or have low test scores.
School Planning and Management; v47 n1 , p88-90 ; Jan 2008

Whiteboards Inc. Interactive Features Fuel Demand for Modern Chalkboards.
http://bit.ly/fyJ0iV
Davis, Michelle R.
Digital Directions; Sep 12, 2007

The Case for Interactive White Boards in the Classroom
http://bit.ly/exatZi
DeCraene, Tom
Scholar Search Associates; 2006

How Can You Use Research Evidence to Enhance your Mathematics Teaching? NCETM 2007
http://bit.ly/htjSGy

Embedding ICT in the Literacy and Numeracy Stages.
Higgins et al. Newcastle University (2005)
http://bit.ly/dWVJSh

Why IWBs?

Originally posted April 20 2008

http://www.whiteboardblog.co.uk/2008/04/why-iwb/

I stupidly got into an argument on the TES forum yesterday with two guys who are not in favour of IWB's and have made their feelings clear on several threads. They wanted to be convinced as to what the IWB could offer over and above just presenting using a laptop and data projector.

I thought it might be useful to add my thoughts here as well.

Here is my response;

I have no doubt that you can do a lot with a PC and a data-projector – even more so if you couple that with a wireless mouse/keyboard and wireless slate which could be passed around the class.

And for showing video clips, PowerPoint presentations etc., this is fine. If you want the students to sit and watch something.

The Review Project, when they looked into the use of IWBs said this

****
Anecdotally, teachers who have taught firstly with a data projector and then with the addition of a whiteboard all say that they would feel very awkward having to return to their computer each time they want to do something on screen. One remarked that he didn't feel part of the class when working on his computer. The students are looking at the screen while the teacher is talking somewhere else in the class. With a IWB the focal point is both the teacher and the screen.
****

With just projector and laptop the lesson is disjointed. Kids are focussing on one area of the classroom while the teacher is in another. An IWB puts the teacher at the focal point alongside the materials

With a laptop and projector there is more chance of the teacher just "presenting" and pupils being spectators. The boards allow better interaction with the materials – annotating over the top.

Unfortunately, due to the lack of training, teachers still use the IWB to present and there is little interactivity.

Like I said, I agree there is other tech out there too – a tablet PC and projector could do a lot of what is done on an IWB in terms of annotation, interaction, but again you still have the disjointed classroom.

And I say again, It's not about the clipart – you're taking a point I made out of context. But for some teachers, having a ready-made resource bank that they can quickly access really helps speed up the creation of lesson materials. The Smart Lesson Activity Toolkit with its interactive flash games, or some of the Promethean flash materials and see how they could be used for lesson starters and plenaries. Yes you can find these online if you know where to look, but many teachers don't have the time to do this

A lot of boards are being used badly, by teachers who haven't been trained on how to get the most out of them, or who just want to "present" to a class rather than interact with them. This needs to be addressed with CPD.

Take a look at the blogs that are appearing from young teachers who have embraced this tech and are doing some amazing things with it to enhance the teaching and learning of whatever subject they are delivering. All agree that there is something that the board adds that makes it more than just a projector

for example Joe Dale's blog: http://snipurl.com/251qt

Thought for the Day

Originally posted June 15 2009

http://www.whiteboardblog.co.uk/2009/06/thought-for-the-day/

This quote from Douglas Adams came up during a radio interview with Baroness Greenfield who has been currently wittering on about computers probably rotting our brains, albeit with a complete lack of evidence or research to back up her "chilling warnings". (http://bit.ly/fB9kvf) – warning, links to the Daily Mail.

It's from "How to stop worrying and learn to love the Internet"

I suppose earlier generations had to sit through all this huffing and puffing with the invention of television, the phone, cinema, radio, the car, the bicycle, printing, the wheel and so on, but you would think we would learn the way these things work, which is this:

1) everything that's already in the world when you're born is just normal;

2) anything that gets invented between then and before you turn thirty is incredibly exciting and creative and with any luck you can make a career out of it;

3) anything that gets invented after you're thirty is against the natural order of things and the beginning of the end of civilisation as we know it until it's been around for about ten years when it gradually turns out to be alright really.
http://bit.ly/hfxAPd

Apply this list to movies, rock music, word processors and mobile phones to work out how old you are. And I think it sums up brilliantly the way a lot of people approach any kind of modern technology – including Interactive Whiteboards, online learning etc. etc.

And if you're interested, Ben Goldacre over at the brilliant Bad Science blog has a nice rebuttal of Baroness Greenfields warning : http://bit.ly/eMtV2r

Why Change?

Originally posted January 14 2008

http://www.whiteboardblog.co.uk/2008/01/why-change/

A little history first. Back in 1998/1999 the school I was working at The Cornwallis School, in Kent which was just starting to flex its muscles as quite a forward-thinking establishment in terms of its use of ICT. Our school was a pilot school for the Microsoft Anytime Anywhere Learning (AAL) project in which we gave 2 tutor groups or year 7 students a laptop each. When people were told we were kitting out 60 kids with laptops there were a lot of raised eyebrows and doubters that the scheme would have any benefits.

As part of the introduction to parents and staff, the Deputy Head gave a presentation that contained some excellent quotes from teachers and educationalists down the years complaining about every new development such as paper, fountain pens and ballpoint pens. It was a very effective argument ☺

I was reminded of that presentation the other day with a post on the blog Learning is Messy. (http://learningismessy.com/blog/?p=396), and much further back is another post with all the quotes the Deputy Head used. (http://learningismessy.com/blog/?p=177)

I'm going to repost them here since I really like them, and I am using this blog partly as a brain dump for myself so I know where to find things in the future.

Students today can't prepare bark to calculate their problems. They depend on their slates which are more expensive. What will they do when their slate is dropped and it breaks? They will be unable to write!"
Teachers Conference, 1703

Students today depend upon paper too much. They don't know how to write on slate without chalk dust all over themselves. They can't clean a slate properly. What will they do when they run out of paper?"
Principal's Association, 1815

Students today depend too much upon ink. They don't know how to use a pen knife to sharpen a pencil. Pen and ink will never replace the pencil."
National Association of Teachers, 1907

Students today depend upon store-bought ink. They don't know how to make their own. When they run out of ink they will be unable to write words of ciphers until their next trip to the settlement. This is a sad commentary on modern education."
The Rural American Teacher, 1929

Students today depend upon these expensive fountain pens. They can no longer write with a straight pen and nib (not to mention sharpening their own quills). We parents must not allow them to wallow in such luxury to the detriment of learning how to cope in the real business world, which is not so extravagant."
PTA Gazette, 1941

Ball point pens will be the ruin of education in our country. Students use these devices and then throw them away. The American virtues of thrift and frugality are being discarded. Business and banks will never allow such expensive luxuries."
Federal Teacher, 1950

For proper attribution, these quotes are apparently from David Thornburg's book Edutrends 2010: Restructuring, Technology and the Future of Education (1992). There is another good blog post over at The Fischbowl that makes the same points. (http://thefischbowl.blogspot.com/2006/09/what-if.html)

This argument was taken further by Ewan McIntosh over at Edublogs over the recent news (http://edu.blogs.com/edublogs/2008/01/its-the-gadgets.html) that a teaching union wanted students not to bring gadgets into school and stick with a pen. While I can understand that shiny new toys can be a distraction and there's a chance of bullying and having them stolen I can also see the benefits of embracing these technologies and putting them to good use.

I don't use a paper diary, I use my (rather battered) PDA. I set reminders to do things on that or on my phone. I have a poor memory for some things, so if I want to remember something (a web address in an article or the details of something I see while out shopping – I use the camera in my phone to take a picture of it to remind me later. I dump web addresses and good websites onto Del.icio.us or onto my forum. I use the technology to help me, why can't we educate the students to do the same?

I don't think I have much more to add to the debate that Karl and Ewan have already eloquently said, only to say I agree with their sentiments and to ask what if we had listened each time someone resisted new technology? Would we still be using slates and chalk?

Pay it Forward

Originally posted July 17 2010

http://www.whiteboardblog.co.uk/2010/07/pay-it-forward/

A few years ago I was on a Train the Trainers day. The chap delivering the training showed us all quite a few nice examples of things to do on Smartboards, one or two I hadn't seen before, and one or two that were nice variations on a theme. At the end of the training we asked him for a copy of his file so we could incorporate it into our own days. He said no. He'd spent ages making them and didn't feel happy giving them away. It would be best if we made our own versions… I was gobsmacked. We were working for same company, it wasn't like we were rival trainers or anything.

I was reminded of this recently when I saw a page I had written appear in someone else's demonstration. It was using a photograph I had taken so was pretty distinctive. More than happy to see that, not a problem. Was quite pleased that they'd liked it so much they wanted to use it. What did surprise me was that when one of the other people in the room asked for a copy, the trainer said no. They'd rather not share something they were using in a current course.

This got me thinking about the way that I share stuff, and expect it to be shared. I've always shared the materials I've written, ever since I started teaching. One of my earliest web sites back in 1996/1997 contained zip files of worksheets I had written (which – scarily – is still online and gathering dust). Sometimes I'd share stuff with the world whether the world wanted it or not! When I moved out of teaching into teacher training I still produced materials and put them on my site to download. That's just what I do. (http://bit.ly/fq2F06)

Anyone coming to any of my training courses will get a CD of resources – often far more stuff than I really should be passing on. You will also find a lot of it on this blog too. But if I can help teachers to get started with using whiteboards and other tech then I'm happy to do that.

But I have an expectation. And maybe I haven't stressed that enough on here, and on my download pages. I've mentioned before that I am a big fan of Creative Commons. I love the idea behind share and share alike. And there's a fantastic community of educators who all share their resources readily with everyone who wants it. It's great to see.

creative commons

Attribution-ShareAlike 2.5 Generic

You are free:

to Share — to copy, distribute and transmit the work

to Remix — to adapt the work

Under the following conditions:

Attribution — You must attribute the work in the manner specified by the author or licensor (but not in any way that suggests that they endorse you or your use of the work).

Share Alike — If you alter, transform, or build upon this work, you may distribute the resulting work only under the same or similar license to this one.

So here's the deal. All of my material is distributed under a <u>Creative Commons license. Attribution/Share Alike</u>. It's always been that way, take a look at the very bottom of the blog, it says so down there, next to the stuff about Guinness and chocolate, that's true too 🙂

I really want you to take what I've done and mash it up. Adapt it for your subject. Rework, adapt and adopt. You get the idea. Or even just use it as-is. Any of that is fine with me. I'm not protective of it – please use it. It's why I share it – for you to use. I want you to have it, and I'm thrilled when I see it used. In no way am I saying – don't use my stuff.

But….

If you use my stuff in your lesson materials, or your training materials, then the deal is that you make it freely available to everyone else who wants a copy. Put in on your school network. Pass it to your colleagues on a USB stick. Put it on a site for download. Use DropBox. Email it to them. Tell them where you got it and give them the link. Whatever. But don't hoard it.

Even better – I'd love to see the stuff you make with it. I want to see some of the ways you adapt them for your own subject. Email me, contact me via twitter or just comment on this blog. I hope, through sharing the stuff on this site, that I can inspire you to make things for yourself. I've been chuffed with the response to posts like my <u>Lesson Starter</u> ideas. If you don't have any webspace and / or don't want the hassle, email it to me and I can host it here.

Become a sharer yourself. **Pay it forward**.

The Need for a Common IWB Format

Originally posted January 23 2011

http://www.whiteboardblog.co.uk/2011/01/the-need-for-a-common-iwb-format/

While SMART and Promethean are still the dominant two companies in the UK Interactive Whiteboard market, there are still plenty of schools out there that are using other solutions. With the increasing numbers of other companies trying to enter the market, as demonstrated at BETT this year, there will be increasing numbers of teachers out there who are not going to be using one of the "big two" interactive whiteboards.

While most IWB software has pretty similar features – pen, text, shapes etc., what becomes the issue is the files it produces.

Teachers changing schools may find that the resources they have diligently been producing over the years for one IWB will now not open in the whiteboard software at their new school. Many schools have several different boards in their school – so teachers hit the same problem just moving classrooms in the course of a week. It's little wonder therefore that some teachers never progress past PowerPoint on their IWB because at least they can future-proof their work. With worksheets, PowerPoint's etc., this isn't an issue as the Office file format is very transferrable.

I work with trainee teachers who are in placement schools while they develop their teaching skills. Most swap schools halfway through the course and suddenly find resources they made for one IWB in one school can't be used in their next school. Or that everything they've made while training can't be used when they get a job and go to a school with a different board.

Plus, selfishly, as a trainer it would be lovely to be able to produce files that I know can be opened by teachers on any type of whiteboard, rather than having to create multiple versions, often from scratch each time.

A few years back it was announced that BECTA were going to work at promoting a common iwb file format (.iwb) that would be supported by all the major IWB software producers – and SMART, Promethean, RM, Hitachi signed up to this. I wrote about this back in 2007, so it's been bubbling around since then.

With the scrapping of BECTA by our lovely coalition government earlier this year the driving force for this format has been lost. But despite this, the .iwb file format has been developed and released into the wild. I noticed that some of the companies displaying software at BETT this year did support the common format, which was a good sign.

I know that RM Easiteach Next Generation already supports the new format. And I noticed with interest that hidden in the SMART press release for Notebook 10.7 was the fact that the new version will support .iwb format. SMART say:

To further support SMART's commitment to interoperability, SMART Notebook 10.7 collaborative learning software – expected by March 2011 – will support the interactive whiteboard common file format (.iwb), enabling users to import and export .iwb files to and from SMART Notebook software.

Promethean's ActivInspire (v1.4) does not support this format. It can import PowerPoint files and Smart Notebook files, but you can only save files in its own .flipchart format. Unlike earlier versions you can't even save as a PowerPoint file now, which is a shame. I have no idea if version 1.5 (currently in beta) will support .iwb files. Does anyone know if Hitachi, Ebeam and Mimio now support these files?

I still foresee a time when Microsoft add an additional "whiteboard" mode to PowerPoint which makes it behave like standard IWB software and then gradually as schools update Office you will see more and more teachers just using that with whatever board/interactive projector/slate they've got in their classroom. PowerPoint wouldn't need to be modified too much for that to happen. I'm still surprised Microsoft hasn't done this yet, to be honest

I know SMART and Promethean are both very protective of their own resources that they have produced themselves. And rightly so – they are great quality and do take time to produce. They both see them as a way of supporting their boards and would not like the idea of teachers buying a cheap board, with cheap software and then downloading tonnes of Smart and Promethean resources. In which case they should be able to "protect" those files to stop them being opened on other boards.

But for the bulk of teachers – they just want a way of ensuring that the resources they produce are not going to become accessible in the future. And until that happens teachers are still going to end up producing PowerPoints.

Anyone know the status of the common iwb format with the other board companies? Please let me know.

ActivInspire for all IWB Users?

Originally posted March 4 2009

http://www.whiteboardblog.co.uk/2009/03/activinspire-for-all-iwb-users/

I've been thinking over the last few days about the implications of the ActivInspire launch for users of other boards. And I think it's pretty big news for everyone who uses an interactive whiteboard.

The launch of the Personal Edition of ActivInspire is quite a major thing and is an interesting development by Promethean to open up their resource library to everyone (http://bit.ly/gg9dGf), something I've always felt that they wanted to protect for their boards only.

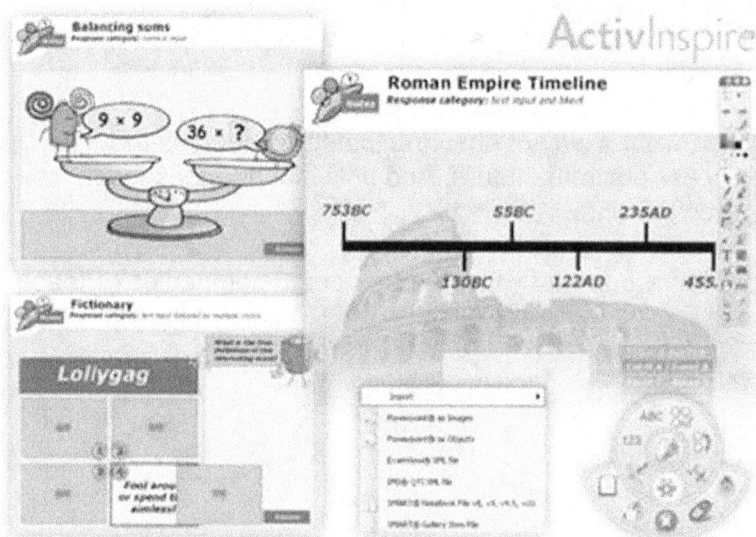

I have always been a big fan of both Smart Notebook and ActivStudio/Primary. I am less of a fan of the software that runs on other interactive whiteboards. They just don't have the usability that I am looking for. I have also found that these the makers of these boards have not really invested in developing banks of resources for their users. Try looking for a Hitachi flipchart anywhere online and you'll see what I mean.

The solution for users of these boards was either to struggle on with the software provided with your board or purchase a third party piece of software such as RM Easiteach. The third option was to use Smart Notebook or ActivSoftware in breach of the user licence – which is not something you should really be doing.

Now it should be possible for the user of any interactive whiteboard to download and run ActivInspire Personal Edition on their board legally. This gives them the basic whiteboard tools, plus more importantly access to open and use all of the Promethean flipcharts available on Promethean Planet, and on other websites (such as mine).

ActivInspire also opens (and converts) Smart Notebook files (for now). So whiteboard users running ActivInspire can pretty much get access to the majority of IWB files available on the Internet. For example on my site I have files I produced only as Smart – those files can now be used by any ActivInspire user. How long it will be before Smart releases a update patch that stops Promethean from opening their files, only time will tell. I hope they don't – I'd like to see resources made more open for teachers, not locked into proprietary formats.

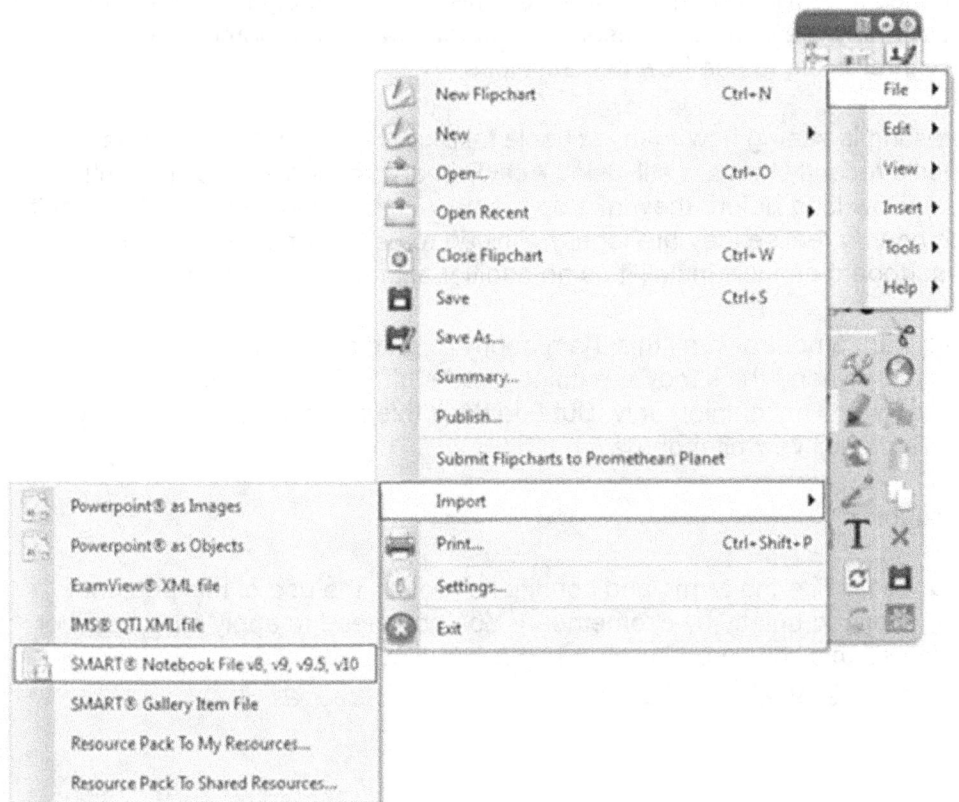

For teachers in schools that have mixed platforms, and I have been in many, it can be a real problem to have materials you have written to use on the Smartboard in your classroom only to find the room you are now timetabled in has a Promethean board – or a Hitachi board etc. Schools could now put the personal version on all computers to give teachers a common platform which they could use if they wish.

It's worth making clear that the Personal Edition of ActivInspire is a cut down version. It does not have all the tools that the full version has. You can see a comparison chart here (http://bit.ly/faLhcj). It does not have design mode, or desktop annotation, or screen recorder. There's no handwriting recognition, or dice tools or on-screen keyboards. But these are often tools people can do without. And if you do like the software the school can purchase the full version of the ActivInspire anyway.

So it's an interesting move. There's no reason now why every school computer connected to an IWB can't be running ActivInspire – and the teachers can be using Smart and Promethean flipcharts on every board.

So what's in it for Promethean? Schools could now buy cheap boards, and run their software? I guess the first thing is that if they can get teachers used to a common format they may be more inclined to buy Promethean boards in the future. It's also a good way of making the Promethean brand more prominent. Promethean can also make money from selling the full version of ActivInspire to these schools.

I think the important thing is that the whiteboard is almost becoming commonplace in schools. Most schools have made their choice about smart or promethean (or Hitachi, or

Cleverboard etc.) and the market is getting saturated. But the next step is the "extras" that come with the boards – voting kits, visualisers, tablets etc. If a Hitachi school has standardised themselves on ActivInspire then they are more likely to purchase Promethean accessories since they just work within ActivInspire. This is the next big market – and Promethean look like they are getting themselves in at the start of the game. This is not a bad thing. It will be interesting to see how this develops.

What will be interesting is seeing how many schools take up the Promethean software. I have been in schools recently that are still using ActivPrimary version 2. They haven't even upgraded to v3 yet. How long before they take up the new version? Will schools that don't have Promethean boards realise they are legally allowed to use this new ActivInspire software? Will Smartboard schools install it as an additional piece of software?

I do need to stress, I am a neutral in all this. I am happy to plug and promote Smart or Promethean (or others) when I think they are doing good stuff. I do not work for Promethean. The above is my opinion only. But I do think this release could be a very good thing for users of all interactive whiteboards.

So..... what do **you** think?

Update May 2010: Looks like the terms and conditions around the use of this personal version have been changed quietly by Promethean. You now need to apply for a Teacher Consent Licence to use this software elsewhere. More details here. http://www.whiteboardblog.co.uk/2010/08/no-longer-activinspire-for-all/

No Longer ActivInspire for All?

Originally posted August 16 2010

http://www.whiteboardblog.co.uk/2010/08/no-longer-activinspire-for-all/

When ActivInspire was released last year there was much trumpeting over the use of the new Personal Edition. I wrote about what a good idea this was in my post "ActivInspire for All IWB Users?" (see previous pages).

I've noticed recently, however, on the ActivInspire website, a section that mentions a change to the terms of the licence, effective 30 April 2010.

Please note that as of 30 April 2010, new licensing terms and conditions apply to the use of ActivInspire Personal Edition software affecting use with non-Promethean products.

You are permitted to use ActivInspire Personal Edition with non-Promethean products **solely for the purpose of operating Promethean approved ActivInspire Publisher Created Resources** available from the Promethean Planet Store or from a Promethean Approved Publisher.

If you do wish to use your copy of ActivInspire Personal edition elsewhere then you need to apply for a Teacher Consent Licence which, according to the site:

The new Teacher Consent Licence allows teachers to use ActivInspire for other purposes with non-Promethean Products.

And if you want a Teacher Consent Licence you can apply for one online (http://bit.ly/hvdmYK) I haven't filled this in myself so don't know what happens after this. It might just allow you to use it, or it might ask for more info. Has anyone done this?

A full copy of the new terms and conditions can be seen here, (http://bit.ly/gHXnHw) which includes this line highlighted in red:

4.4 Use with Competitive Products: If You wish to Use the Software with any third party products which are comparable with or similar to Promethean Products (other than as provided in Clause 4.1), including but not limited to any projectors, interactive whiteboards, slates, tablets or learner response devices, then you must purchase a Professional Licence.

So it looks like quite a change from the initial promise of this software, which I am guessing comes from a large number of people downloading ActivInspire to use on cheap Chinese IWB's (or Hitachi boards) or the IWB-free projectors.

I can see why they have done it, but I'm rather concerned that most people I speak to still think the old terms and conditions apply and that you can run the cut down version of ActivInspire Personal on any IWB. I wonder how many users have been made aware of this change.

Now – if you are using ready-produced materials from the Promethean Planet website, then you are fine. Likewise if you've bought Promethean Flipcharts from a publisher. But technically you can't open any of my flipcharts for example....

Of course, if you have a cheaper board and want to run ActivInspire then it's best to purchase a licence for the Professional edition, so you get all the features of the software. It's well worth upgrading to the full version as you get so much more than the free version.

Thoughts?

From what I can tell Smart have made similar changes to their licence. I'm trying to track down an announcement about that too.

Update – I found out Smart's changes, they're covered on the next page.

Smart Notebook Licence Update

Originally posted August 16 2010

http://www.whiteboardblog.co.uk/2010/08/smart-notebook-licence-update/

Further to the article about Promethean's licence changes, I've managed to locate the new Smart Notebook licence as of 21 June 2010. You can download the pdf file here: http://bit.ly/g6T3XO

Basically, like Promethean, Smart are tightening up on what you are allowed to do with Smart Notebook software. The ability to install it on staff machines for preparation purposes is still there. But what they are being more explicit about is what you cannot use Smart Notebook on. To quote from the letter sent out by Smart in June.

A SMART Notebook licence is included with a SMART licensed product (IWB, voting set, slate etc.) and you are permitted to use the software on any computer connected to these Licensed Products. SMART Notebook software may also be used on a reasonable number of computers associated with your authority or school that are not connected to pen or touch-enabled devices. This permits teachers to use the software at home to create lessons for use on their Licensed Products in the classroom.

The licence agreement does not, however, normally permit the use of SMART Notebook software when a computer is connected to a restricted pen- or touch-enabled device ("Restricted Product"). Restricted Products include, but are not limited to, any touch-enabled or pen-enabled devices that are not on the Licensed Products list above, including the following:
· Interactive whiteboards
· Interactive projector systems
· Display screens
· Screen digitising devices or slates

The only exception to this is if you use a non-SMART slate/graphics tablet. You are allowed to use this if another Smart product is attached. But if you are using a wireless slate with a projector, you're not allowed to use Smart Notebook.

What Smart do make clear is that if you do with to access Smart Notebook files, then you can use their SMART Notebook Express web application, which can be found at http://express.smarttech.com/

So if you are using Smart Notebook on a non-Smart product, you are in breach of the licence. This hasn't changed, it's been like that for quite a while, but now they're being more explicit about it. At present I don't know of any way of buying additional licences for Smart Notebook to use on other boards or devices (IWB-free projectors) but maybe that will be something that will develop soon.

Don't forget – if you have Smartboards in your school, the licence does allow for staff to have it installed elsewhere for preparation of lesson resources (on a *"reasonable* number of machines"*, whatever that means…). Make sure you do this – it is a much better way of making resources to use in the lesson. You'd be amazed how many schools I go into where the staff have not been told this.

Promethean Flipchart Search Tool

Originally posted February 23 2010

http://www.whiteboardblog.co.uk/2010/02/promethean-flipchart-search-tool/

Just a quick post. You may not be aware that it's now possible to use the power of Google to search only for Promethean flipcharts using this custom search engine: http://bit.ly/fRHSG9

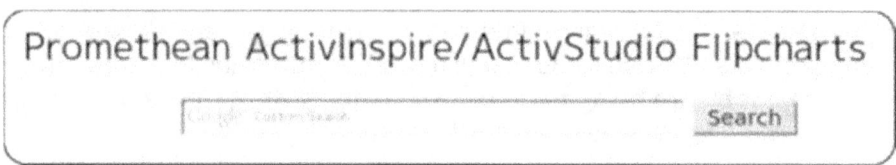

Smart Notebook Search Tool

http://www.whiteboardblog.co.uk/2009/07/smartboard-updates-gallery-collections-and-notebook-search/

If you are looking for Smart Notebook files produced by teachers around the world, it's now possible to search by keyword using SMART Notebook Lesson Search. This is powered by the Google Custom Search service.

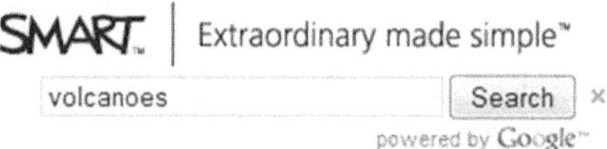

Update Jan 2011 – this is no longer active – sadly. But you can search the Smart Exchange here : http://exchange.smarttech.com

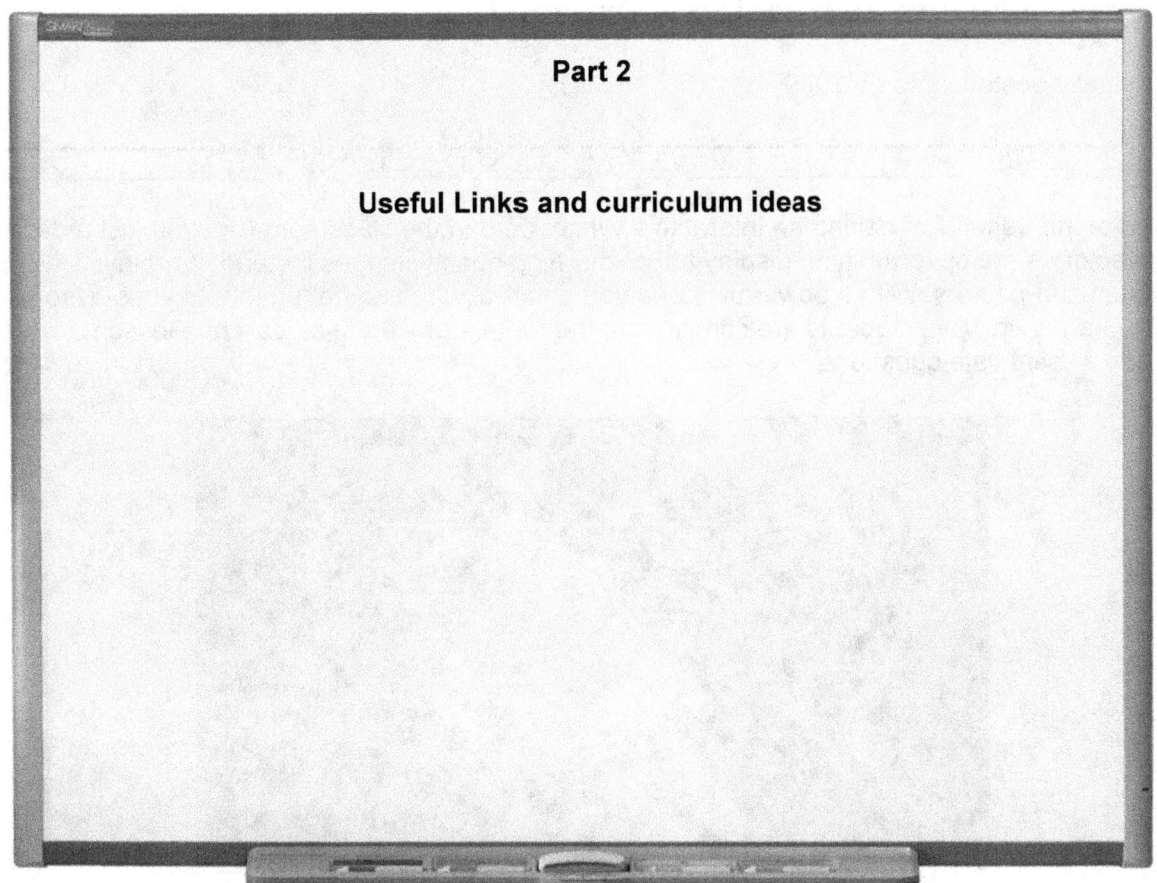

Part 2

Useful Links and curriculum ideas

Powerful Images to Give Lessons Punch

Originally posted June 23 2009

http://www.whiteboardblog.co.uk/2009/06/powerful-images-to-give-lessons-punch/

One of the benefits of having an Interactive Whiteboard in the classroom (or even just a data projector) is the opportunity to display full colour high quality images instead of grainy acetates or posters. With a powerful image you can really add some "punch" to your lesson. Put images up while students are coming into the room – use them as part of a lesson starter – stimulate questions.

http://www.flickr.com/photos/nasacommons/5134455469

What is going on here? Why is the astronaut wearing that suit? Why is it white? What would happen if he/she wasn't on that robotic arm? What do you think it would be like to be up there? What do you think he is thinking? Should we be sending people into space? What is keeping him up there? What do we mean by Orbit? etc. etc.

The Big Picture

One of my favourite sites for these kind of inspirational images is The Big Picture from the Boston Times. Every few days they post another set of images which never fail to make me go "wow".

Here is just a selection of the great images that you could use in different curriculum areas. This post is link heavy, so please head to the original to click them all : http://bit.ly/h9W9jD

- For Science; Mercury Images, Robots, Hubble Images, International Space Station, Earth and Environment, Animals, Zoos, Swine Flu.
- For Citizenship powerful images of the protests in Iran, Also Life in Iraq,
- For Geography – images of Cyclones, Earth Observed, Hurricanes from Above, Hurricane Ike
- For RE – Carnival, Easter, Holy Week, Hindu festival of colours, The Hajj, Christmas,
- For Art – La Princesse, Festival of Lights,

For Literacy – any and all of them could have a role in stimulating story writing, or class discussion on different topics.

And there are many more, plus it's growing every week with more images being added.

In a similar vein, The BBC website also has an "In Pictures" section which covers events in the news (http://bbc.in/eSyGnF) As does The Times (http://thetim.es/gFg4ee), The Telegraph (http://bit.ly/gwRFki) and The Guardian (http://bit.ly/ftSXH4). All worth bookmarking and checking from time to time.

Remember to attribute the source of these images when you use them in your lessons. These are still the copyright of the photographer so you need to be careful how you use and distribute these images.

Flickr

For those of you who are into photography – Flickr is the YouTube of photographs. Several thousand photos get uploaded to Flickr every minute. The quality can be patchy, but there are thousands of excellent photographers sharing their works on Flickr. (and a few dodgy photographers, like me!)

What makes Flickr useful is the ability to add a Creative Commons licence to your images which says how they can be used. Many people allow their photos to be used anywhere, as long as you attribute them as the source of the image. Many will also let their images be used commercially in this way as well. In my presentations I now use a lot of images from Flickr and always link the image back to its original Flickr page by way of acknowledging the photographer.

Flickr also has an area for Public Photo Collections which you can search here: http://www.flickr.com/commons/tags/

To help find creative commons images, there are several tools now which will let you search Flickr for CC images. My Favourite is FlickrCC – enter a tag to search for and it will return 36 thumbnails. Click on a thumbnail to see more information and to visit the original page on Flickr. http://flickrcc.bluemountains.net/

Other tools include; Compfight, Flickr Storm, and Simple Flickr CC Search.

The Creative Commons website now also provides a CC search engine for images and other resources as well as listings of tonnes of CC Image sites. http://search.creativecommons.org/

If you want to know more about Creative Commons, I have written a short guide which you can read on Scribd: http://scr.bi/f5omKb

You are free:

 to Share — to copy, distribute and transmit the work

 to Remix — to adapt the work

Under the following conditions:

 Attribution — You must attribute the work in the manner specified by the author or licensor (but not in any way that suggests that they endorse you or your use of the work).

 Share Alike — If you alter, transform, or build upon this work, you may distribute the resulting work only under the same, similar or a compatible license.

E2BN Gallery

Another useful gallery is the E2BN Educational Gallery of images. It's not anywhere near as comprehensive as Flickr, but some schools may block access to Flickr since there are adult images on there. http://gallery.nen.gov.uk/gallery-e2bn.html

Google Image Search

It would be wrong to talk about image searching without mentioning the Google Image search, which I use quite a lot. The drawback of the images it produces is that on the whole they are usually copyrighted images, or that the copyright of the image is unclear. This makes them tricky to use in educational resources that you want to redistribute.

A new addition to the Google Search is the ability to select the colour you are looking for. So instead of just looking for Flowers, you can look for only red flowers... It's a neat addition.

In summary, there is a wealth of image sources on the Internet that you can use to provide punch to your lessons.

Remember to not to choose images that are too small, or that look blocky when stretched to full screen. Test them out before the lesson to make sure they look OK. Show them as big as you can for maximum impact. Think about how you want to use them — what questions could you ask to stimulate your students thinking processes?

Update — Found this great blog post **with a few more images sources: 7 Awesome Newspaper Photoblogs.**

http://www.petapixel.com/2009/08/04/7-awesome-newspaper-photoblogs/

12 Useful Image Search Tools

Originally posted December 21 2010

http://www.whiteboardblog.co.uk/2010/12/12-useful-image-search-tools/

The internet is awash with fantastic images. The problem is finding images that are not breaching someone's copyright, which is often the case. For student projects is also good practice to have them attribute the source of their images.

Here's a few ways of getting images that let you find ones you are actually allowed to use.

Google Image Search

Google Image Search is excellent for finding images and is often the first place people check, but in its default setting it has a scattergun approach to copyright, pulling images in from everywhere. It is possible to change the settings of the search to look for images that are able to be reused. Go to Google Image Search, and below the search box click on **Advanced Search**.

Then under "**Usage Rights**", select "**Labelled for Reuse**". Images that are then returned in the search should then be able to be reused in projects and on blogs safely. Always remember to credit the original source of the image though.

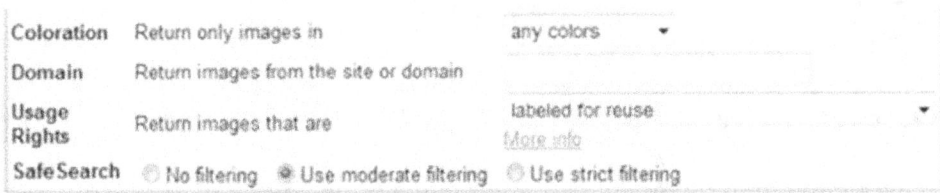

Flickr Commons and Wikipedia

Both Flickr and Wikipedia maintain libraries of creative commons/public domain images that are well worth a look. Flickr hosts images for many publicly-held photo libraries from museums around the world.

Wikipedia Commons : commons.wikimedia.org

Flickr Commons : www.flickr.com/commons

Flickr Search Engines

To help find creative commons images, there are several tools now which will let you search Flickr for CC images. My Favourite is FlickrCC (http://flickrcc.bluemountains.net/) enter a tag to search for and it will return a load thumbnails. Click on a thumbnail to see more information and to visit the original page on Flickr.

Alternatives to FlickrCC Include:

- Compfight : http://www.compfight.com/
- FlickrStorm : http://www.zoo-m.com/flickr-storm/
- Simple Flickr CC Search : http://johnjohnston.info/flickrCC/index.php
- Flickr Creative Commons Search : http://flickr.com/creativecommons/

Pics4Learning

Pics4Learning (http://pics4learning.com/) is a copyright-friendly image library for teachers and students. The Pics4Learning collection consists of thousands of images that have been donated by students, teachers, and amateur photographers. Unlike many Internet sites, permission has been granted for teachers and students to use all of the images donated to the Pics4Learning collection.

Veezzle

Veezzle (http://www.veezzle.com/) is a free stock photo search engine. The site pulls in images from many different stock photo sources, as well as Flickr. Click on the "download in HQ" button to view the image in its original site/page to be able to attribute correctly. Worth a look.

The Open Clip Art Library

The Open Clip Art Library (http://openclipart.org/) is a good source of open-source/public domain clip art resources. Registration is required for some of the features of the site, but it's free to join. You can browse without registering.

Also check out School Clip Art http://www.school-clip-art.com/

Searching for images on your IWB – a warning!

A quick tip if you are doing an image search live – on your IWB – in front of a class. Although you might be searching with the best of intentions – sometimes even the most innocuous search can throw up images that you may not want the students to see. Some search engines have a "safe search" filter, and the school filter may block them, but it's always best to cover yourself just in case.

Check your Projector remote for a **Blank** or a **Freeze** button (most should have at least one or the other) and freeze/blank the screen while you do the search on the computer. You can see the search on the regular monitor and check that nothing untoward is being displayed.

7 Sources of Creative Commons Audio For Podcasts

Originally posted January 19 2011

http://www.whiteboardblog.co.uk/2011/01/7-sources-of-creative-commons-audio-for-podcasts/

A podcast sounds better with a bit of music in it. Or some special audio effects. But the problem is that legally you can't just use any mp3 file from your music library since you will be breaching the copyright of the original artist. So move away from using your favourite bands – and look into the wide range of "pod-safe" or creative commons audio that are out there on the web.

Here are several websites that are worth a look – some provide whole music tracks, others provide sound effects.

Music Sites

Jamendo
http://www.jamendo.com/en/
Jamendo is a community of free, legal and unlimited music published under Creative Commons licenses. You can search by genre and style. Over 280,000 tracks on the site at the time of writing.

Free Music Archive
http://freemusicarchive.org/
The Free Music Archive is an interactive library of high-quality, legal audio downloads.

AudioFarm
http://en.audiofarm.org/
Like the two sites above, AudioFarm is an interactive library of audio downloads. As well as music it also hosts radio shows/podcasts from around the world.

CCMixter
http://www.ccmixter.org/
ccMixter is a community music site featuring remixes licensed under Creative Commons where you can listen to, sample, mash-up, or interact with music in whatever way you want. If your students are into sampling, remixing and mash-ups they can use the files from the site to remix, then upload back into ccMixter, for others to enjoy and re-sample.

Sound Effects

Soungle
http://soungle.com/
Soungle is a free site for finding all kind of sound FX and musical instruments samples from their online library. Search results of a keyword search are displayed ten to a page. Clicking on play icon allows you to preview a file. Download button instantly downloads the sound effect or musical instrument sample file.

FreeSound
http://www.freesound.org/
The Freesound Project is a collaborative database of Creative Commons licensed sounds. Freesound focuses only on sound, not songs. You need to register to download, but it's free.

Soundbible
http://soundbible.com/
SoundBible.com is the encyclopaedia of free sound clips, offering free and royalty free sounds. They update regularly.

In addition

Don't forget the Creative Commons Search Engine : http://search.creativecommons.org/ which you can use to search many different creative commons sources from one page.

10 avatar generators for profile pictures

Originally posted 22 Jan 2010

http://www.whiteboardblog.co.uk/2010/01/10-avatar-generators-for-profile-pictures/

With the release of the James Cameron movie (which I highly recommend you see, by the way) everyone has now heard the word Avatar. In computing, an avatar is often the name used for the little picture you use on profile pages for things like blogs, twitter etc.

If you are blogging with students – it's recommended that you don't use real photographs of the students. A fun alternative is to create a cartoon avatar instead.

Here are 10 websites that you can use to create fun avatars. Some allow you to save the finished creation as a jpg for free. If not, then use the print screen button to copy the screen, paste into a paint program, crop and save as a jpg.

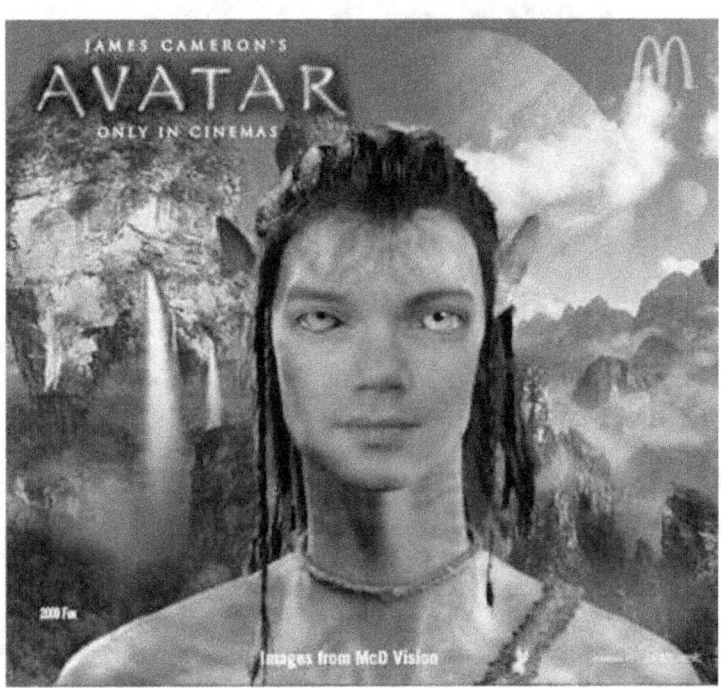

1. WeeMee -Create a mini version of yourself, add accessories. There's plenty of scope for customisation of your avatar. http://www.weeworld.com/

2. South park studio – turn yourself into a South Park character http://www.sp-studio.de/

3. HeroMachine 2.5 – Turn yourself into a super hero character. This would also be great as a part of a digital storytelling resource or story starter. http://bit.ly/e0aKPD

4. FaceYourManga.com Create a character in the style of a manga comic book http://www.faceyourmanga.com/homepage.php?lang=eng

5. Ultimate Flash Face v0.42b a bit like a police photofit. http://www.faceyourmanga.com/

6. Make yourself in lego – Produce a lego character that looks like you. Or turn yourself into a Stormtrooper wizard. Is up to you 😃 http://bit.ly/e59YJ3

7. Simpsons Movie – Ever wanted to be a Simpsons character? Now you can create your own yellow-skinned doppelganger in the style of the Simpsons. http://www.simpsonsmovie.com/

8. Mr. Picassohead – become an abstract piece of work in the style of Picasso. Put your eyes and ears wherever you want! http://www.mrpicassohead.com/

9. BuiLD YouR WiLD SeLF – Create an avatar out of bits and pieces of humans and other animals – head, arms, legs, clothes, eyes, mouth, tail, wings, shells ... just pick the parts you like and assemble them together http://www.buildyourwildself.com/

10. My Mii Avatar Generator – create a Mii in the style of the characters found on the Wii computer console. http://www.myavatareditor.com/

If you want more of these sites, the full list can be found on my Delicious list here: http://delicious.com/dannynic/avatar

Plus – since writing, the Avatar generator from the James Cameron "Avatar" movie is back up at: http://www.avatarizeyourself.com/

Make a Monster

Originally posted February 25 2009

http://www.whiteboardblog.co.uk/2009/02/make-a-monster/

Yesterday I decided to dust off my rudimentary Flash skills and have a go at making a new flash resource to use on an interactive whiteboard with younger pupils.

I wanted to make something that could be used to stimulate writing or discussion like the Superhero generator etc. So I had a go at a Make a Monster activity. You can view it here: http://bit.ly/eZvMVt

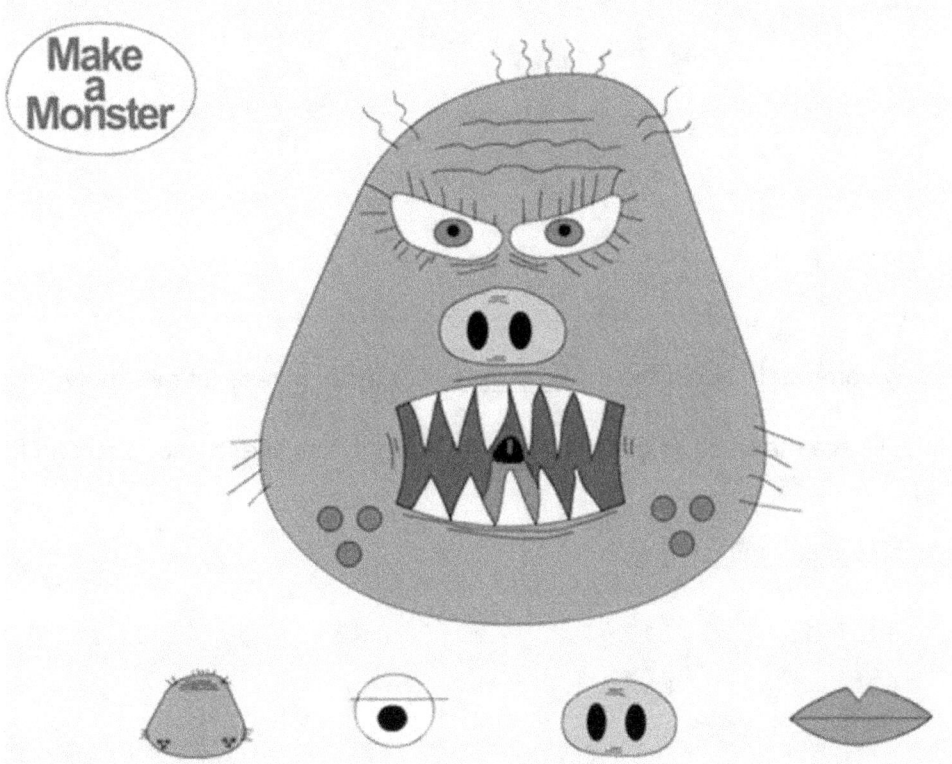

Click on the icons at the bottom of the screen to change the face, eyes, nose and mouth. I've put the icons at the bottom of the screen to make it easy to reach.

Once you've built your monster you could use the IWB screen capture tools, or Print Screen button and paste a copy into your software of choice. Pupils could then write about the monster.

You could write key words to describe your monster on your page – then drag them to another page where you have a partially completed writing frame. If you have Smart Notebook you can view both pages at the same time by clicking the Dual Page button, but you could just drag the words onto the next page using the Page Sorter in both Smart and Promethean.

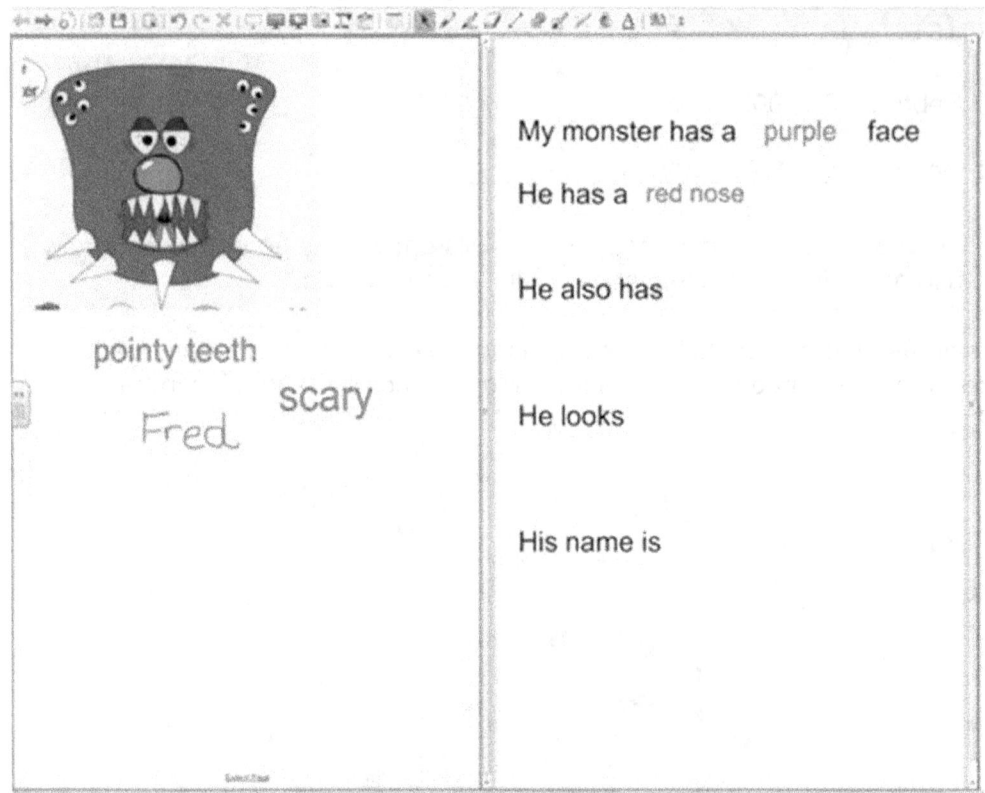

If you have any comments about the Make a Monster game, please let me know.

If you like this, I have made other games which you might also like to use. You can find them all on my Think Bank website. :

http://www.think-bank.com/iwb/flash/

20 Interactive Whiteboard Resources for Teachers

Originally posted July 19 2009

http://www.whiteboardblog.co.uk/2009/07/20-interactive-whiteboard-resources-for-teachers/

Interactive whiteboards are a great way for teachers to engage classrooms in learning. These tools are also cost effective. The Internet has tons of free sources to help teachers learn about and use IWBs with students. Here is a list of 20 interactive whiteboard resources and activities guaranteed to stimulate learning:

General Resources

TeacherLED
http://www.teacherled.com/
TeacherLED is a site dedicated to making the use of Interactive Whiteboards (IWB) easier and more productive. This comprehensive site features resources to use with IWBs in math, English, and geometry.

SMART
http://exchange.smarttech.com
This SMART Board interactive whiteboard site provides several lesson plans and activities for teachers to use in the classroom. SMART lessons are available for a variety of ages and subjects.

Topmarks
http://www.topmarks.co.uk/INTERACTIVE.ASPX
With some of the best free educational materials for IWBs, Topmarks is a great resource for finding IWB lesson plans and activities. This educational site also features teacher resources, educational sites for classroom, and homework help.

Interactive Whiteboard in the Classroom
http://www.fsdb.k12.fl.us/rmc/tutorials/whiteboards.html
This site for whiteboard users features tutorials, interactive websites, and software.

Eduscapes
http://eduscapes.com/sessions/smartboard/
This guide to interactive whiteboards explains different activities and resources that can be used with IWBs. Eduscapes is a good starting place for teachers who are just beginning to use this technology in the classroom.

Games and Activities

PBS
http://pbskids.org/smartboard/
PBS provides a collection of fun, interactive SMART Board games. All of the games featured on this site are age appropriate and screened by educators.

MathFrame.co.uk
http://www.mathsframe.co.uk/
This site, created by a school teacher, houses several interactive math games specifically designed for IWBs. All activities are aimed at reinforcing mathematical concepts and skills.

BBC History Game
http://www.bbc.co.uk/schools/famouspeople/
BBC offers several interactive activities that can be used with interactive whiteboards. This Famous People history game is a great way to teach elementary children about historical figures.

Scholastic
http://www.scholastic.com/interactivewhiteboards/
Scholastic provides interactive whiteboard lessons for phonics, math, science, and history. This site also features a search engine for finding more lessons across North America.

Crickweb
http://www.crickweb.co.uk
Crickweb.co.uk provides free resources for use with interactive whiteboards. These math activities are designed to teach elementary students the basics of math.

Math Playground
http://www.mathplayground.com/mathtv.html
The Math Playground offers interactive math activities for middle schoolers. These games and activities work well for teachers who want to engage the entire class.

Classbrain
http://www.classbrain.com/
This games site features several interactive math games that work with IWBs. A fun game worth trying with students is Regrouping.

Funbrain
http://www.funbrain.com/
Funbrain offers several interactive educational games for use with IWBs. These fun games cover a range of subjects and grades.

Kerpoof
http://www.kerpoof.com/
Kerpoof is an educational interactive website from the Walt Disney Company that can be used with IWBs. This site is a great way for children to create, discover, and learn.

Skeleton of the Beast
http://dsc.discovery.com/convergence/beasts/build/jigsaw.html
This interactive game from Discovery Education is a useful learning tool for IWBs. Skeleton of the Beast features four skill level timed games that teach children about prehistoric animals.

Xpeditions
http://www.nationalgeographic.com/xpeditions/atlas/
Xpeditions from National Geographic provides an atlas that can be used on interactive whiteboards. This atlas explores every region of the world.

Periodic Table
http://periodic.lanl.gov/default.htm
This interactive periodic table site was designed for educational use by elementary to high school students. The site works with interactive whiteboards to introduce and engage children in learning the element table.

Archiving Early America
http://www.earlyamerica.com/series.html
Archiving Early America features a range of short videos on American history that are perfect for use on IWBs.

Memorial Hall Museum
http://www.memorialhall.mass.edu/home.html
This free online museum features a complete interactive website for teachers. IWB teachers can view collections, online exhibits, and games.

Place the State
http://bensguide.gpo.gov/flash/states_puzzle_lines2.html
Place the State is an interactive geography game from Bensguide.gpo.gov. This resource can be used with IWBs to teach students about U.S. states.

10 More Cool Teaching Resources for Your Whiteboard

Originally posted February 11 2010

http://www.whiteboardblog.co.uk/2010/02/10-more-cool-teaching-resources-for-your-whiteboard/

Engaging students in some classroom topics can be difficult. But with the help of your interactive whiteboard you can get and keep your students interested in what you are trying to teach them. Here are 10 especially cool whiteboard resources for grades K-12.

Stellarium
http://www.stellarium.org/
This free planetarium software is perfect for astronomy lessons. Stellarium displays a realistic 3D sky, complete with planets, major moons, more than 600,000 stars, and constellations from 10 cultures.

Illuminations
http://illuminations.nctm.org/
Created by the National Council of Teachers of Mathematics, Illumination provides more than 100 interactive math games and activities for students in grades pre-K through 12.

FreeRice
http://www.freerice.com/
FreeRice is an amazing trivia game from the United Nations World Food Program. Rice is donated to hungry people every time visitors answer trivia questions correctly. Trivia categories include art, chemistry, math, English vocabulary and grammar, geography, and language learning.

Signed Stories
http://www.signedstories.com/page/index.cfm
Signed Stories features videos of stories being told with sign language and subtitles. Although the site is designed primarily for deaf children it would be useful to any classroom interested in learning more about sign language.

Sheppard Software
http://www.sheppardsoftware.com/web_games_menu.htm
Sheppard Software provides a wide range of free educational web games for students. Covered topics include animals, science, chemistry, health, history, math, and vocabulary.

Fit Brains
http://www.fitbrains.com/
Designed by a clinical neuropsychologist and brain health expert, Fit Brains is an online gaming platform with puzzles and other "brain games." Players can track their progress and win trophies and achievements when they do well.

Tutpup
http://www.tutpup.com/
Tutpup is a competitive game site that allows students to play interactive web games with other children around the world. All of the games on Tutpup focus on math or spelling.

Spelling City
http://www.spellingcity.com/

Spelling City is a free online learning platform with 10 learning games and more than 40,000 spelling words. The site also offers how-to videos to help teachers integrate Spelling City into the curriculum.

The Eco Zoo
http://ecodazoo.com/

The Eco Zoo is a 3D environment that can be used to teach students about environment, ecology, and eco-friendly living. Content can be viewed in Japanese or English.

NASA Space Place
http://spaceplace.nasa.gov/en/kids/

This award-winning NASA website is a good place to find videos, animations, and games that teach kids about space science and technology. Nearly all of the materials on this site would work well with an interactive whiteboard.

11 Ideas for Music Lessons on Your Interactive Whiteboard

Originally posted July 24 2009

http://www.whiteboardblog.co.uk/2009/07/11-ideas-for-music-lessons-on-your-interactive-whiteboard/

I've been asked several times recently on Twitter to recommend ideas for Music lessons that involve the interactive whiteboard.

So here are 10 free resources, and one excellent paid-for resource, that will help you make music on your interactive whiteboard. More can be found on my delicious list.
http://delicious.com/dannynic/music+iwb

MoodStream
http://moodstream.gettyimages.com/

Moodstream is a really interesting tool. It combines images (from Getty Images) and audio tracks to suit your mood. Would be good to investigate how different sounds and tunes affect our how we feel. Choose from combinations of happy/sad, calm/lively, warm/cool etc. Is really interesting to leave running for a while and see what it does.

Shaun the Sheep's Bleat Box
http://bbc.in/gcZwl0

Make music with Shaun the Sheep of Wallace and Gromit fame. Click on a sheep to make them bleat! Great fun. Includes a free play mode or a memory game.

Making Music from Help Kidz Learn
http://www.helpkidzlearn.com/creative/making_music.html

Simply press a piano key or run your finger down the keys on a touch screen, to play the notes. Mouse users can click on the keys. The keys are in different bright colours and marked with the note they play.

Virtual Drum Kit
http://www.kenbrashear.com/

Ken Brashear has made a giant drum kit that you play simply by hitting the different hotspots on the image. Very therapeutic.

Music Match Game
http://www.y8.com/games/Music_Match

This game helps you learn how to play the piano and read music. You can learn the notes, learn the keys or both.

Drum Machine
http://www.onemotion.com/flash/drum-machine/

An interactive drum machine that lets you build up different beats to create your own drum track which you can then export as a swf file.

Poisson Rouge Piano
http://www.poissonrouge.com/piano/index.htm

A simple interactive piano that lets you produce a tune and then play it back. Will show the musical notation at the same time.

Muxicall
http://www.muxicall.com/

A collaborative "wall of music" Click on the notes to play a track, but other people can also be using it at the same time and play music between you!

Toy Theatre Music
http://www.toytheater.com/music.php

4 different games here. Compose your own music, create drum beats, music maker and piano puppet. Try them out!

Musical Monsters
http://www.q-and-d.co.uk/musicalmonsters1.htm

A paid-for resource that is wonderful for KS1 is Musical Monsters from Q& Multimedia. Create rhythms and melodies by putting the singing creatures onto the music board, then listen to – and watch – the results.

And finally... **Reindeer Orchestra**
http://dingo.care2.com/cards/new/0422/Do-a-rain-deer.swf

Probably best left until close to Christmas, but click on the reindeer's noses to make them sing. Choose from several Christmas carols, or free play mode.

More links can be found on my delicious list at: http://delicious.com/dannynic/music+iwb

Update: Following this tweet from GirlfromPBO on twitter:

girlfromPBO @*dannynic* *great links in your post & bkmks but you're missing our wiki full of teacher made lessons from across the US! mustech.pbworks.com*

So for some more good ideas for music – also head over and check out their wiki at: http://mustech.pbworks.com

12 Art Resources for your IWB

Originally posted 8th March 2010

http://www.whiteboardblog.co.uk/2010/03/120-art-resources-for-your-iwb/

There's nothing better than playing with an art program on an interactive whiteboard and literally drawing with your finger. It really works like a massive graphics tablet. And there are some excellent, free, online drawing packages. Some are quite simple, and others really mimic real-world art materials.

For the entire list, check out my Delicious page under Art + IWB, but here are a few of my favourites:

Sumopaint
http://www.sumopaint.com/home/
This is an excellent resource – a free, fully featured paint package in your browser. Very impressive. http://www.sumopaint.com/home/

Sketchpad
http://mugtug.com/sketchpad/
Another paint package demonstrating the capability of the new HTML5 – this doesn't use Flash, which is quite interesting. If that last sentence made no sense, don't panic. Just have a play and paint something!

Livebrush
http://www.livebrush.com/
Another free paint package, that should work well on an IWB. The size of the brush stroke depends on the speed you drag across the page, the faster you go the broader the brush stroke. Needs Adobe Air, so check you can install it at school.

Dreezle
http://www.dreezle.com/
A simple, java-based paint application.

Aviary
http://aviary.com/home
A fantastic site. Aviary contains a stack of great free tools, it even has a sound editor!

Sketch
http://www.onemotion.com/flash/sketch-paint
The brush tool gives a really realistic effect and you can alter lots of different variables if you want – or just paint away!

Crayola Digi-Colour
http://www.crayola.com/coloring_application/
Choose from a variety of Crayola products including crayons, pencils and stamps. If you want to do something more off-line then there are colouring pages to print out as well. The Crayola site also has a lot of information for teachers including lesson plans here:
http://bit.ly/i8HBAk

Bomomo
http://bomomo.com/
I love this. It's brilliant for making abstract drawings. Some of the pens are really fun. Quite hypnotic to watch

Imagination Cubed
http://www.imaginationcubed.com/
This has been around a while, but it's still really fun. You can even collaborate with friends on a joint drawing.

Splashup
http://www.splashup.com/
An online paint package very similar to Sumo Paint. (There's also a Lite version too for netbooks and less powerful computers)

Mondrimat
http://www.stephen.com/mondrimat
Create blocks of colour in the style of Piet Mondrian.

This is Sand
http://thisissand.com/
Another odd, but very hypnotic application. Make pictures by piling up sand. Fun.

As a bonus, check out these three extra sites:

Artpad - a quick and simple paint package. Share and see what others have painted in the gallery. http://artpad.art.com/artpad/painter/

Jackson Pollock : http://bit.ly/hG7D2f

Do Ink: http://www.doink.com/

10 Primary Science Resources for your Whiteboard

Originally posted February 1st 2010

http://www.whiteboardblog.co.uk/2010/02/10-primary-science-resources-for-your-whiteboard/

Here are 10 websites that will prove useful to any teacher of Primary Science looking for things to use on their interactive whiteboard:

The Children's University of Manchester. Several excellent interactive resources for Primary Science. http://www.childrensuniversity.manchester.ac.uk/

NGFL Cymru : Early years, KS1 and KS2 Science resources from the Welsh Grid for Learning. http://www.ngfl-cymru.org.uk/eng/vtc-home/vtc-ey-home/vtc-ey-kuw

Simple Science : I love these excellent science song videos. Great for lesson starters or reinforcement of key facts. http://www.simplescience.net/index.html

IWB.org.uk: KS1 and KS2 interactive science resources (and other subjects) http://bit.ly/gt64Bg and http://bit.ly/fEjqWH

BBC Bitesize. Always worth a visit, there are some excellent resources here for Ks2. http://www.bbc.co.uk/schools/ks2bitesize/science/

BBC Learning Zone - lots of videos to use in Science and other lessons. http://www.bbc.co.uk/learningzone/clips/

Birmingham Grid for Learning – some excellent resources here, and links to other sites. http://www.bgfl.org/bgfl/15.cfm?s=15&p=249,index

Crickweb – great flash-based games for KS1 and Ks2 Science. http://www.crickweb.co.uk/ks2science.html

Fossweb - US site with some interesting interactive science activities. http://www.fossweb.com/

Primary Resources – Home to some great resources – IWB files, powerpoints, links and more! Also worth checking out is Teaching Ideas, which is on very similar lines. http://www.primaryresources.co.uk/science/science.htm

Don't forget, if your school subscribes to Espresso, there are some excellent resources for EYFS, KS1 and KS2 in there. (OK, so that makes 11, but Espresso is well worth a look): http://www.espresso.co.uk/

10 Secondary Science Resources for your Whiteboard

Originally posted February 11th 2010

http://www.whiteboardblog.co.uk/2010/02/10-secondary-science-resources-for-your-whiteboard/

As a companion post to 10 Primary Science ideas for your Whiteboard, here are 10 secondary school Science websites you might enjoy:

Absorb Learning from Yenka
http://www.absorblearning.com/en/Free_online_Absorb_resources/
Hundreds of free IWB animations for KS4/KS5 Chemistry and Physics.

ARKive
http://www.arkive.org/
thousands of free wildlife videos and photographs, including great Darwin resources.

FreezeRay
http://freezeray.com/
large bank of interactive Science animations for KS3 and Ks4.

Periodic Table of Videos
http://www.periodicvideos.com/
videos of all the different elements of the periodic table.

Centre of the Cell
http://www.centreofthecell.org/lessonplans/index.php
cell biology interactive resources.

Skool.co.uk
http://lgfl.skoool.co.uk/index.aspx
excellent science animations and interactives for KS3/4 Science.

PhET – interactive simulations
http://phet.colorado.edu/en/simulations/
fun, java-based physics simulations.

Astronomy Picture of the Day
http://apod.nasa.gov/apod/
Provide the Wow factor with some of these images.

KScience
http://www.kscience.co.uk/animations/anim_1.htm
Animations for KS3/4 Science.

Biology in Motion
http://www.biologyinmotion.com/
Animations for KS4/5 Biology.

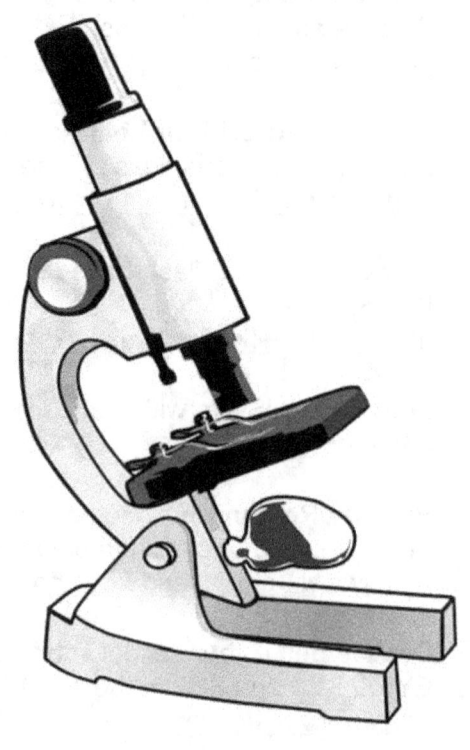

Biology on the IWB: 10 Quick Ideas

Originally posted March 21 2008

http://www.whiteboardblog.co.uk/2008/03/biology-on-the-iwb-10-quick-ideas/

Here are some quick ideas for using an IWB for Biology teaching.

1. Sequence the stages in Mitosis or Meiosis using images or statements

2. Drag and Drop animals and arrows to create Food Chains and Webs

3. Label diagrams of the various body systems using images captured from the Internet or from the gallery.

4. Investigate genetic crossing using drag and drop punnet squares. In Smart you could use the Infinite Cloner on the B and b, or just stack several letters on top of each other so when you drag one down, the rest remain.

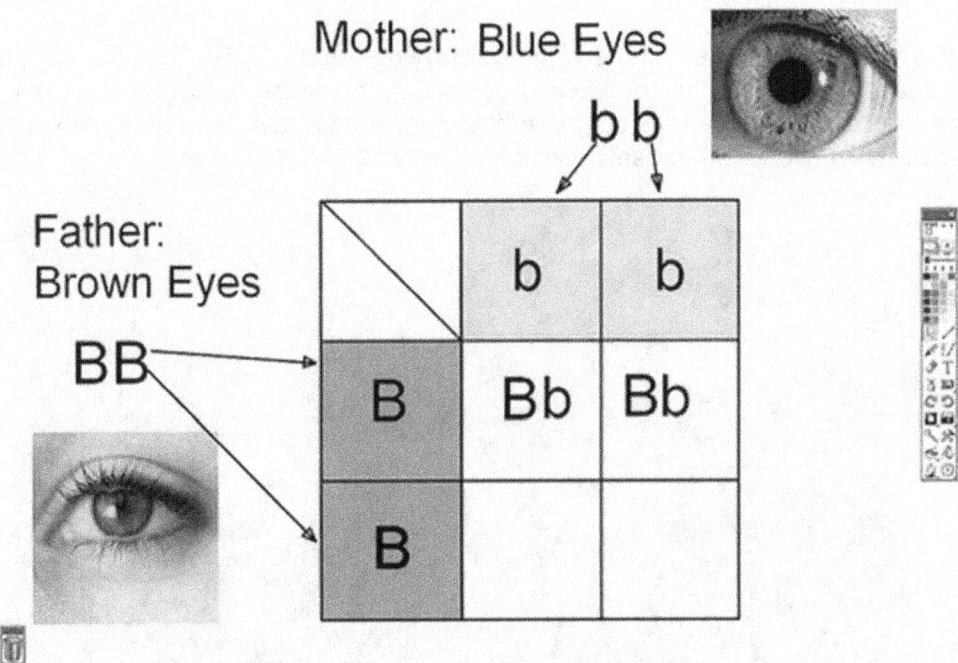

5. Use the camera to capture pictures from the internet to illustrate a lesson on the dangers of alcohol and smoking. Or use the Inside Body PowerPoint presentations from the ASE as a source of images. http://bit.ly/gl75iJ (archived on STEM site)

6. Sort foods into 'healthy' and 'unhealthy' foods, then use as basis for a discussion about whether there is actually any such thing as an unhealthy food.

7. Simulate how to use a quadrat before going out into the field using random dots and a square annotation, or the square spotlight tool.

8. Combine the IWB with a digital microscope to demonstrate and label slides as a whole class.

9. <u>Keyword Plenary</u> – pupils choose keywords from a selection, drag them into the middle of the screen and use them to explain one thing they've learned from the lesson.

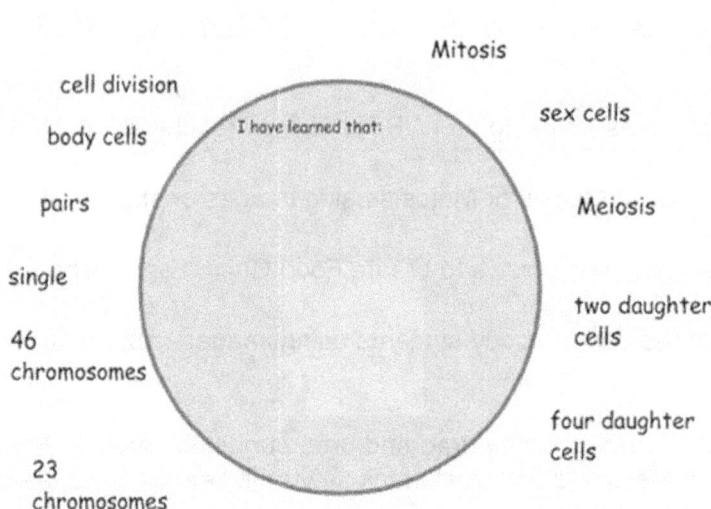

10. Use a visualiser (Document camera) when carrying out dissections of the heart or flowers to make it easier for the whole class to see what is going on. Use the camera tool to capture images during the various stages of the dissection and add labels to the images. A cheaper alternative would be to use a webcam clamped to a retort stand

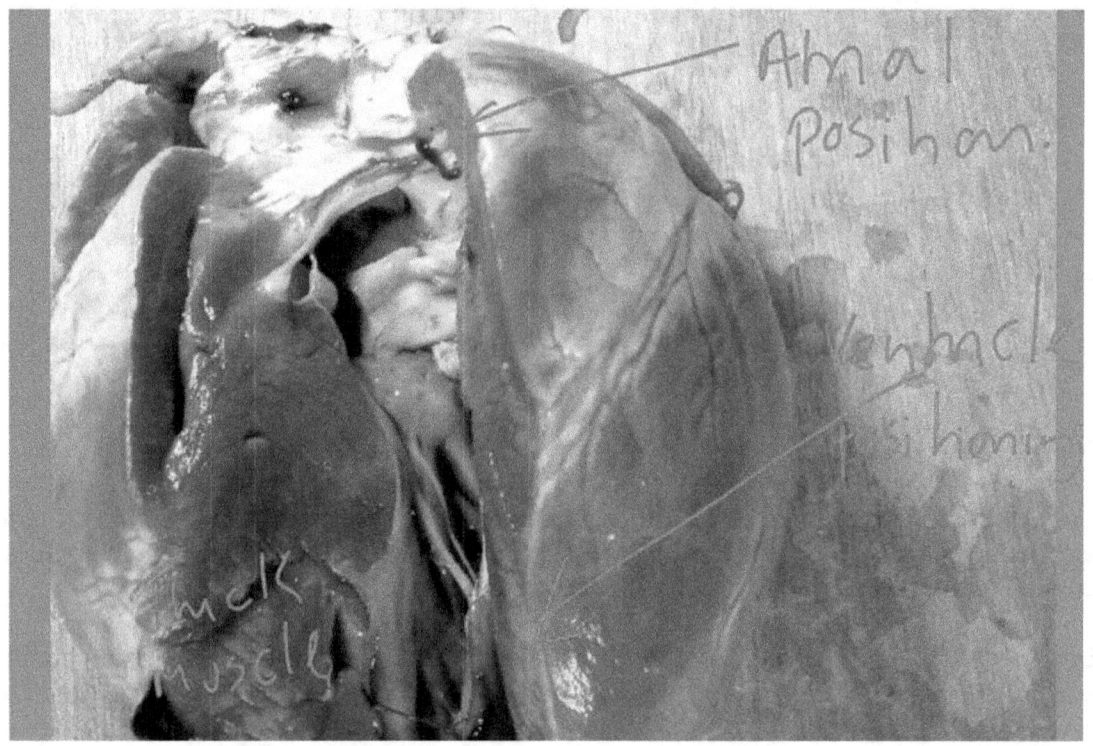

Science Notebook Files

Originally posted March 18 2008

http://www.whiteboardblog.co.uk/2008/03/science-notebook-files/

Two years ago I produced a pack of Smart Notebook files for Steljes, the distributors of Smartboards over here in the UK. They formed part of a teacher's pack that was distributed to schools around the UK.

The files were also available via the Steljes Software site. For now, that site is no longer up, and the files are no longer available online.

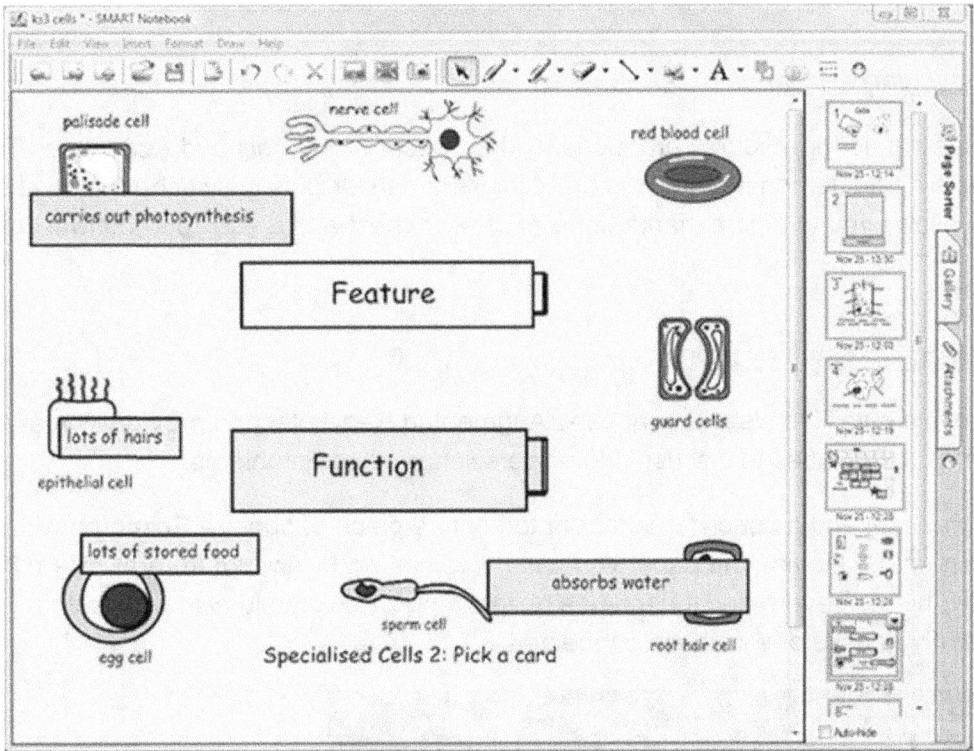

I have copied the files onto my Think Bank website so that Smartboard users can still access them. Each file has a corresponding teachers' guide in pdf format.

The six lesson packs cover the following topics:

- The Blast Furnace (KS4)
- Cells (KS3)
- Forces (KS3)
- Metals (Ks3)
- Muscles and Joints (KS4)
- Reflection and Refraction (KS4)

To download the files, and the corresponding teachers guide, visit:
http://think-bank.com/iwb/steljes.html

3 Augmented Reality Tools for Science

Originally posted January 5 2011

http://www.whiteboardblog.co.uk/2011/01/3-augmented-reality-tools-for-science/

Augmented reality makes use of a webcam to superimpose animations over the world you usually experience. When the webcam sees special markers printed on paper it replaces them with a 3d model which you can move and manipulate simply my moving the piece of paper around.

Here are three augmented reality tools that would be useful for science teaching:

LearnAR

http://www.learnar.org/

LearnAR is a paid-for resource produced by the Specialist Schools and Academies Trust, but there is a free demonstration version of their Human Organs activity on their website. This tool allows you to hold a marker in front of your chest and a see your internal organs.

SciMorph

http://scimorph.greatfridays.com/

Scimorph is a cute little website that uses Augmented Reality tech to provide Primary school pupils with opportunities to discuss and solve science-based problems.

Using a webcam and a special marker printed onto a piece of paper – Scimorph will appear on the screen. By moving the paper you can move him and view him from all sides. It's a little fiddly, but persevere and it becomes quite simple. This should also work with a visualiser if you have one of those connected.

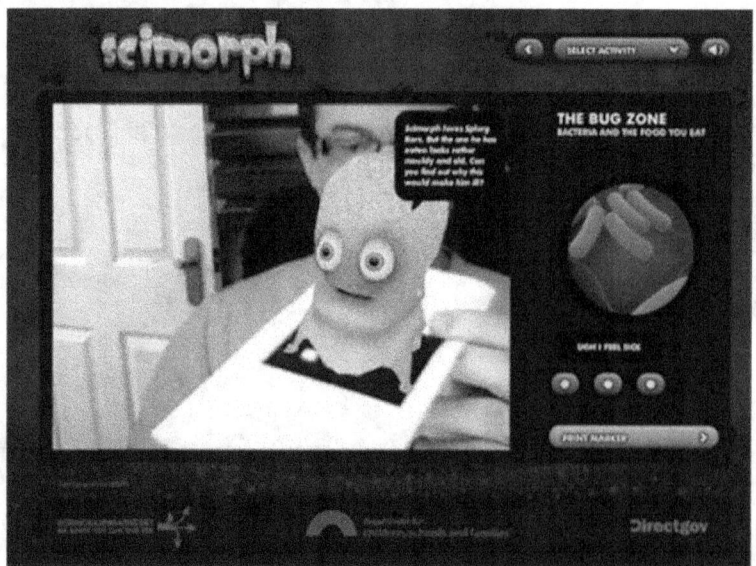

There are several scimorph zones you can investigate – The Bug Zone to look at microbes, Gravity Pulls and The Vibe Zone to investigate sound.

Each zone provides a series of questions or scenarios. Scimorph is not a complicated simulation or anything like that. The main purpose is to promote discussion between children about the science underlying the different situations.

Guidance on how to use the resource can be found here. It does provide a useful introduction to Augmented Reality technology and is worth checking out if you want to try something a little different with your class. Visit it here: http://scimorph.greatfridays.com/

Rainforest Life / Loris the Lemur

http://bit.ly/e0aBKh

Produced by London Zoo, Rainforest Life gives you the chance to have your very own Augmented reality lemur, Loris, sitting in the palm of your hand.

Loris doesn't do a lot, and you can't really interact with her. But she's very cute.

As before, you'll need a webcam to get this to work, and you'll need to print out a special marker on a page for the camera to detect.

The Great Plant Hunt

Originally posted January 22 2010

http://www.whiteboardblog.co.uk/2010/01/the-great-plant-hunt/

To mark the 200th anniversary of Charles Darwin's birth the Royal Botanic Gardens, Kew, commissioned and funded by the Wellcome Trust, has created The Great Plant Hunt. This project will encourage Primary school children to explore the natural world around them and join other schools in the biggest ever school science project.

http://www.greatplanthunt.org/

The Great Plant Hunt invites primary school children to follow in the footsteps of Darwin by going on nature walks in and around their school grounds. They'll find out more about plants and in the process learn key scientific skills. There is a lot more information, and links to resources in the Teacher Area of the site.

In addition to the activity ideas, there are also interactive resources to use on an IWB such as Plant or Not?, Herby Havoc and Sunflower Survival.

All teaching materials and resources are available to download – so you can make your own Treasure Chest of resources to run The Great Plant Hunt completely free.

http://www.greatplanthunt.org/

The History of Vaccines

Originally posted October 4 2010

http://www.whiteboardblog.co.uk/2010/10/the-history-of-vaccines/

Here's a site that will be of interest to GCSE and A Level Biology teachers. The History of Vaccines is an informational, educational website created by The College of Physicians of Philadelphia, the oldest professional society in the United States.

http://www.historyofvaccines.org/

The College has created The History of Vaccines to provide a chronicle of the history of vaccination, from the time before Edward Jenner, to the defeat of polio in the Western Hemisphere, to cutting-edge approaches to novel vaccines and vaccine delivery. The site aims to increase public knowledge and understanding of the ways in which vaccines, toxoids, and passive immunization work, how they have been developed, and the role they have played in the improvement of human health.

Interactive resources demonstrate how vaccines work, how vaccines are made, how to visualize risk, and more. Explore these activities to discover the past, present, and future of vaccination and infectious disease.

The site includes media-rich timelines on yellow fever, polio, smallpox, measles, diphtheria, and other diseases; the educational activities on how vaccines work, how vaccines are made, and how the scientific method is employed; the variety of articles on social and medical issues surrounding vaccination; and the gallery, which houses over 400 images and videos.

The History of Vaccines offers resources for use in biology and health courses. The content is targeted to high school students but can be adapted for use in other settings. Lesson plans are included - http://bit.ly/frkpTS .

It's an excellent resource that's well worth bookmarking: http://www.historyofvaccines.org/

Algodoo – 2D Physics Simulator

Originally posted April 9 2010

http://www.whiteboardblog.co.uk/2010/04/algodoo-2d-physics-simulator/

I've been a big fan of some of the real world physics games that have appeared on the PC in recent years, and also on the iPhone, making use of its touchscreen.

One of my favourite pieces of software is called Phun, which is a brilliant 2D physics sandbox for PC, Linux and Mac. You can hand draw shapes, pin them in place, join them together with chains and springs and much more. You can create some very complicated systems.

Phun is freeware, and you can get the latest version from here: www.phunland.com.

Phun was developed by Emil Ernerfeldt in his MSc thesis project at the Department of Computing Science at Umeå university, Sweden. Emil now works for Algoryx Simulation AB – and he has continued to work on Phun – and has now produced a commercial version designed for education market called Algodoo which you can get from www.algodoo.com

As well as springs and gears, Algodoo also deals in light and optics – which starts to make it a rival to other software such as Crocodile Physics.

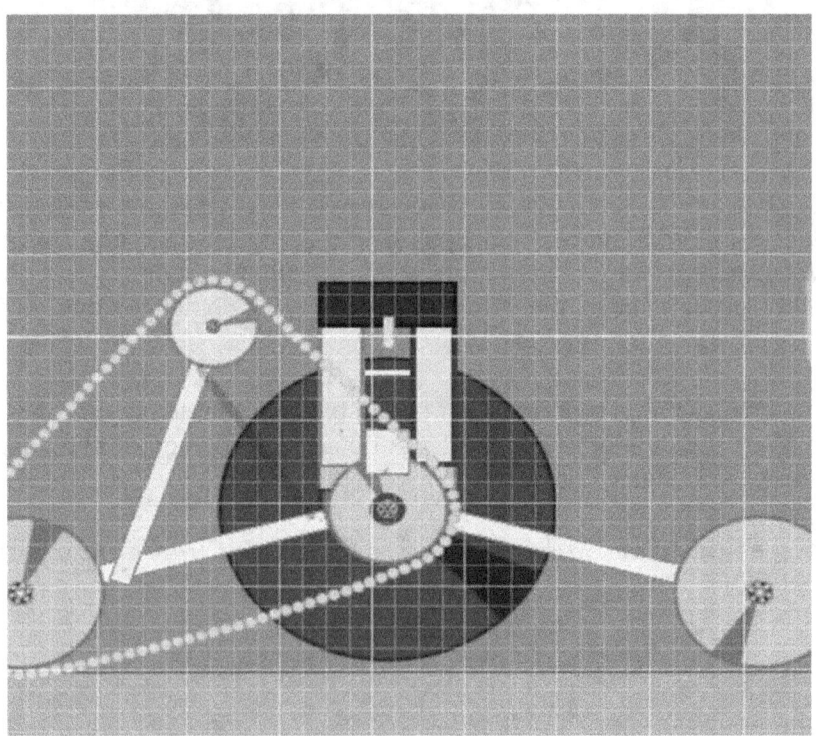

They've produced plenty of ready-made scenes that you can download and try out, as well as lesson plans which cover KS1 up to KS4.

Pricewise it looks very good- a single license is about €29, with bulk deals bringing that down quite a lot. You can also get a trial version of Algodoo as well to see what if can do.

Phun is still freeware – so try that to see if you like it. If you don't want all the bells and whistles then stick with Phun.

It is a very cute bit of software and works brilliantly on an interactive whiteboard – but would also be good with a graphics tablet.

www.algodoo.com

See also:

http://www.whiteboardblog.co.uk/2008/04/phun-phun-phun/

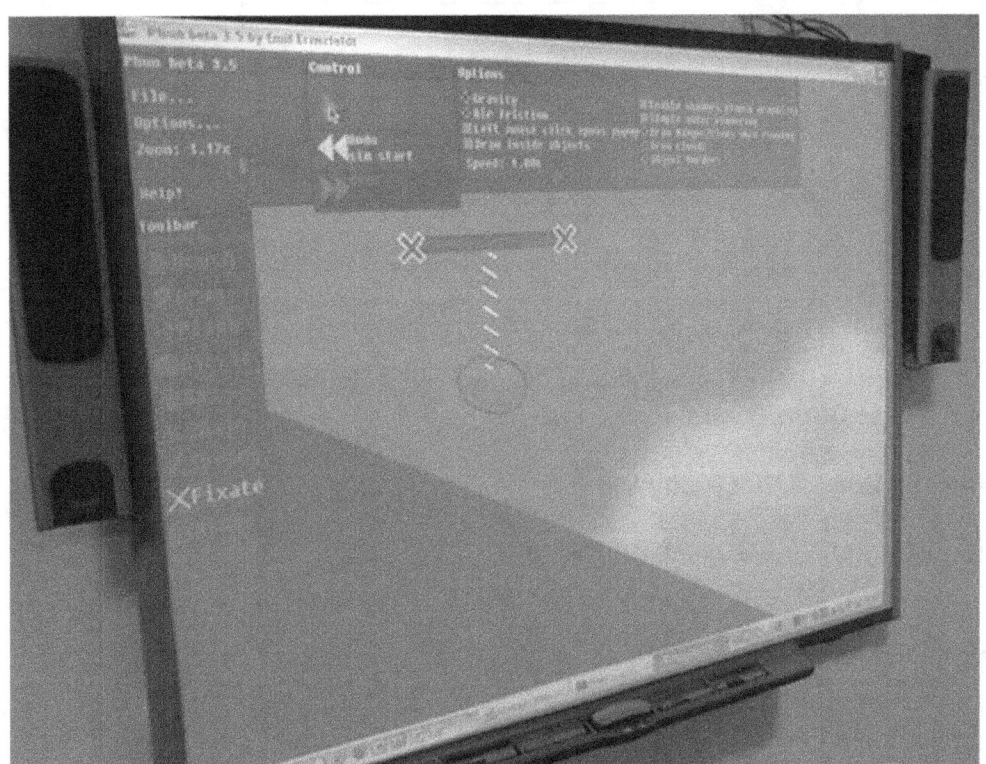

Electricity and Circuits KS2

Originally posted June 19 2008

http://www.whiteboardblog.co.uk/2008/06/electricity-and-circuits-ks2/

Here are some handy links for teaching Primary Electricity on an IWB

This is something I haven't seen before. Looks quite fun

The Blobz Guide to Circuits : http://www.andythelwell.com/blobz/

From the BBC:

http://www.bbc.co.uk/schools/scienceclips/ages/6_7/electricity.shtml

http://www.bbc.co.uk/schools/ks2bitesize/science/activities/conductors.shtml

http://www.bbc.co.uk/schools/ks2bitesize/science/activities/changing_circuits.shtml

Other Links

Make an Electric Circuit Online : http://gwydir.demon.co.uk/jo/elect/index.htm

BBC Learning Zone – Electricity Videos : http://bbc.in/fFI94H

PhET Circuit Builder : http://bit.ly/fyUQKO

Cleo Circuit World : http://bit.ly/g1Wgbe

For a quick 10 minute preview, that explains some aspects of circuits. Go to Furry Elephant http://bit.ly/fpSfKj

Link to other Links Pages

TopicBox – Electricity : http://bit.ly/eVFNe1

Science Resources from BP

Originally posted February 19 2010

http://www.whiteboardblog.co.uk/2010/02/resourcesfromb/

Thanks to fellow twitterer Sophie Bessemer for tipping me off about these science resources from BP Educational Services, the education department of the energy company.

Secondary Science teachers might want to check out the Carbon Footprint Toolkit. This teaches students about carbon emissions and their impacts, choices for carbon reduction and alternative energy supplies. The Toolkit includes an interactive school carbon calculator, quick-fire activities, factsheets, energy animations, a picture gallery and teachers' notes. It could be used as part of both KS3 and KS4 science lessons, as well as geography.

You can access a preview of the toolkit here. http://bit.ly/dZJutM And login to order it for free.

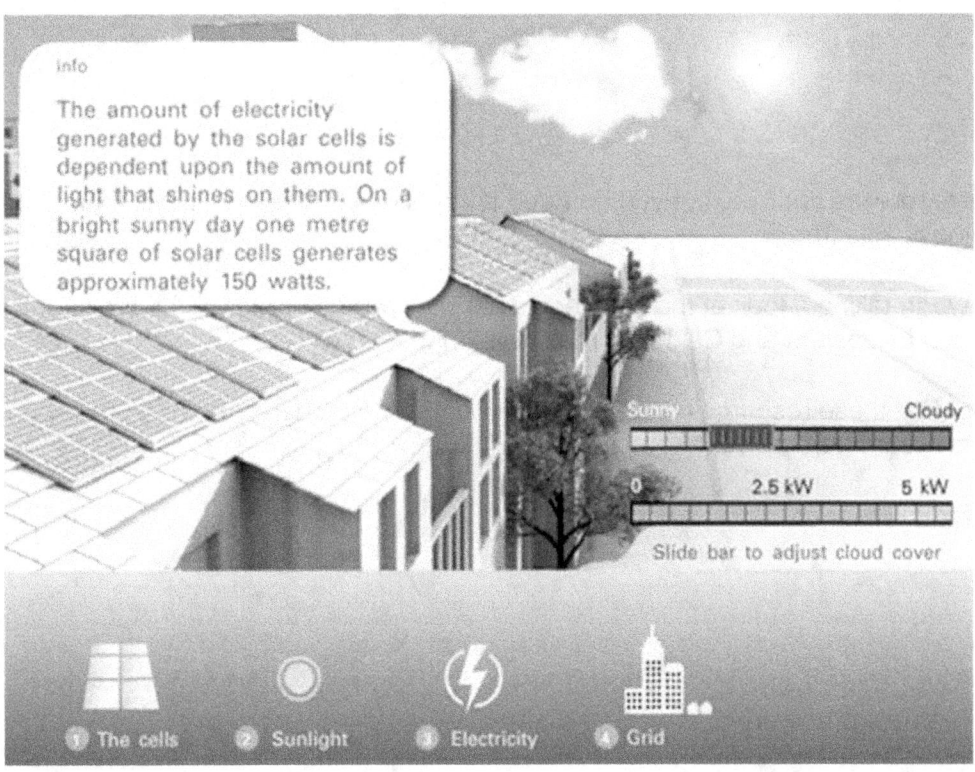

For Primary Science, there are some great resources in the Young Science Investigators series (http://bit.ly/i5uGsc) aimed at KS2 pupils. These resources include the following modules:

- Energy
- Our Environment
- Online Experiments

All these resources are free, but you do need to register with the site to get them although registration is also free.

It's also worth taking a look at the free resources that you can order and have sent to your school such as posters and CD-ROM materials. http://bit.ly/euQqND

Take a look at these resources and see what you think. Could they be used to support science on your Interactive Whiteboard?

Science Skills Resources from BP

Originally posted October 26 2010

http://www.whiteboardblog.co.uk/2010/10/science-skills-resources-from-bp/

Science Skills is a free online teaching resource with six challenges drawn from the real-life context of BP's business. Students can use video briefings, interactive experiments and information sheets to answer questions and ultimately solve the challenges :
http://bit.ly/fu5Ais

Each challenge is based around a core topic from the Key Stage 3 and 4 curricula and the Scottish Curriculum for Excellence and helps to develop science skills.

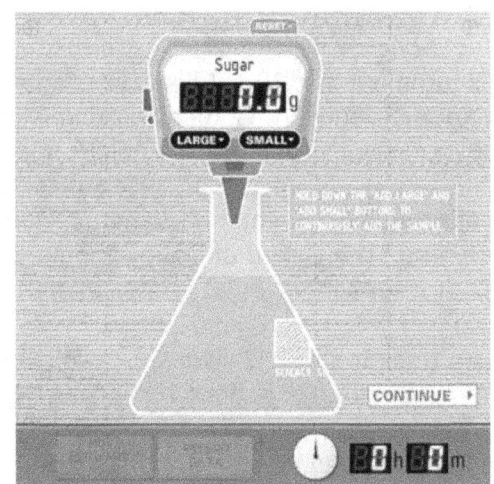

The topics include:

- Speeding up a reaction
- Bioethanol
- Energy from Wind
- Energy from the Sun
- Crude Oil
- Energy from Fuel

The teachers version of the resource (http://bit.ly/hqsnSD) includes lesson plans, notes and other guidance. You need to register with the site to access the teacher area, but it is free. Students can access the main resources without a login.

This is a great resource for teaching various aspects of How Science Works along with important investigative skills.

In addition BP have also produced a "Science at Work" resource which provides real world science for 14–16 year olds. This free teaching resource comprises seven case studies from BP's business, seven student challenges, a student sheet on science in the workplace, a short film about the work and skills of BP scientists, and teachers' notes. http://bit.ly/guqd5H

http://www.bp.com/genericResource.do?categoryId=8043&contentId=7044216

There are plenty of other resources on the BP site for primary and secondary teachers. You can check out the main content page at http://bit.ly/euQqND

Science Songs from They Might Be Giants

Originally posted July 27 2009

http://www.whiteboardblog.co.uk/2009/07/science-songs-from-they-might-be-giants/

I've always been a fan of using songs to introduce science concepts, and there's tonnes of possibilities to choose from. From proper "commercial" songs to stuff like Simple Science Videos.

Two I liked to use include They Might Be Giants – Birdhouse in Your Soul (electricity/energy) and Particle Man.

Well, it turns out that They Might Be Giants are releasing a new CD / DVD of Science songs and videos called Here Comes Science with catchy tunes about the periodic table, photosynthesis, the planets, the colour spectrum and more.

Song titles include "Meet the Elements," "Roy G. Biv," "Photo Synthesis," "Speed and Velocity and "The Ballad of Davey Crockett in Outer Space". The CD will come bundled with a DVD of videos too.

Here's a track they did previously – Why Does the Sun Shine
http://www.youtube.com/watch?v=Zbgul1NpEA8&

There's an updated version of Why Does the Sun Shine with the line -" The Sun is a miasma of incandescent plasma" 😃
http://studio360.org/flashpop.html?playlist=/stream/xspf/136670

I can't find mention of the album on the usual UK sites I buy CD's from, so it may be something to look for on import from the US. It's definitely worth looking out for when it gets released sometime in the Autumn.

Thanks to Jennifer Ouellette and David Bruggeman for the heads-up on this via their blogs.

For other songs – how about "Danger High Voltage" by Electric Six for an electricity lesson (**but don't show the video**). For space lessons "Supermassive Black Hole" by Muse or "Man on the Moon" by REM. Simon and Garfunkel's "The Sound of Silence" for a lesson about Sound – or Slade's "Cum on Feel the Noize"?

Play them as the students come into the room 😃

Data Handling with Census at School

Originally posted December 3rd 2010

http://www.whiteboardblog.co.uk/2010/12/data-handling-with-census-at-school/

The CensusAtSchool Project (http://www.censusatschool.org.uk/) is an online survey that the Royal Statistical Society Centre for Statistical Education (RSSCSE) established in 2000 linked to the UK population census of 2001. Since then, new questionnaires have been launched each year and it now comprises over a million lines of data responses from learners in the UK and overseas.

The best bit is that samples from these databases can be downloaded and you can use them in your classroom along with resource packs and worksheets.

The site will be of interest to teachers of many different subjects, Maths obviously, but also science, geography, history, citizenship, ICT and others.

The Random Data Selector lets you draw random samples of the raw data collected from CensusAtSchool, in the UK and some of the other nations taking part. You may choose to select from all data or you can choose responses from a particular region, age or gender depending on which database you choose. http://rds.censusatschool.org.uk/

Another very useful part of the site is their built-in Data Handling Tool which lets you choose which sets of data you want to look at and then takes you through the steps of producing different kinds of graph and chart to display the results. For example this example looking at link between height and foot length:

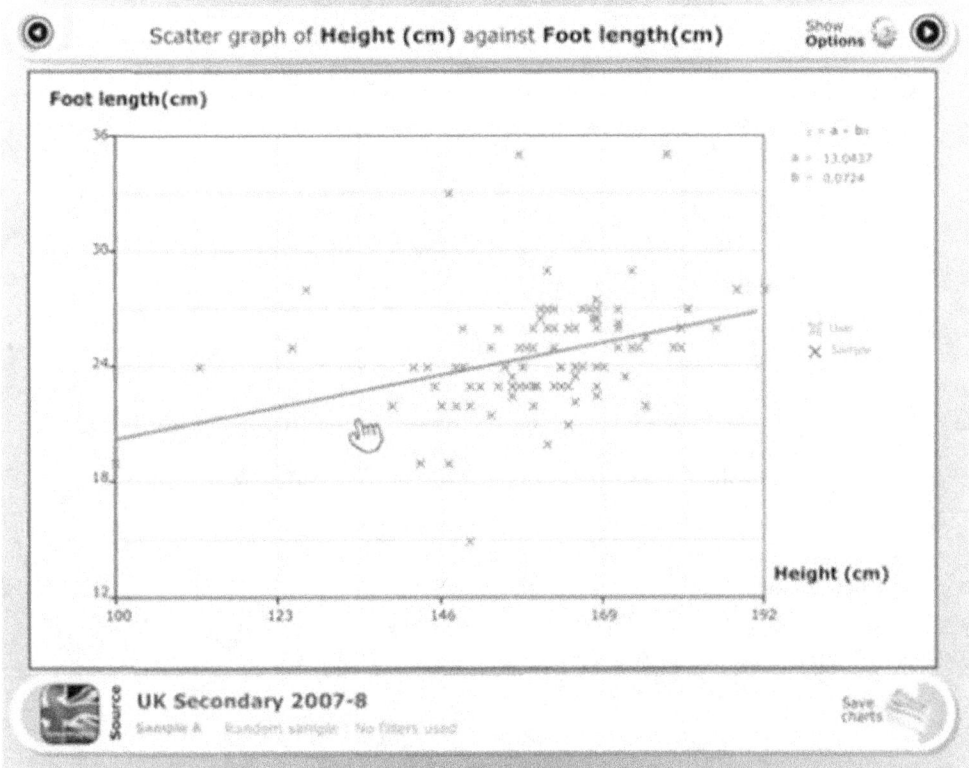

It definitely takes out some of the problems in extracting and processing large amounts of data in Excel, if you only want to focus on the analysis skills and looking at graphs and charts. If you want to use the raw data then the Random Data Selector will be the thing to go back to. http://datatool.censusatschool.org.uk/datatool.swf

There are lots of different teaching resources that are available for download. Most of these come with worksheets which contain sample sets of data and link to different parts of the curriculum such as maths, history, science, geography etc.

There is also an international version of Census at School, with links to the different versions in Canada, USA, Australia, New Zealand, Ireland, South Africa and Japan: http://www.censusatschool.com/en/links

Planet Orbits

Originally posted April 4 2009

http://www.whiteboardblog.co.uk/2009/04/planet-orbits/

Here's a link to a cool website that lets you view how the planets in the Solar System move around the Sun : http://www.gunn.co.nz/astrotour/

You can run it automatically, and change the speed. or pause it and step through slowly. You can choose to view the whole thing with the sun at the centre, or to follow a particular planet around.

The controls at the side let you zoom in so you can see a few planets more closely. You can also make the planets bigger to make them easier to see on an IWB.

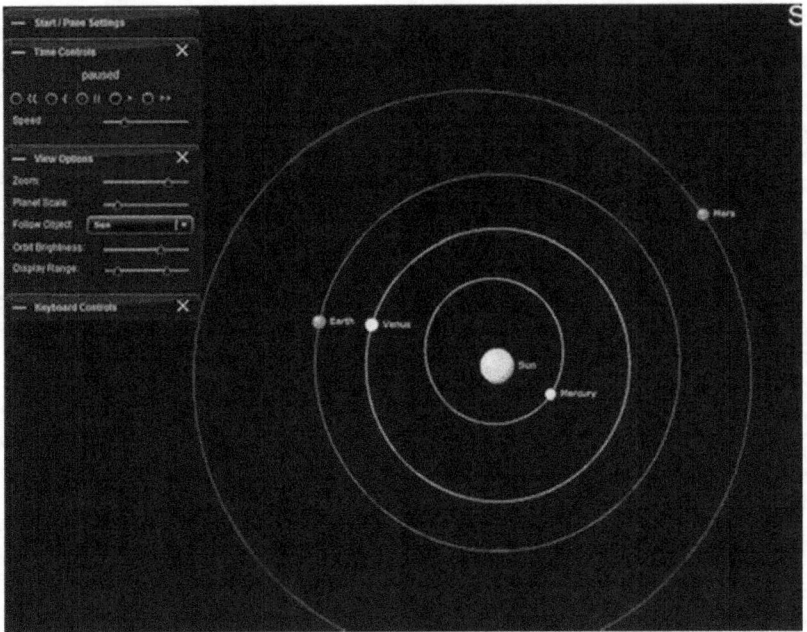

Another nice touch is that if you click and drag any planet, all the others will move in time with it.

This is a neat little tool to show how the planets orbit the Sun. You can see how some move faster than others and use the dates to calculate how long it would take some of the outer planets to complete one orbit. Visit the site now and have a play!

http://www.gunn.co.nz/astrotour/

Science Lesson Activity Generator

Originally posted June 12 2009

http://www.whiteboardblog.co.uk/2009/06/science-lesson-activity-generator/

I was inspired by John Davitt's excellent Learning Event Generator (http://newtools.org/showtxt.php?docid=737) and wanted to produce a similar version for Primary Science. Partly because I wanted to create some fun ideas for science and also because I wanted to try to brush up my Flash programming skills (or lack of them)

The end result is the beta version of the Primary Science Lesson Activity Generator. This is very much a beta, and I may be tweaking the events that can be produced in the future. But at present there are over 3,600 possible permutations – click the generate button to produce a new lesson idea.

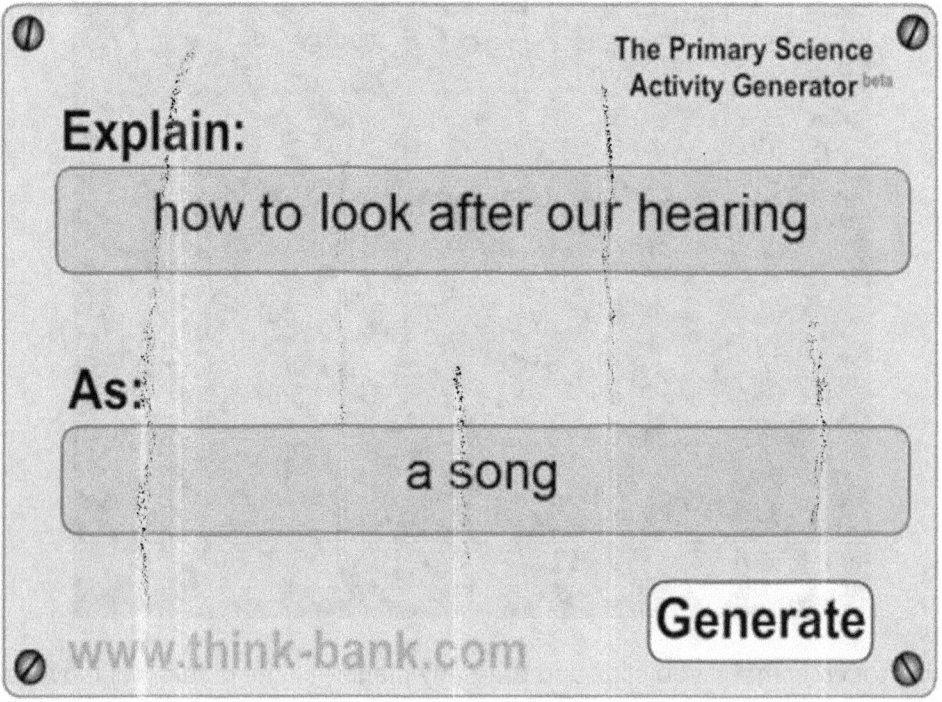

http://think-bank.com/lessongenerator/

I hope you like the ideas that it generates.

Please also be sure to visit Johns other versions of the generator. You can now also get his activity generator as a rather cool iPhone application. I don't currently have an iPhone, but if I did I'd definitely get this application! http://www.newtools.org/slist1.php?Subject=5

Ricky Goes to Antarctica – a Primary Science Resource

Originally posted September 11 2010

http://www.whiteboardblog.co.uk/2010/09/ricky-goes-to-antarctica-a-primary-science-resource/

This is Ricky. Ricky is very lucky in that he will soon be going on an expedition to Antarctica alongside a teacher called Lisa Woods, sponsored by the Fuchs Foundation. He leaves in November and will be there for 5 weeks! He's already packing for his trip, but I think he'll need a little help first to see what clothes he should be bringing!

You can follow Ricky's adventures via his blog :
http://antarcticapuppet.primaryblogger.co.uk/

Teachers could use Ricky's problems as a stimulus for talk and investigations, as well as to encourage children to raise questions.

There are two main sections to the blog – both of which will of interest to teachers who want to use Ricky in their lessons.

"Ricky's Diary" – this is Ricky's record of his preparation and his trip. He started writing his blog entries over the summer holiday and will add to these when he gets responses to his problems or new things happen to him. You can help to solve the problems in whatever order you wish, either by following Ricky's posts in date order, or dipping into them as you choose. You might decide to focus on one issue such as what Ricky should eat or how to keeping warm. You might choose something that could help Ricky even though he hasn't yet thought about it.

You can post questions for Ricky, and ideas for investigations to be carried out before he goes or during his Antarctic adventure. He will try to respond to most ideas or questions. He will also choose some of the interesting ideas and questions from children to explore when he goes on his adventure in November.

"How can you help Ricky?" – this section contains idea for how to solve Ricky's problems linked directly to the posts in Ricky's Diary. There are also links to other support materials where relevant.

The Fuchs Foundation arranges for young teachers of science and geography to undertake scientific expeditions to the Antarctic and Arctic. The charity was re-launched in 2005 to coincide with the 50th Anniversary of Sir Vivian Fuchs' Commonwealth Trans-Antarctic Expedition 1956-58, There is more information about the Fuchs Foundation expeditions on the Fuchs Foundation website. www.fuchsfoundation.org and you can watch teachers on the 2007 expedition recorded by Teacher's TV

If you're looking for a way to make Primary Science a little more fun and interesting then you might like to incorporate Ricky and his Antarctic adventures into your curriculum. It would be a nice way to introduce investigative work and become a stimulus for talk, as well as to encourage children to raise questions. It would also have some fun cross curricular activities such as creative writing.

Good Luck to Ricky and Lisa on their expedition. I look forward to reading more about it.

http://antarcticapuppet.primaryblogger.co.uk/

http://www.freezingteachers.com

The Science of Scams

Originally posted May 5 2010

http://www.whiteboardblog.co.uk/2010/05/the-science-of-scams/

The Science of Scams was a set of hoax videos produced by Channel 4 in association with the amazing Derren Brown. In total there were 7 hoax videos which appear to demonstrate paranormal phenomena. In fact they're all based upon real scientific principles.

http://www.scienceofscams.com/

This hoax footage was been posted all over the internet in an attempt to find out if people would either accept it as genuine or question it in an attempt to discover the real truth. These include evidence of ghosts, telekinesis and much more.

On the Science of Scams website they show the original hoax videos, then go through the process of explaining and debunking the scams behind them.

These videos could all be used to generate discussion around Critical Thinking skills for KS3 and Ks4 and promoting healthy scepticism of what they see on the internet. Would provide interesting discussion matter if handled correctly.

In addition, 5 of the videos could link themselves to Scientific Investigation in the classroom. Students could develop experiments to test and replicate these videos.

Here's how you might link some of the videos to the Science curriculum

Ghost on Film

This is a great way to introduce the famous Peppers Ghost experiment – Recreate with model room and a toy plus a sheet a glass. Linked to Ks3/Ks4 Mirrors and Reflection. Investigate properties of glass / mirrors. ICT Opportunity – use video camera inside the model to recreate what an observer might see.

Psychic Wheel

Linked to KS4 – Convection currents & Energy transfer and also link to particle theory – expansion of gases and density. Students could try and build their own wheel – try with different heat sources.

Brick Breaking

Linked to forces and pressure Ks3/Ks4. The experiment could be mocked up safely using a melon instead of someone's head. Also linked to materials (using "fake" bricks that look same as normal brick)

Chi Energy

Linked to KS4 Chemical Reactions as an example of Exothermic reaction. Investigate experiments which generate heat – test out – measure heat of reaction. Datalogging opportunities in measuring temperature changes.

Telekinesis

Linked to Magnetism and Static Electricity. Look at how static can make objects repel / attract. Interestingly "psychic" Uri Gellar does a similar thing with a magnet in a false thumb tip (videos showing this keep getting removed) Could look at how different materials can hold different charges – insulators such as plastics

There are two other videos which cover Psychic Readings and the Ouija Board – would leave out as not linked to "Science" as such – but could still have critical thinking component perhaps. It may be best to leave that Ouija boards alone in a school setting just to be safe from parental complaints.

http://www.scienceofscams.com/

Xtranormal in Science Lessons

Originally posted December 6 2010

http://www.whiteboardblog.co.uk/2010/12/xtranormal-in-science-lessons/

Here's a different idea for getting pupils to write up science practicals that makes a change from the usual method/results/conclusion format using a website called Xtranormal. (http://www.xtranormal.com/)

Xtranormal is a website which makes it very easy to create a simple animated movie. You can choose between one or two people and then write the dialogue. The website uses text to speech technology to read your script out, so there's no need to use microphones.

The obvious use would be for MFL or English teachers to write short pieces of dialogue. (See Jose Picardo's blog to see how it's being used in languages) But there's no reason why it can't be used for other subjects too. (http://www.boxoftricks.net/?p=1381)

So for Science, one character could be explaining what they have found out to a second character. Like this: (http://www.xtranormal.com/watch/7956245/)

You could also just have one speaker. Maybe make it into a news report explaining their findings. It could also be used to explain scientific concepts or to model important points in a debate about a controversial issue in Science.

The voices are a little stilted, but for those pupils who are too embarrassed to record their voices using microphones, it's the next best thing.

The finished videos are hosted on Xtranormal, and you can embed them into blogs/VLE etc. You can also upload your videos to YouTube too if you wish.

(http://www.youtube.com/watch?v=Fonym6AYHwQ)

You can't use Xtranormal if you are under 13, according to their terms of service, so this activity would have to be done with KS4 or Post-16 students. Also be aware that not everything on the site is free.

But if you are looking for something different to do with a class, then this might make a change from always presenting the results of an experiment the same way.

If you do use Xtranormal for something like this, I'd love to see what your pupils have produced!

Yenka Science and Maths Resources

Originally posted February 12 2008

http://www.whiteboardblog.co.uk/2008/02/yenka-science-and-maths-resources/

Yenka is a new resource from the people who produced Crocodile Clips. It's based on their Absorb range of online teaching materials that originally were released alongside Crocodile Physics and Chemistry.

The whole library is going to be a subscription service, but on release they have produced 700 resources which can be used free-of charge. : http://www.yenka.com/freecontent/

These resources cover aspects of science and maths and should work very well on an interactive whiteboard. Well worth a visit.

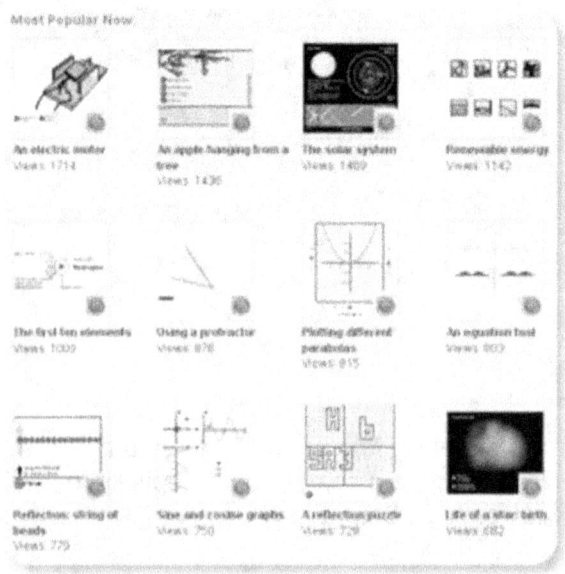

7 Mythbusters Clips for Science Teachers

Originally posted August 31 2010

http://www.whiteboardblog.co.uk/2010/08/mythbusters-clips-for-science-teachers/

If you ever put the Discovery channel on, the chances are that very soon you'll encounter an episode of Mythbusters. It's one of my favourite shows on TV at the moment. OK, the kid in me never tires of watching large explosions, but there is some very good science going on too. They put movie myths, old wives tales, urban legends, thought experiments and internet viral videos to the test. If you've ever wanted to know if you can find a needle in a haystack, or teach an old dog new tricks then this is the show for you.

I'm still amazed when I meet science teachers who have never heard of the Mythbusters. In every situation the team use proper scientific method to break down each myth and put it to the test. Often they go one step further on busted myths to see if they can replicate the intended outcome of the myth (which is usually where the explosions happen!)

There are plenty of clips from the shows up on YouTube that are perfect for use in Science lessons to illustrate concepts or to demonstrate thought experiments. Here are a few of my favourites:

Note – on the original blog I linked to YouTube videos, but the nature of the internet is that often these videos get taken down. I'll try and give a keyword or phrase to do a YouTube search with to get the video rather than give a link that will almost certainly be broken.

Bullet Drop

A classic thought experiment. If you fire a bullet from a gun, and at the same time drop a bullet straight down from the same height, will they hit the ground at the same time. Physics says yes, but most peoples common sense says no. The Mythbusters put it to the test.

YouTube Search Phrase : Mythbusters Bullet Fired Dropped

Throwing an object from a moving car

If you have a car travelling at 60mph, and you throw an object out the back at 60mph, will the two velocities cancel each other out and the object appear to an observer to fall straight down?

YouTube Search Phrase : Mythbusters soccer ball shot from truck

Can you really build a lead balloon?

If you do it right, can you build a balloon out of lead that can actually float?

YouTube Search Phrase : Mythbusters lead balloon

Thermite and Ice

If you combine the thermite reaction with a lump of ice, it turns into something a lot more explosive!

YouTube Search Phrase : Mythbusters thermite vs ice

Alkali Metals (Debunking the Brainiac video)

This is the Mythbusters take on the famous (and sadly faked) Brainiac video of alkali metals in a bathtub (http://bit.ly/hAcCra)

YouTube Search Phrase : Mythbusters threequel alkaline metals

Water on a chip pan fire

An amazing video which demonstrates exactly why you don't pour water onto a chip pan fire. Scary.

YouTube Search Phrase : Mythbusters greased lightning

Can you cut down a tree with a minigun?

OK, not a lot of science here (although could demonstrate friction) – but I just love this clip of Kari cutting down a tree with a minigun

YouTube Search Phrase : Mythbusters minigun chop tree

There are loads of other great examples out there. If you haven't seen the Mythbusters before, go check them out!

Mythbusters channel : http://www.youtube.com/show?p=maoKMJHUScs

Alkaline Metals Videos for Science

Originally posted January 31 2010

http://www.whiteboardblog.co.uk/2010/01/alkaline-metals-videos-for-science/

One of the benefits of using videos on an IWB in Science lessons is for those moments when you want to demonstrate something that is just too dangerous to do in the classroom.

This is particularly true when demonstrating the reaction of Alkali Metals with water. You can demonstrate small pieces, but it's a little dull. And when the kids ask "go on Sir, throw in a bigger bit" you still can't use too big a bit for obvious safety reasons.

Which is why it's good to then turn to a good video to demonstrate the reaction.

An old favourite of mine was from the TV show "Brainiac": http://bit.ly/hAcCra

But sadly this is actually a fake experiment. If you look carefully you can even see a wire going into one of the bathtubs which sets off the regular explosive.

Last night I watched a Mythbusters episode that I must have missed previously where they test out the scenario in the Brainiac video and prove that it didn't happen the way it was show. It's a nice way of demonstrating how to actually test something you see on screen to see if it is actually real.

Their take on Alkali metals in water is in two parts.

Here's part one: http://www.youtube.com/watch?v=xyY6wg1Jl1w

And here's part 2 : http://www.youtube.com/watch?v=hqbwPxZsgHs

Awesome stuff. I think I now have a new favourite Alkali Metal explosion video to show.

An alternative is to check out the Sodium Party videos from Theodore Gray. Big lumps of sodium in a lake. Fab http://bit.ly/hIJiIv

And remember – don't try this at home….

Update: if links are broken – Do a YouTube search for "*MythBusters Viewers Special Threequel: Alkaline Metal Explosion*"

Furbles – a fun maths tool

Originally posted November 21 2010

http://www.whiteboardblog.co.uk/2010/11/furbles-a-fun-maths-tool/

Furbles is an old favourite of mine that I'd forgotten about until recently (thanks Lara!). Furbles started life as an idea for teaching statistics in an interesting way with children from KS1 to KS3. The original version was published in 2003 online, and its popularity spread.

Furbles was originally devised as an innovative way of imagining statistics and the depiction of statistics. You have a variety of creatures of different colours and shapes which you can move around on the screen. You can then arrange them into different charts and graphs to show simple frequency data. The children can see the Furbles move into the correct groups, and are then replaced by the corresponding bar graph, pie chart etc. It's lovely and visual.

You can find out more here: http://ptolemy.co.uk/furbles

The old 2003 version is still freely available – and it's well worth bookmarking: http://ptolemy.co.uk/furbles/furbles03 And if you like it I think the retail version is still available. Link should be on the website.

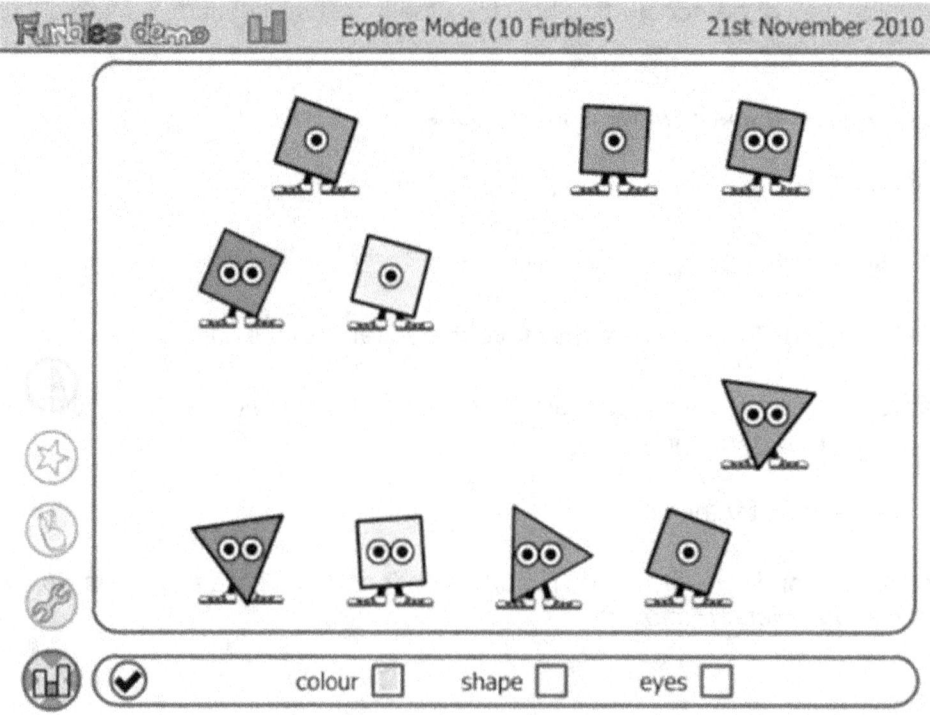

MathsFrame IWB Resources

Originally posted June 5 2009

http://www.whiteboardblog.co.uk/2009/06/mathsframe-iwb-resources/

Here's a nice website for Primary teachers to use in their maths lessons.

Mathsframe.co.uk was created by a primary school teacher who "thought it ridiculous that he spent most of his Sunday evenings searching for resources to use on his interactive whiteboard". So he made his own resources instead.

Their aim is to provide simple, high quality maths resources for interactive whiteboards. To make resources that allow for effective differentiation and progression, and to make planning easier (and less time consuming) for teachers.

All the activities are clear and simple to use and understand. They are designed as tools for teachers to use to teach. All activities are linked to a key objective/objectives from the Primary Framework. They are ideal for reinforcing and practicing the key mathematical skills and concepts.

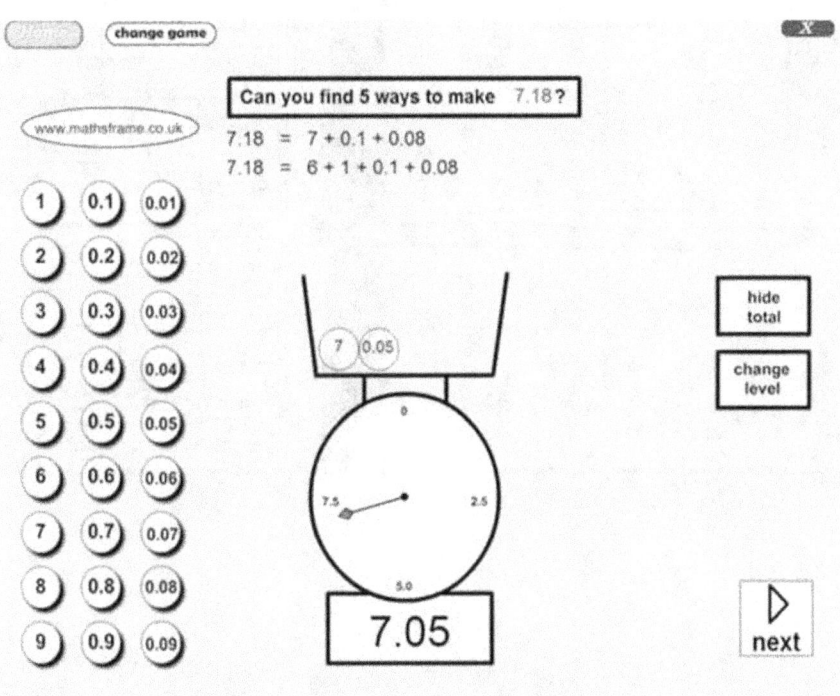

There are free resources on the site. If you like them, you can buy a site licence for a pack of resources and install them onto your own machines.
(http://www.mathsframe.co.uk/free_resources.asp)

It's well worth adding to your list of bookmarks for those times when you need something to use for a lesson starter or plenary.

Fridge Magnet Poetry

Originally posted February 20th 2009

http://www.whiteboardblog.co.uk/2009/02/fridge-magnet-poetry/

Here's a fun activity from the Magnetic Poetry website – Fridge Magnet poetry. There are several sets of words to choose from. Drag the words and phrases onto the page to create your own poems. This is an activity you could make yourself in your IWB software with a lot of text boxes, but this site saves you having to think of all the words.

http://www.magpo.com/kidspoetry/playonline.cfm

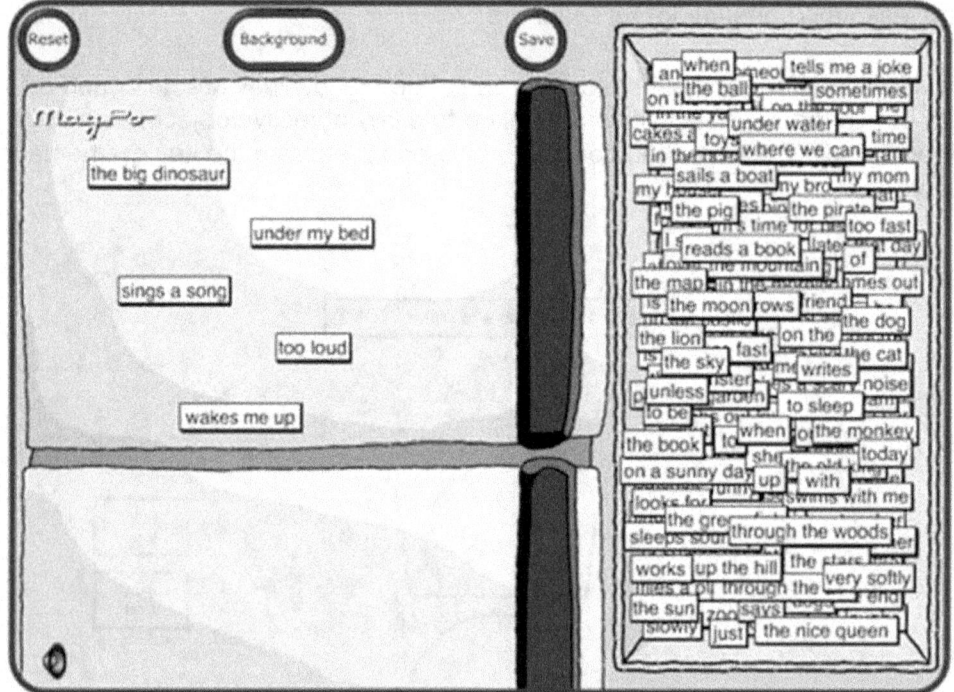

Storynory and Smartboard / Promethean resources

Originally posted July 27 2009

http://www.whiteboardblog.co.uk/2009/07/storynory-and-smartboard-promethean-resources/

Storynory (http://storynory.com/) is an online treasure trove of audio stories. The site contains a mixture of new stories, fairy tales, and specially adapted myths and histories. They have published an audio story every week since November 2005 which are free to download and use.

The stories are read by Natasha Gostwick and her clear story-telling voice has won a place in the hearts of children and adults all over the world. The amazing artwork is produced by a friend of mine, the very talented Sophie Green. (http://www.sophie-green.com/)

StoryNory allows you to download their audio files to use in your classroom. It's well worth a visit. You could add these stories to your own IWB resources if you wanted to.

image © Storynory and Sophie Green

I have been given special permission to use the images and sounds from Storynory to produce an Interactive Whiteboard resource. I have only produced one for now, as a proof of concept, but if it goes down well then I'll make some more. The resources include the large images with sound, plus the text of the story as well as some pages to provoke class activities and discussion.

You can find the download page on my Think Bank website. I've produced a PowerPoint version as well as an ActivInspire (note, not earlier versions) and Smart Notebook 10 version. http://think-bank.com/iwb/storynory.html

The audio and images are copyright StoryNory so please check their website for their terms of use. And thanks again to Storynory for giving me permission to use their material in this way! Go check out their site now! http://storynory.com/

Online Audio Stories

Originally posted May 11 2010

http://www.whiteboardblog.co.uk/2010/05/online-audio-stories/

Online Audio Stories provide free downloadable audio books for children.
http://www.onlineaudiostories.com

With a wonderful selection of short stories for kids and bedtime stories, their free storytelling audio books for children are a delight. You can download the audio as an mp3 file and play on a computer, or transfer to a portable mp3 player.

Stories include classic tales from Aesop, Brothers Grimm, Edward Lear and Hans Christian Andersen. It's well worth a visit. Take a look http://www.onlineaudiostories.com

And don't forget if you like these, you'll also like StoryNory: http://storynory.com/

Read All About It!

Originally posted May 3 2008

http://www.whiteboardblog.co.uk/2008/05/read-all-about-it/

Here's a fun little tool that could liven up the way you present information – or make a class writing task a little more fun.

The **newspaper generator** lets you put your own text into a few boxes, and then generates an authentic looking newspaper article containing your text.

http://www.fodey.com/generators/newspaper/snippet.asp

The finished product is very authentic, and quite impressive.

You have to save your image and host it elsewhere if you want to use it online, but it is a very quick process to host it on Flickr or similar.

Year 6 Literacy Ideas

Originally posted May 6 2009

http://www.whiteboardblog.co.uk/2009/05/year-6-literacy-ideas/

I was emailed over the weekend by a year 6 teacher who wanted some ideas for using ICT with his class, and in particular for literacy.

I set up an Etherpad to collate ideas and threw the question out to my network of Twitter friends. I invited them to visit the Etherpad and add their thoughts.

The etherpad has since been taken down with the closure of the etherpad website – but the ideas were saved before it was lost.

Thanks to @kvnmcl, @joysimpson, @LynnShellard, @AllanahK @pam_thompson, @psycho65 for their comments. Thanks to anyone else who didn't add their name!

Here is a summary of the ideas that were shared

Flat Life
http://www.youtube.com/watch?v=HjjaJ4csfS4
It's not a website however Flat life available via You Tube is a great 10 minute animation that can lead to a range of writing development and own animation am currently using with my year 6 class.

PicLits
http://www.piclits.com/compose_dragdrop.aspx
Writing to go with pictures – lovely.

Wordle
Wordle is a great tool for developing comprehension skills in literacy. Wordle the first paragraph or two of a text and see if you can work out what you think the big ideas might be about in the text. You can also see if you can group words together and then give them a heading. Both activities will help tune children into a text. http://www.wordle.net/

Mind Mapping

I am just in the middle of blogging about myWebspirations at
http://www.mywebspiration.com . It is a fantastic tool for collaborating on mind-maps and
creating a plan for a piece of writing.

VoiceThread

Using Voice Tread http://www.voicethread.com is particularly good for gathering opinions
about a book, illustrations etc. and for generating ideas to write about. For instance if writing
a persuasive text as series of related images can be uploaded and then children can then
add their opinions, information etc. about each one. This then provides a resource for ideas
when writing.

Podcasting is a great way of enabling children to share what they are learning. Podomatic is
great but if it doesn't get through the school filter then create in audacity and upload to gcast.

Blogging

For some ideas about what you could blog about see this post
http://literacyresourcesandideas.edublogs.org/2009/05/12/what-might-you-write-about/

If you want to generate lists of resources and communicate with children through
microblogging then try www.Edmodo.com. This is great for setting challenges for the
children, reminding them about homework, creating lists of useful websites for a project and
generally communicating with each other whether in school or at home.

For another way to do online discussion – try http://www.think.com – or look at what your
VLE already provides in-school.

Digital Storytelling

Digital storytelling is a great project and any number of tools could be used for this:
http://literacyresourcesandideas.edublogs.org/tag/digital-storytelling/

You can't go wrong with collaborative writing and nothing beats a wiki for this purpose. I use
pbworks at http://pbworks.com but there are several wikis that are good for school use. The
world is your oyster here. Create a collaborative document about anything.
@joysimpson

Animoto

Animoto http://animoto.com/education is great for year 6 and you can apply for an 'education
account'. All you then need is a google mail account and you can create accounts for each
child.

With Animoto you can make mini music videos… my class are making videos for leavers
assembly.

Story Starters

Another site worth looking at is http://bit.ly/h89HMY, according to their blurb "Scholastic
Story Starters are a quick, fun way to inspire students to write." I have a class of reluctant
writers and they enjoy this so I guess that's a good recommendation… anything to get EBD
kids to write works for me.

PhotoStory 3

http://bit.ly/hpdhap
PhotoStory3 is fab, free and easy to use combining photos, text and music

Monkey Jam Animation
http://bit.ly/fObkP4
If you've got time animation using freeware such as monkey jam is very effective – 2D with cut paper is quicker than 3D models!

Be Funky
I've just been using http://www.befunky.com/ with my class (year 5) this morning to upload some photos from a school trip yesterday. You can apply various effects to these including adding text and speech bubbles. The class enjoyed doing this and want to continue.

You could then use www.animoto.com to create a 'movie' slide show of the images and http://audacity.sourceforge.net/ could be used to record the voice over.

You could use http://www.stupeflix.com/ for slide show presentation combining voice overs and music, http://www.glogster.com/ for creating a poster wall of information including movies and recordings.

Writing Fix – Story Ideas
http://writingfix.com/traits_primary.htm#forkids
Scroll down for the interactive random writing ideas. My Year 6/7 students loved using these and were very amused by some of the combinations they were presented with. (Pam Thompson)

Telescopic Text
http://www.telescopictext.com/
We had great fun using this very simple site. It really made students think about the value of words. We then used it as a collaborative writing task with another school using Etherpad. (Pam Thompson)

Persuasion Map
http://www.readwritethink.org/materials/persuasion_map/
This tool from ReadWriteThink is a great way for students to organise their thinking as they plan a piece of persuasive text, whether oral or written. (Pam Thompson)

Web Links
I have Year 4/5 so these websites will generally be close to what you might want.
http://delicious.com/AllanahK/Literacy

Also http://www.delicious.com/dannynic/digitalstorytelling

Also check out:

http://www.lancsngfl.ac.uk/curriculum/literacyresources/index.php
http://www.sgfl.org.uk/englishandliteracy/primary/y6network
http://www.teachingideas.co.uk/english/contents.htm
http://www.twomilehill-jun.bristol.sch.uk/literacy.php
http://thedowns.wikispaces.com/

Five Card Flickr

Originally posted February 23 2009

http://www.whiteboardblog.co.uk/2009/02/five-card-flickr/

Here's another nice idea for using the internet as an inspiration for creative writing; Five Card Flickr. (http://web.nmc.org/5cardstory/flickr.php)

Five Card Flickr draws from nearly a thousand photos on Flickr tagged with "5cardflickr"

You are dealt 5 random photos from Flickr and you choose one to add to your story. You then repeat this 4 more times until you have 5 photos that you can then use to tell a story.

Flickr photo credits: (1) Rachel Smith (2) bmllnrob (3) cogdogblog (4) D'Arcy Norman (5) Dawcomecy1

You can then write your story on the blog itself, or you could display them on the IWB for students to write their own stories individually.

If you have photos on Flickr that you'd like to add to the pool of images used, then just tag them with 5cardflickr.

The 5 Card Flickr idea is based on a game called 5 Card Nancy where you create a 5 frame story using old comic strips. Here's an online version of that game which you might also like to use. (http://www.7415comics.com/nancy)

Or if you're looking for a non-ict activity and have a stack of old comics or magazines, then here are the rules on playing it for yourself.
(http://www.scottmccloud.com/4-inventions/nancy)

A related, but slightly different way of doing things, is the "Tell a story in 5 frames" group in Flickr. Take 5 photographs to tell a story. Again this could be a nice activity to do with students and some digital cameras. (http://www.flickr.com/groups/visualstory/)

If you are looking for new ways to use technology to tell stories, then here are 50+ Ways to tell a story, collated by CogDogRoo. (http://cogdogroo.wikispaces.com/50+ways)

Flickr Poet – Turn poems into pictures

Originally posted December 23 2009

http://www.whiteboardblog.co.uk/2009/12/flickr-poet-turn-poems-into-pictures/

Here's a great little link I got from the PetaPixel photography blog this morning. (http://bit.ly/i9vYsO)

Flickr Poet is a quick way of turning a poem, sentence or chunk of random text into a sequence of Flickr photographs. **FlickrPoet** is part of _**Stories In Flight**_, an ongoing exploration of storytelling in the age of the Internet.

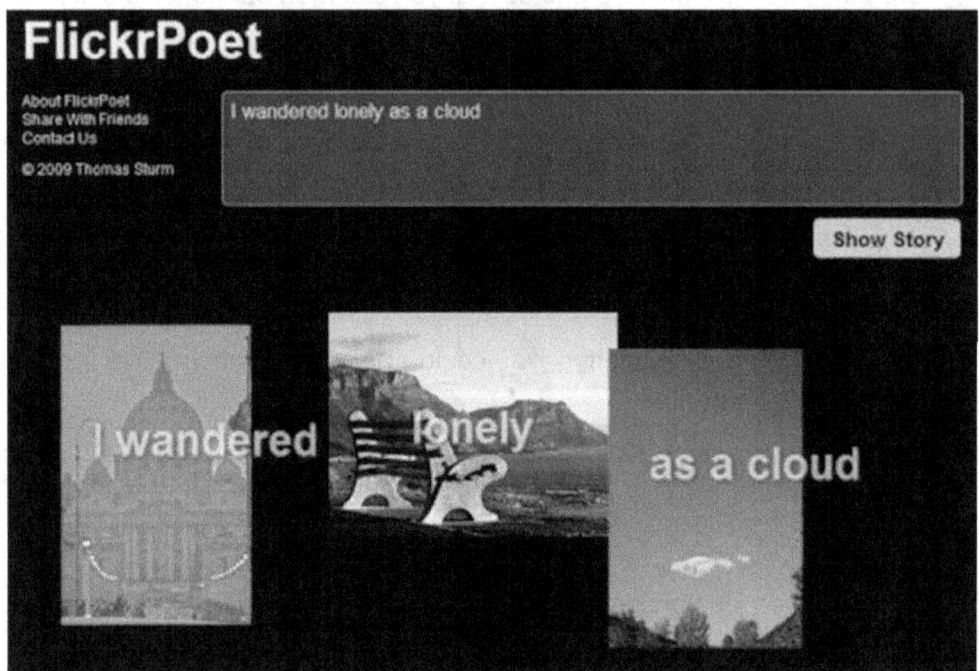

It would be nice if you could specify creative commons images perhaps and also produce a permalink (or a gallery) so you could share your creations. But if you are using IWB software you could use the camera tool to capture your creation and put it into your notebook file (or the good old Print Screen and Art Program like I did to create the image above)

Go try it out now : http://www.storiesinflight.com/flickrpoet/

Shoofly

Originally posted January 28 2008

http://www.whiteboardblog.co.uk/2008/01/shoofly/

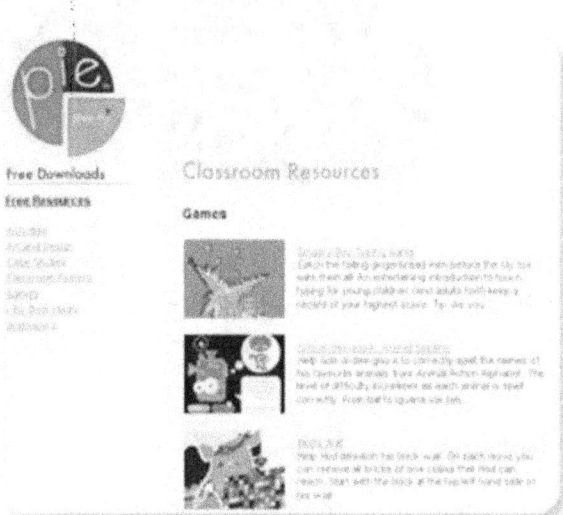

One of the highlights of the BETT exhibition for me was **ShooFly**. This is a small independent company, their stand was tucked away upstairs at the exhibition, but I was really impressed with the quality of their resources. http://www.shooflypublishing.co.uk/

A lot of companies are beginning to produce electronic resources to be used on Interactive Whiteboards. But a lot of these are either the equivalent of a PowerPoint presentation or bigscreen games. Both of these have a place in the market but what ShooFly have produced is something that is much more than this.

At a basic level they produce big books or animated stories using Flash to provide the interactivity. These on their own are great and some of them, especially the secondary resource Angel Boy is amazingly atmospheric and visually brilliant.

But what you also get with ShooFly resources is a massive bank of additional material for the teacher to use. Smart Notebook and Promethean Flipchart files of the book pages as well as clipart galleries of all the images used which can be used in any application. They also come with a teacher's guide and activity pack that puts the resource into a cross-curricular context with links to many other subjects.

They also have a website called Shoo Fly Pie which gives some free resources which you can download to use on your own whiteboards. Well worth a visit.

My particular favourite is the one that caused all the fuss in the press last week (http://bbc.in/g0hKae): The Three Little Cowboy Builders. I had never seen anyone attempt to make a 3D PopUp book on an IWB before, and it works brilliantly. The story is very funny too with the Three Little Pigs building their houses before the Big Bad Housing Inspector comes round.... great stuff.

http://www.shooflypublishing.co.uk/

Google Sky

Originally posted March 14 2008

http://www.whiteboardblog.co.uk/2008/03/google-sky/

Previously only available via Google Earth, which you had to download and run locally, Google have now made Google Sky available online to access anywhere with an internet connection.

http://www.google.com/sky/

Now you can browse the night sky and zoom in on any interesting galaxies or star clusters that you like.

If you haven't tried them, also check out Google Mars and Google Moon for surface maps based on information from various Moon and Mars missions.

http://www.google.com/mars/

http://www.google.com/moon/

Remember you can use the camera function in your interactive whiteboard software to make any screengrabs from any part of the map and bring it into your IWB software to annotate over the top. You can also put these images into your resource library/gallery for later use.

World Wide Telescope

Originally posted May 13 2008

http://www.whiteboardblog.co.uk/2008/05/world-wide-telescope/

Microsoft have finally released the public beta of their World Wide Telescope project, and I just had to write about it. It's a must for any Science teacher, or anyone interested in astronomy.

Basically, its Microsoft's version of Google Earth/Sky and if you've used the Google version in the past then you'll pick this up very easily.

The software provides a virtual planetarium and lets you study the night sky with great detail. Some of the images are astounding. You can also switch the view to study planets and moons such as Jupiter and Io.

When looking at the stars, right clicking will bring up a star identifier which tells you the name of the star (if known) and some information about it. You can even link direct to the relevant Wikipedia page.

Maybe a quick activity would be to search for their star sign (I looked up Aries) and find the names of the stars in the constellation. Maybe even find out how far away they are from Earth.

You can also point the camera downwards and study the Earth instead just like Google Earth, although not in as high resolution. A nice feature is the Earth at Night view which shows just where all the populated areas are. Interesting to use for Geography perhaps?

This is highly recommended and would be an excellent piece of software for anyone who has to teach about the Earth and space.

Download it from here: http://www.worldwidetelescope.org/

Google Earth Version 5

Originally posted February 3 2009

http://www.whiteboardblog.co.uk/2009/02/google-earth-version-5/

Yesterday, Google announced the launch of Google Earth version 5, the brand new version of the already excellent Earth viewing tool. For those of you that have never played with it, I can highly recommend it. It's free, and you can download it here. : http://earth.google.com/

As an application to use on your interactive whiteboard, this really is an essential piece of software to have. Combine it with your desktop capture/camera tool and you can grab images from anywhere in the world and annotate over the top.

The obvious use would be for Geography lessons – it gives you an amazing globe at your fingertips which you can spin, zoom and see pretty much everything on Earth. The search facility lets you find a place almost instantly. You can also add weather information, radar images and recent cloud cover information. One of the new features is an ocean view where you can explore the sea floor and obtain information files about ocean life.

History teachers might want to take tours of Rome, or Athens and see where the monuments are. Many famous buildings are rendered as 3d structures. Street level view even lets you take tours of some of these areas from a visitors eye view – visit the Colosseum from the comfort your classroom!

For Science teachers I love the Sunlight feature, where you can view light/dark areas over time. Drag the slide to change the time and see how the area of light and dark moves. This is really nice for showing how we get night and day (use alongside a demo with a torch and a football/globe)

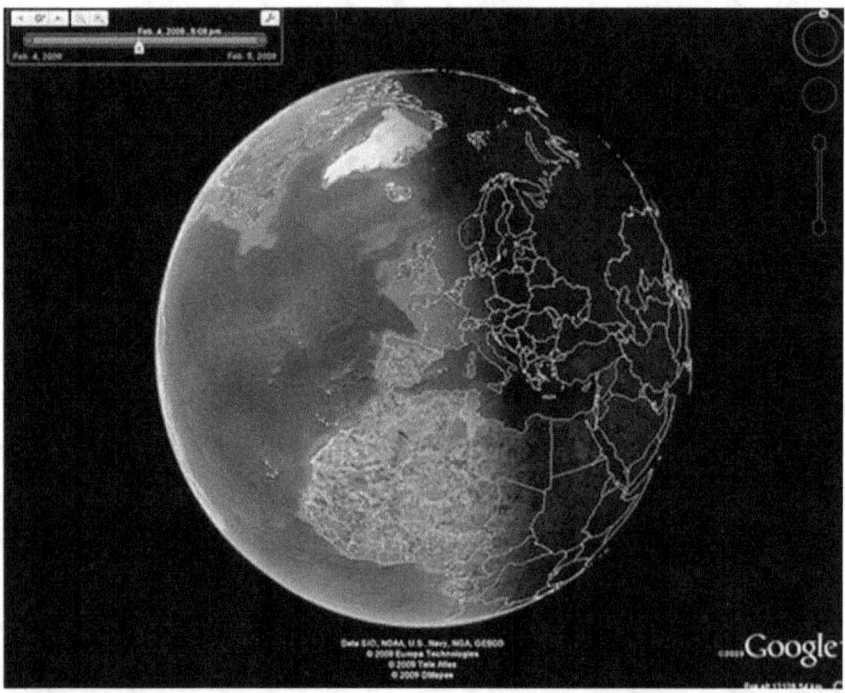

For some inspiration on how to use this feature here's an excellent idea from Tom Barretts blog (http://bit.ly/hcPuw2) He used his Twitter network to tell his class where they were in the world. The students then had to find where they were using Google Earth and to then use the shadowed layer to find the length of the day at that point. This was a great way of making the search relevant since they were looking for places that real people had suggested.

As well as views of Earth, Google Earth also has a detailed map of Mars which can be explored, as well as a fully featured Sky mode which lets you explore the universe. Again it's fully searchable and perfect for Earth and Space or Our Place in the Universe areas of the curriculum.

Another new feature is Historical View which lets you view past images of an area, if they exist, to see what it would have looked like in the past. This works better in some areas than others and does depend on how many times that area has been photographed. For example the area where I live has been surveyed last year, and in 2005 so I can toggle between seeing how my house looked before and after I moved in 😊

You can find out more about Google Earth from the Google Earth blog (http://googleblog.blogspot.com/).

And also from Tom Barrett, here's 22 interesting ways to use Google Earth. (http://bit.ly/gUKE9p)

Google Earth v6 Released

Originally posted December 1 2010

http://www.whiteboardblog.co.uk/2010/12/google-earth-v6-released/

Google have released version 6 of their amazing Google Earth software. As an application to use on your interactive whiteboard, this really is an essential piece of software to have. Combine it with your desktop capture/camera tool and you can grab images from anywhere in the world and annotate over the top. (http://www.google.com/earth)

New features include Street View that will be familiar to users of Google Maps, which lets you see what these places look like from a visitors eye view. The History view is less obvious, so you can look back over past images for an area, and you can also see trees at street level which is less useful, but quite impressive.

So using street level view, here's my hometown of Southend. Standing on the seafront at the top of Pier Hill looking at the longest pleasure pier in the world ☺

To see the History Tool in action; here's the Anglia Ruskin University campus in Chelmsford where I occasionally work. This is how it looks today.

And here is how it looked in 2000, before they built the new wing, using the History slider.

This is a great way of looking at different areas and seeing how they changed. You can go back quite a way, depending on the images available. If there are local developments near your school you might be able to see what the area looked like before they were built.

The obvious use of Google Earth would be for Geography lessons – it gives you an amazing globe at your fingertips which you can spin, zoom and see pretty much everything on Earth. The search facility lets you find a place almost instantly. You can also add weather information, radar images and recent cloud cover information. There is an ocean view where you can explore the sea floor and obtain information files about ocean life.

History teachers might want to take tours of Rome, or Athens and see where the monuments are. Many famous buildings are rendered as 3d structures. Street level view even lets you take tours of some of these areas from a visitors eye view – visit the Colosseum from the comfort your classroom! It doesn't beat visiting places for real, but it's the next best thing.

Modern Language teachers could use the Street Level view to take tours of foreign towns and cities and look at street signs, shop signs etc. Try using it as a way of giving directions in a different language

For Science teachers I love the Sunlight feature, where you can view light/dark areas over time. Drag the slide to change the time and see how the area of light and dark moves. This is really nice for showing how we get night and day (use alongside a demo with a torch and a football/globe).

Google Earth is free to download, and it adds a whole new level to the regular Google Maps website. It's definitely well worth getting hold of a copy. http://www.google.com/earth/

Google Squared in the Classroom

Originally posted June 22 2009

http://www.whiteboardblog.co.uk/2009/06/google-squared-in-the-classroom/

Google have recently rolled out a new twist on their search engine in their continued bid for world domination – Google Squared.

Google Squared takes a category and creates a starter 'square' of information, automatically fetching and organizing facts from across the web and producing them in spreadsheet format. You can then add additional columns and rows to this grid of information (if more info is available)

To see how this differs from a normal Google search, try this search for Chemical Elements

http://www.google.com/squared/search?q=chemical+elements

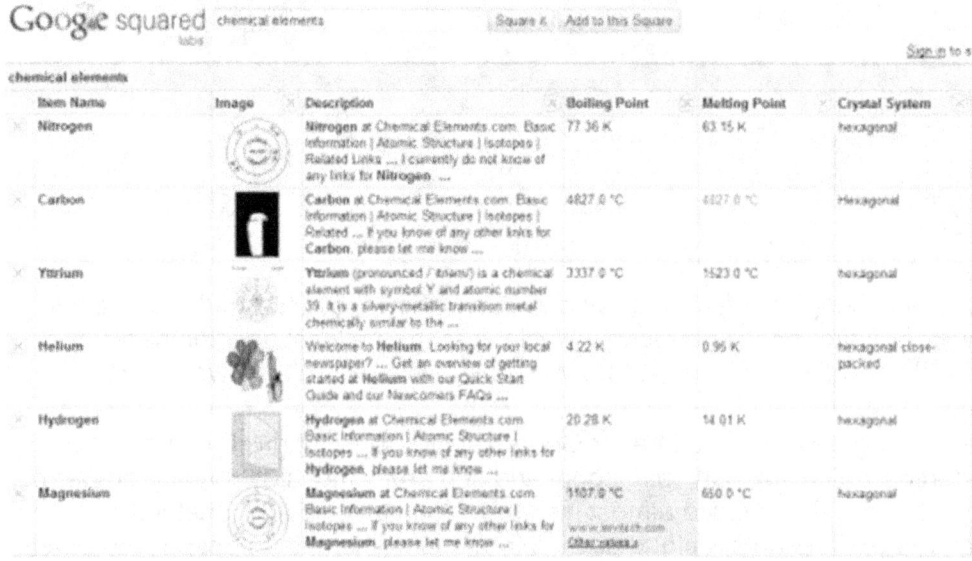

How about just The Noble Gases, or Halogens, or Transition metals?

or Women Scientists , Black Scientists, Space Probes, and many more! (http://bit.ly/fRYt2o)

With my Science hat on, there's loads of ways you could use this. Thinking of the whole curriculum there's even more: English Kings, Capital Cities, US States, etc. etc.

It's a really interesting way of displaying the results from a search and it could be very handy for quickly summarising data from any number of sources; including Wikipedia and others.

It would also be useful for comparing prices and spec on items you want to buy such as Digital Cameras or NetBooks.

13 sites for MFL teaching with your Interactive Whiteboard

Originally posted 29 July 2009

http://www.whiteboardblog.co.uk/2009/07/13-sites-for-mfl-teaching-with-your-interactive-whiteboard/

Foreign languages, I am ashamed to say, are not one of my strong points. I did scrape B's at GCSE in French and German, but I am not very good. I can order a beer in most languages though. I was asked recently if I could run a Smartboard training day in France, in French which my wife thought was most amusing. I didn't take up the offer, "Voici le tableu blanc" is about as much as I could muster. And I don't even know if that's correct ☺

Anyway, here are some useful sites that could be used to teach Modern Foreign Languages on your Interactive Whiteboard. If you can recommend any others, please put them in the comments!

Pic-Lits
http://www.piclits.com/compose_dragdrop.aspx
Drag words onto photographs to describe the scene or mood. The default language is english, but could be used in other languages in freestyle mode.

Word magnets
http://www.triptico.co.uk/flashFiles/wordMagnets/WordMagnets.html

This resource from Triptico could again have uses in many different subjects since it is quite open-ended. Use it to create drag and drop sentences in your chosen language.

MFL Sunderland
http://www.sunderlandschools.org/mfl-sunderland/resources.htm

Some excellent resources from a group of MFL teachers in Sunderland. Contains resources for all key stages in French, German, Spanish and Italian. Worth a visit.

Teachers TV MFL Resources
http://bit.ly/goPNri

I often forget to check Teachers TV for resources, but there are quite a few on there for many different subjects. These videos are designed to be used in class and would be perfect on the IWB. Register for a free account and you can download them to your computer. Remember to play full-screen!

WatchKnow – videos
http://watchknow.org/Default.aspx?Category=198

Simple videos to introduce languages at Primary level. Includes pronunciation guides. Like this one: http://www.youtube.com/watch?v=aafd2a9FHHY

Newbury Park – Language of the month
http://www.newburypark.redbridge.sch.uk/langofmonth/
Short video clips that would be ideal to introduce different languages in Primary schools from Newbury Park school in Ilford.

Ashcombe School – GCSE French Videos
http://bit.ly/dTmlNp

Some very useful videos here for French teaching from Ashcombe School in Surrey. Also check out their Primary MFL resources. Videos are a little small, but come with a quiz. May be better for self-study rather than IWB use. Right click on the video to play it full-screen.

Anna Graingers – MFL Resources
http://www.mflresources.org.uk/index.html

Visit Anna Graingers site for powerpoints, game templates and worksheets.

CrickWeb Spanish / French
http://www.crickweb.co.uk/ks2spanish.html
http://www.crickweb.co.uk/ks2french.html

Crickweb has a wealth of great resources for all subjects, and that includes languages. Check out their KS2 Spanish and French resources.

Northumberland Grid MFL
http://ngfl.northumberland.gov.uk/languages/

Northumberland Grid for Learning has some very good primary MFL resources that are well worth a look. Including traditional story books in different languages.

If you have a Smartboard, they also have some year 1-4 Smartboard files to download.

BBC Learning Zone clips
http://www.bbc.co.uk/learningzone/clips/

The BBC is always a good place to look for video resources for classroom teaching. They have videos on all subjects, including French, German and Spanish at both Primary and Seconday level.

Bleu, Blanc, Rouge…
http://www.teachnet.ie/clane/index.html

Bleu, Blanc, Rouge is a website for teachers wishing to access resources for teaching French in the Primary School. The site contains songs & rhymes, language games, art & seasonal ideas, tongue twisters, recipes & links to French stories on the net.

World of Teaching
http://www.worldofteaching.com/

Lots of powerpoints to adapt and adopt for language teaching (and other subjects)

For a full list of sites for MFL teaching that I've found, check out my Delicious list on:
http://delicious.com/dannynic/mfl+iwb

MYLO – a new site for MFL Teachers

Originally posted November 4 2010

http://www.whiteboardblog.co.uk/2010/11/mylo-a-new-site-for-mfl-teachers/

MYLO is a new website designed to engage young people in learning languages, to raise their competence, and to encourage them to continue studying languages. It launched today – so is pretty new on the block! http://mylo.dcsf.gov.uk/

MYLO is organised into a series of challenges. Each challenge is designed to offer a fully-rounded and self-contained learning experience, promoting language learning through creativity, problem-solving, decision-making and enquiry.

Challenges are structured to include:

- Context – a short video sequence sets the scene for the learner, explaining what the challenge is about, and how to succeed.
- Practice activities – a number of bite-size activities and materials designed to encourage learners to develop new skills or refine those they already have.
- The Challenge – challenges can be started and work saved. Examples of good practice, from other learners, are available.
- Support – an ever-present collection of support materials, such as a dictionary, key phrases and cultural background notes are available for reference.
- Submit – if a school is registered with MYLO then learners submit their completed challenge to the teacher for assessment. Teachers can choose to publish this work to the wider MYLO community.

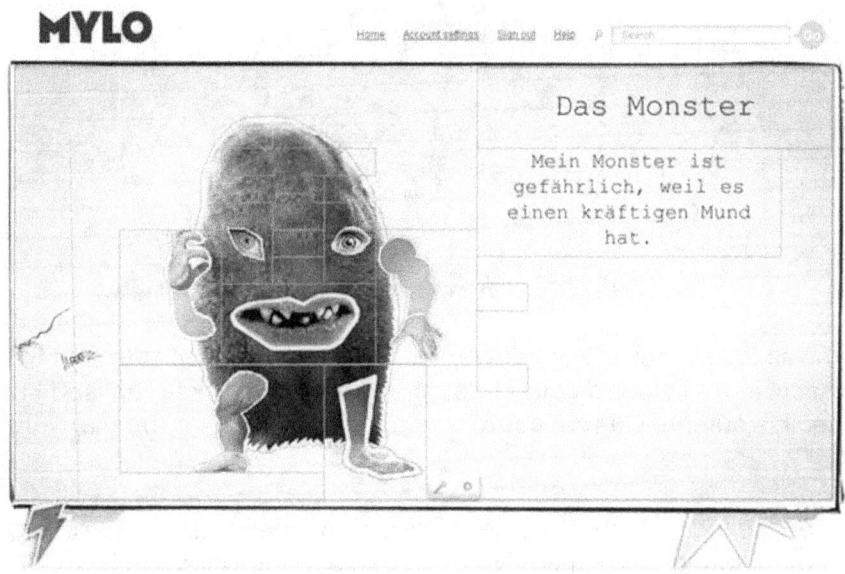

From its launch in November MYLO will cover the most popular languages : French, German and Spanish– the ones most commonly taught at school or spoken on holiday: In addition they've also included Chinese as it is already offered in many secondary schools and is predicted to become a popular choice!

It's free to register with MYLO as an individual, or as a school. MFL departments should definitely take a look. http://mylo.dcsf.gov.uk/

Finger Friendly Websites

Originally posted February 20 2009

http://www.whiteboardblog.co.uk/2009/02/finger-friendly-websites/

Last week I was at a college running a session on how to use a Smartboard. One of the questions I was asked was if I knew of any good 'finger-friendly' websites that I could recommend. I demonstrated a few during the course, but this got me thinking about producing a decent list of these kind of websites.

What I wanted was to list sites that work well with a finger (but also with an IWB pen) and were very interactive. As I started going through my delicious links I realised I had quite a lot of sites that met this criteria. Current count is about 50 of them, far too many than for just one blog post.

If you want to see the whole list, I have gone through my delicious links and tagged anything that fits the bill with the tag "fingerfriendly" – you can see the whole list here; http://delicious.com/dannynic/fingerfriendly

I'll try and produce some blog posts that summarise some of the best for different subjects.

Collaborative Digital Storytelling with Storybird

Originally posted Dec 23 2009

http://www.whiteboardblog.co.uk/2009/12/collaborative-digital-storytelling-with-storybird/

I've just got back from a Smartboard trainers gathering up in Leeds. It's always great to get together and share new stuff that we've found with everyone else, and learn new things too. Vicki from Shoofly (http://www.shooflypublishing.co.uk/) demonstrated Storybird, a website she'd found, and I just had to share it here http://storybird.com/

Storybird provides a very user-friendly way of combining images and text to tell a story, and then share that story with other people. You choose images from a huge bank of ready-drawn pictures which also help to provide inspiration for story ideas.

You can also have several users all working on the same Storybird story, which would be a great classroom activity

The three little pigs decided to get away from it all

When you have created a Storybird you can send it to others (via weblink) or use the embed code to embed it into a blog / wiki etc.

See : http://storybird.com/books/emilie-and-her-dreams/

You can also read the stories produced by other people, if you want a little inspiration. It's a really cute little website and it would be an excellent way of making Big Books to use in the classroom on your IWB.

Go check it out http://storybird.com, and thanks again Vicki for sharing the link.

Update – Thanks to @valleseco for sharing this great wiki of MFL Storybirds created by @wizenedcrone. : http://mfl-storybirds.wikispaces.com/

Blitz Resources from History Pin

Originally posted September 9 2010

http://www.whiteboardblog.co.uk/2010/09/blitz-resources-from-history-pin/

Seventy years ago this month the Blitz began. It started with the bombing of London for 76 consecutive nights, and soon cities and towns across Britain were suffering attacks, from Aberdeen to Coventry, from Birmingham to Hull.

Many homes, high streets and famous landmarks were dramatically altered by the bombings, in some cases beyond recognition. By the end of May 1941, more than a million homes had been destroyed or damaged in London alone.

HistoryPin (http://bit.ly/g6P6Fm)

HistoryPin has a selection of images of the Blitz, many superimposed over modern day streetview images of the area such as this image of bomb damage in Broadgate, Coventry (http://bit.ly/gwVR7s). If you've not seen History Pin before, it is one of a series of projects created as part of We Are What We Do's campaign to get generations talking more, sharing more and coming together more often. It's an excellent resource bank, and still growing.

This would be a lovely resource for History teachers when teaching about World War 2.

History Lessons from the National Archive

Originally posted May 5 2010

http://www.whiteboardblog.co.uk/2010/05/history-lessons-from-the-national-archive/

The National Archives is the UK government's official archive, containing over 1,000 years of history. We give detailed guidance to government departments and the public sector on information management and advise others about the care of historical archives.

http://www.nationalarchives.gov.uk/education/

The National Archives Education Service brings history to life through an award-winning programme of taught sessions and online resources. Their website contains a huge range of online learning resources to support the National Curriculum in history from key stage 1 to 5.

There are many large-scale topic sites packed with original sources and activities, as well as more than 50 lessons based on documents from our collections, a podcast series and an award-winning film website called Focus on Film with a film archive and teaching activities.

There are some fun games and activities for students to play. Ranging from Tudor Joust, Build a Bomb Shelter and Victorian Crime.

A comprehensive teacher guide can be downloaded which explains everything a teacher needs to know to be able to make the best use of the website and its resources. You can get it here. http://bit.ly/hfg1lh

History teachers should make sure this site is in their favourites list!

http://www.nationalarchives.gov.uk/education/

Animated Storybooks

Originally posted April 27 2010

Thanks to Anne Marie (http://annemarie80.edublogs.org/)for making me aware of Frank Asch and his website.

http://www.frankasch.com/animatedbooks.html

Frank Asch is an author whose work includes the Moonbear picture books . He has a great website which contains five animated story books complete with audio such as I Met a Penguin. http://bit.ly/enaMWa

He also has his own channel on YouTube where you can also access his animated stories.

Watch his animated books here : http://www.frankasch.com/animatedbooks.html

Grapholite – Diagram and Chart Tool

Originally posted November 6 2010

http://www.whiteboardblog.co.uk/2010/11/grapholite-diagram-and-chart-tool/

Grapholite is a new service for creating diagrams and flowcharts online, via your browser. You can create new diagrams from scratch or use the sample templates provided by Grapholite. It's another good example of a cloud-based application which does not require you to install anything on your computer.

Grapholite will work on both Windows and Mac computers, in Internet Explorer, Firefox, Chrome and Safari.

It looks pretty useful, and would work well on an Interactive Whiteboard, as well as standalone computers.

As well as flowcharts and diagrams, this would be good for producing MindMaps (of a sort) for revision or brainstorming activities.

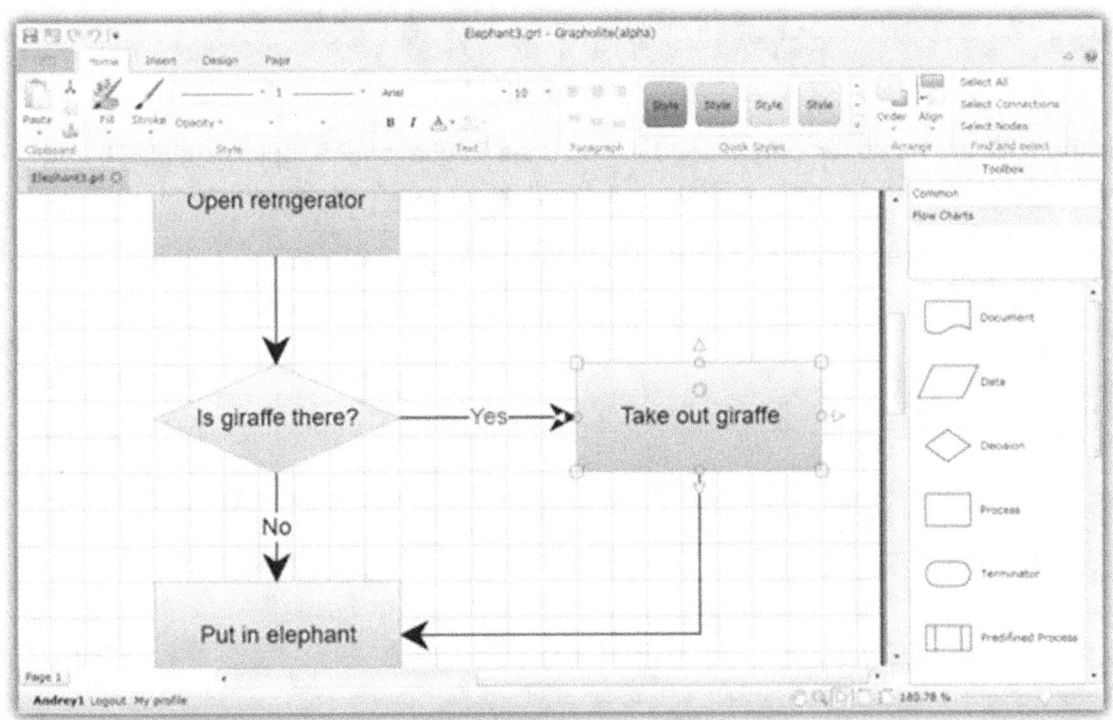

Check out Grapholite here : http://grapholite.com/

Thanks to Richard Byrne at Free Technology for Teachers, for bringing Grapholite to my attention.

iBoard – Free Interactive KS1 resources

Originally posted February 5 2010

http://www.whiteboardblog.co.uk/2010/02/iboard-free-interactive-ks1-resources/

iBoard first caught my eye last year at the BETT exhibition. They produce an excellent bank of interactive resources for Reception, Year 1 and Year 2 classes in several subjects, including literacy, numeracy and science.

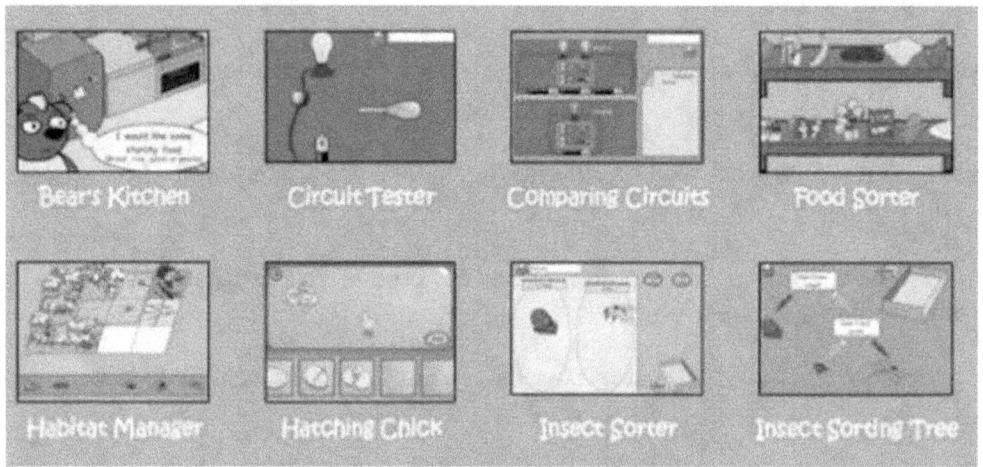

Since then, iBoard has been purchased by the Times Educational Supplement (TES) and made available free of charge to all teachers, which is an excellent development.

You can access the resources here: http://www.tes.iboard.co.uk/

Teaching Resources from the TES

Originally posted September 20 2010

http://www.whiteboardblog.co.uk/2010/09/teaching-resources-from-the-tes/

On 6th September 2010, a new version of the TES Resources website was launched, making it easier for teachers to find and use some of the brightest lesson ideas posted online by the teaching community.

http://www.tes.co.uk/teaching-resources/

TES Resources is one of the biggest websites in the UK made up of content that is created by its user community. Teachers can access the site to download and share more than 50,000 free resources to freshen up their teaching and add colour to the classroom. Those tools that are rated most highly by other teachers appear at the top of the targeted search so in just three clicks, a teacher can find exactly the right resource.

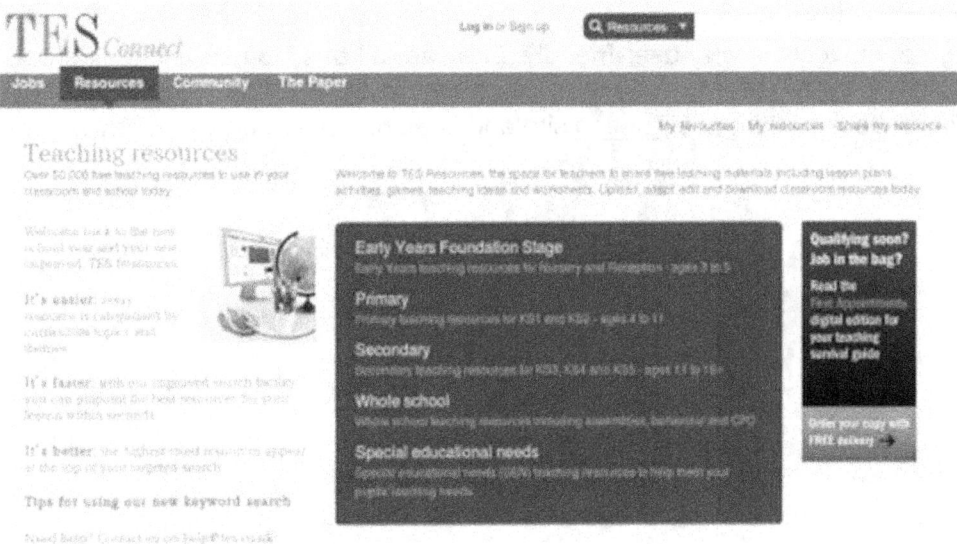

For example – here's a Lesson Starter Generator: "120 starters all in one place! The Starter Generator has enough starters for you to shake a stick at. All come with pictures to aid recall and enjoyment and are explained, often with examples. Nearly all are generic and can be used across subjects." : http://bit.ly/dVnpA8

To access the resources you will need to sign up for a login, but it's free to do so.

Triptico – Free IWB Tools

Originally posted June 11 209

http://www.whiteboardblog.co.uk/2009/06/triptico-free-iwb-tools/

I have written about this site in the past when it was XML Education. The site has a new look, and a new name. It's now called Triptico and you can find it here: http://www.triptico.co.uk . The site is produced by two teachers over here in the UK, and the resources they have produced so far are really handy.

There are nearly 20 cool flash utilities on the site which are free to use.

There's the Word Magnet tool which lets you paste a sentence into a text box, then break it up and move the words around.

The site also includes a number of different spinners for choosing things at random, as well as timers, score keepers and memory games.

The design of the tools is very user-friendly. They are all easy to use and look great.

It's well worth bookmarking the Triptico site and keeping an eye on what they add in the future.

True Tube – PSHE, RE and Citizenship Videos

Originally posted November 8 2010

http://www.whiteboardblog.co.uk/2010/11/true-tube-pshe-re-and-citizenship-videos/

TrueTube is a FREE, award winning education site for schools, designed to support the teaching of PSHE*, Citizenship and RE at Key Stages 3 and 4. Science teachers may also find some of the videos useful for teaching some of the controversial issues in science such as Global Warming.

TrueTube has hundreds of high quality short films on a wide range of social, ethical and moral issues including; Eating disorders, faith, poverty, depression, sexuality and crime.

Some of the films are personal, some provocative or opinionated, some objective and factual; all of them are brought together here, to highlight different angles on the issues which affect young people in modern society.

Some videos come with lesson plans, and there are also some newly-added assembly plans for download which covers topical subjects such as Diwali and Remembrance.

Check it out here : http://www.truetube.co.uk/

(*for non UK readers, PSHE is the abbreviation for Personal Social Health & Economic education which has been proposed to become a statutory part of the curriculum in England)

Teachable

Originally posted February 6 2009

http://www.whiteboardblog.co.uk/2009/02/teachable/

When I went to the ASE conference in January I was given a demonstration of an excellent website called Teachable. (http://www.teachable.net/)

Teachable.net is a high quality resource sharing website for teachers, where you can browse, download and adapt Powerpoints, worksheets and other interactive material for your class. All the files are contributed by other teachers, and have been quality-checked and tagged under easy-to-find categories.

There are over 1000 different lessons to download, ranging from high impact KS3 starters, to in-depth interactive A-level worksheets.

Unlike some other sites, Teachable is not free. Access costs from just £15 for a 10 file bundle, or there is a special offer for schools for access up to 400 files and get some training bundled for free. Charging does mean they can employ people to check the quality of the uploaded resources, which is fair enough.

Alternatively if teachers submit their own resources to the site they can get credits which they can spend on download other resources. And if your resources sell to other teachers then you will get a cut of the proceeds as well. So there is a benefit to sharing your materials with the world!

You can preview everything before you download the full version, and when you do download the full version they grant you a Creative Commons license the right to copy and share the resource (for educational use).

At present the site deals mainly in PowerPoints and Word files. There's no facility to upload Smart Notebook or Promethean files. I discussed this with the representatives of Teachable at the time and they say they've had no call for this facility yet. Teachers are sticking with PowerPoint. While a lot of the PowerPoint's I saw were interactive with the use of Macros and suchlike, this did seem like an opportunity missed.

So, if you do have any high quality Smart Notebook files or Promethean flipcharts then I suggest you get in touch with Teachable to create some demand. In the meantime check out the bank of resources that are already there and perhaps share some of your good work too.

Teachable also runs a cool blog that is also worth adding to your RSS reader. From a post recently here are 10 Top Physics Videos. (http://bit.ly/ecCuq2) Well worth a look.

Teaching Videos

Originally posted January 18 2010

http://www.whiteboardblog.co.uk/2010/01/teaching-videos/

Teaching Videos is a great new free website from Mark Warner – you may know him from other educational websites such as Ideas to Inspire, Display Photos, and Teaching Ideas.

- http://www.ideastoinspire.co.uk/
- http://www.displayphotos.co.uk/
- http://www.teachingideas.co.uk/

Teaching Videos is intended to be a place where teachers and view and share educational videos that can be used in the classroom. Whilst you can browse YouTube, Vimeo or Google Video to find a wide range of videos, Teaching Videos allows you to see videos which other teachers have recommended as suitable for education. In the future you will also be able to register and add videos to the database yourself!

The site is just starting out, and is beginning to grow. It will be well worth keeping an eye on it, and checking it out when you are looking for videos to use in the classroom.

http://www.teachingvideos.co.uk/

Please be aware that some school networks might block YouTube or other embedded videos, so check this before your lesson!

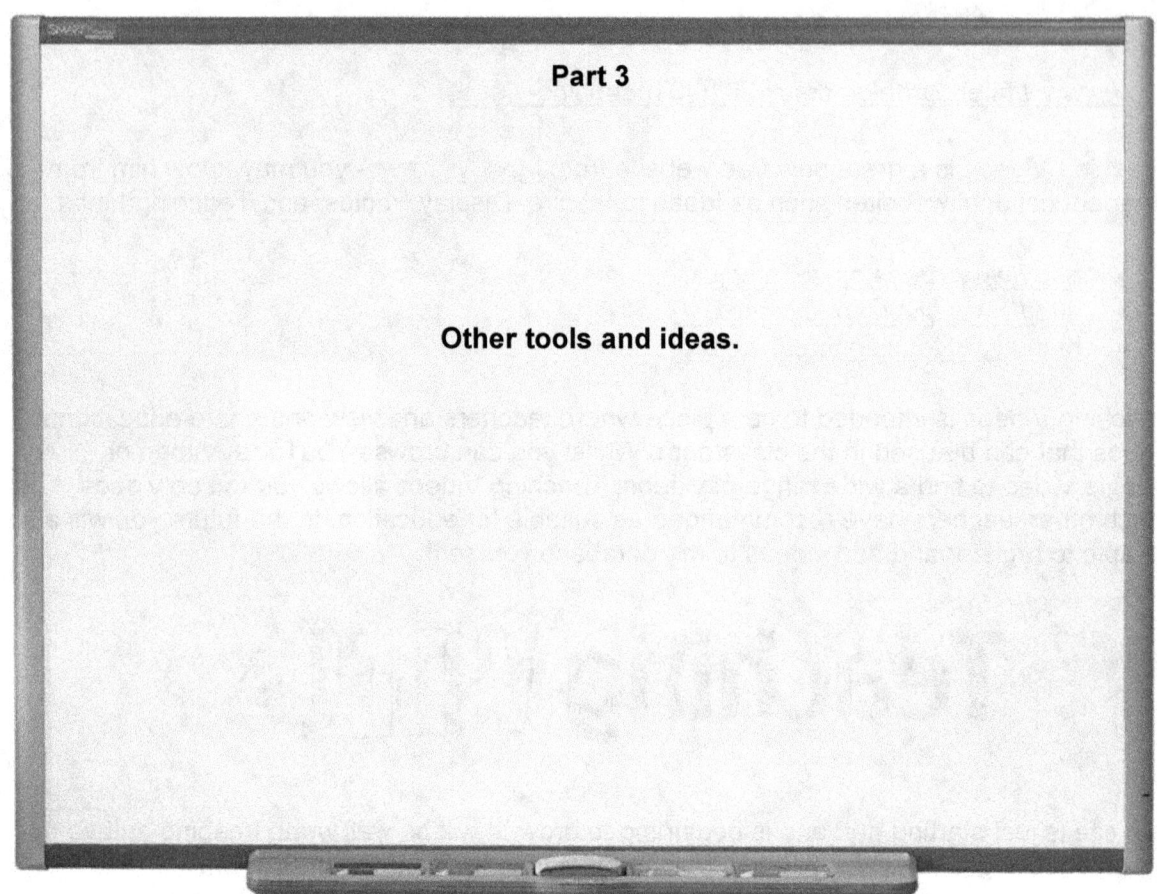

Part 3

Other tools and ideas.

Make Easy Screenshots with Aviary

Originally posted July 5 2009

http://www.whiteboardblog.co.uk/2009/07/make-easy-screenshots-with-aviary/

Here's a new website that will make it easier to take screenshots of other sites to save to your desktop or to embed into your blog or your wiki.

It's called Aviary (http://aviary.com/) And it's a neat, free, image editing application. You can create images from scratch, and share them with others online.

But as well as that, it has a screen capture feature.

If you use Firefox you can get "Talon" an Aviary plug in that puts a small button onto your toolbar. Just click that button and select the area you want to grab. You then get the option to save that image to your desktop, copy to the clipboard or have it hosted on Aviary to easily embed online.

Like this:

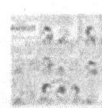 Swanny203 thanks to @dannynic and @jameshollis for sources of chem animations....
about 16 hours ago from web

 mathwhiz RT @jameshollis: Got a #smartboard? Looking for Physics games? Check it out! http://www.physicsgames.net - Thanks @dannynic
about 19 hours ago from TweetDeck

kltheobald RT @jameshollis: Got a #smartboard? Looking for Physics games? Check it out! http://www.physicsgames.net - Thanks @dannynic
about 20 hours ago from TwitterGadget

 kellyhines RT @jameshollis: Got a #smartboard? Looking for Physics games? Check it out! http://www.physicsgames.net - Thanks @dannynic
 about 20 hours ago from TweetDeck

Which was a pretty painless way of grabbing a section of my Twitter page.

You need to sign up for an Aviary account, but it was free to do so (there are pricing plans for more advanced use of the site)

Aviary also lets you edit and manipulate images online once you've captured them – or upload your own images to edit.

As well as the Firefox button, Aviary has just launched its easiest feature yet!

You can capture any webpage at all, from any browser, by simply putting **Aviary.com/** in front of the URL!

For example, say you want to capture Google's homepage:
Just change http://www.google.com to Aviary.com/http://google.com.

Very simple.

Edit – if you like this – Lifehacker has just reviewed the Five Best Online Image Editors, and Aviary is on the list, along with Sumo Paint, Photoshop Express, Pixlr and Picnik. I'd probably also add Splashup to the list.

Making Music with the Myna Sound Editor

Originally posted September 23 2009

http://www.whiteboardblog.co.uk/2009/09/making-music-with-the-myna-sound-editor/

I've written about Aviary before. If you haven't seen it, Aviary provides a suite of online tools that allows you to take screengrabs and edit / host images. For free.

Twitter has been buzzing this week with talk of their latest addition to their application suite. They've called it Myna, and this time they are entering the world of music and audio editing.

Again, the application runs in a browser window – so nothing needs to be installed on your computer. Just visit the Aviary website, click on Audio Editor and off you go.

The software allows for multi-track editing. A wide range of audio loops are provided in different musical styles from Rock to Electronica.

In addition you can import your own sound files and also record your own straight into the application.

Using Myna, it would be very simple to produce your own Podcasts or music mixes, much in the same way that you could with Audacity or Garageband.

Once saved – you can "Mixdown" your creation and share it with others via the Aviary site. This would be a good way of hosting your podcasts, which can sometimes be tricky. Aviary provides a link to the hosting page, or you can use an embed code to put it into your blog/VLE.

Myna is free, but you can upgrade to a pro account for $25 or so.

I'm very impressed so far. And will be interested to see how many people make use of this instead of something like Audacity. I do like the free music samples which can give students a very quick start up time if you just want them to look at how to mix different tracks together.

Myna is well worth checking out. And the rest of the Aviary suite too. Go take a look now! http://aviary.com/

Class Projects on the Internet

Originally posted July 9 2008

http://www.whiteboardblog.co.uk/2008/07/class-projects-on-the-internet/

Here's a little bit of history. I found this while trawling through my hard drive. Back in 1995, when I was a young green teacher, I was just starting out with creating simple web pages in Notepad. The World Wide Web was really in its infancy, and not many schools had their own websites yet.

I wanted a new angle on the "make a class folder" style project – so I decided I'd get kids to make a set of web pages instead. It was a slight cheat because I added the few html codes instead – but the text and the images were created by the kids. I still think this was one of the first times this was tried in the UK and I had the article published in the ASE journal Education in Science in November 1996.

Sadly the school website was revamped many years ago (I left the school in the Summer of 1996) although I did carry the work on at my new school – The Cornwallis School in Maidstone. I became the school webmaster and we won a national competition from RM for using the web to support learning in the school.

Nowadays you could tailor a similar project around a class wiki or blog

Apologies for some of the language – which in the very early days of the internet seemed to be needed but now, in the age of wikis, blogs and web2.0 seems rather unnecessary. Remember, this was written 12 years ago.

I can remember when all this was just fields.....

****

Class Projects on the Internet

Danny Nicholson: Education in Science (ASE Journal) November 1996

The World Wide Web (WWW) is composed of millions of pages of information held on computers across the world. Each of these pages can contain images and sounds, as well as text. This is termed Multimedia. Each page can contain 'links' to other pages; for example if this article was a web page you could click your mouse on the word NASA and you would be connected to their web pages.

Last year as part of a topic on energy, I organised a class project on renewable energy sources. The idea behind this was that the class was split into groups, each researching a different topic. The finished pieces of work were then combined into a booklet. The activity provided the students with the chance to practice a number of skills, which included:

• increasing their knowledge of renewable energy sources;

• working as a group and having to delegate the various tasks themselves;

• using the library, CD-ROM, and my own resources to collect relevant information;

• using word processing software to produce the finished pages.

With hindsight, I became aware of a number of drawbacks with presenting the project as a booklet. Many of the students used a computer painting package to produce some great pictures, but these lost their impact when printed on our black and white printer .

The other limitation was that, even one year on, very few people have actually seen the book. So this year I wanted to repeat the activity, but to find another medium for presenting all their hard work. I had recently become involved with the Internet and was interested in the potential of the WWW. It seemed like a logical step to take the files that the students had written on the computer and turn them into a series of web pages.

I passed round a questionnaire asking the students how they felt when I first told them about the project going on to the Internet. Comments I received included; 'I was amazed that we were going to be on the Internet', quite a few were 'excited', one was 'delighted', one girl wrote 'I felt happy and excited because the whole world could see our work', and one commented 'I felt surprised that our work would be good enough!'. The general opinion was one of interest because most of them had heard about this thing called the Internet, but most had never had anything to do with it. I felt that this provided a very good motivator to many of the students.

Starting the project

Over the next six lessons the project began to take shape. The students were given free reign as to the content of their specific section. I provided some guidance if they were stuck for things to write, but on the whole everything was up to them. By the end of our sessions in the computer room each student had produced at least one piece of text or a picture. I then encoded the pages into HTML (Hypertext Markup Language). HTML contains codes that produce special effects when viewed with a web browser program. There are also special codes to insert pictures as well as links to other pages.

It would have been possible to create the whole project as a single document, but this would have too cumbersome for a visitor to read. To make it easier, the document was divided into seven pages; one page per energy source plus an introduction page. The introduction page described the rationale behind the project and gave the names of all the students involved. A special link was included that let the viewer send a message to the students by e-mail. The six energy sources that we looked at were: Solar, Nuclear, Tidal/Wave, Geothermal, Wind and Hydroelectric. Each page consisted of information about the given energy source, plus a number of computer-drawn pictures. At the foot of each page were links so that the visitor could choose which page to visit next.

Responses

The end result was put on to the school pages just before the Christmas holidays and the site was advertised on many of the Usenet education newsgroups. Usenet is a giant bulletin board where messages can be posted on the Internet for anybody to read. I was overwhelmed with the response it produced. In the first three weeks over 200 people had visited the site and many of these sent me e-mail messages to say how good they found it. The site has been used by some teachers as a source of information for their classes tackling the subject of energy. I have even heard from a teacher in Italy, who was using it to help her students to learn English (this was one use that had not occurred to me when I started out). Messages came from as far away as Palm Springs, Sydney and Seattle. Not bad for a small school stuck in the far south east of England!

I passed on these messages to the students, many of whom were amazed that somebody in Australia or America would be interested in their work. One lad has asked me for a copy of the messages so that he can show his mum!

Evaluation

I asked the students to evaluate the project for themselves. I asked them if they enjoyed working on the project and all but two said that they did. When asked what they liked about it, most said that they enjoyed working on the computers. I felt that this was important because often many students do not get enough practice at using IT. Quite a few enjoyed using the painting programme, and many were quite adept at using it. One student told me he enjoyed researching in the library, and another thought it was good to be able to work as a group. Dislikes were few, one student said she did not enjoy the topic she had been asked to do.

Every student was pleased with the way the project looked; 'better than I thought' said one. All the students thought it was a good idea that the project could be seen by people around the world. One said that it was good 'because other people could use our project to learn' showing that a few were realising that they were doing something worthwhile and that they had something to offer other people.

On the whole I was very pleased with the way the project was received. I had no idea when I started that so many people would respond so positively to it. I will certainly try to repeat the process with a different group and another topic. There is not that much that I would alter, if I could do it again. I think it may help to give the students more guidance at the start so that they know what sort of information they could be providing, but then again the fact that the whole direction of the project was left up to them lends the project more of a student-centered feel; it becomes less like a text book.

I have also put the seeds of ideas into the heads of my colleagues in the science department, who are keen to make more use of the schools' IT resources. Other departments have also shown interest; and a history project has just been completed.

Easi-Speak Sound Recorders

Originally posted May 18 2009

http://www.whiteboardblog.co.uk/2009/05/easi-speak-sound-recorders/

Here is an excellent gadget to use for recording student voices without having to be tied to the laptop or PC.

The Easi Speak USB mic is a handheld microphone that lets you record directly onto the device, a bit like a dictaphone. They are very portable and would be ideal for taking on school trips.

You can play the recorded files back directly from the microphone (it has a small speaker built in, or you can use the headphone socket) for immediate feedback. Or you can flip the cap off the bottom of the microphone to reveal the USB connector and plug it in to your computer to offload the files.

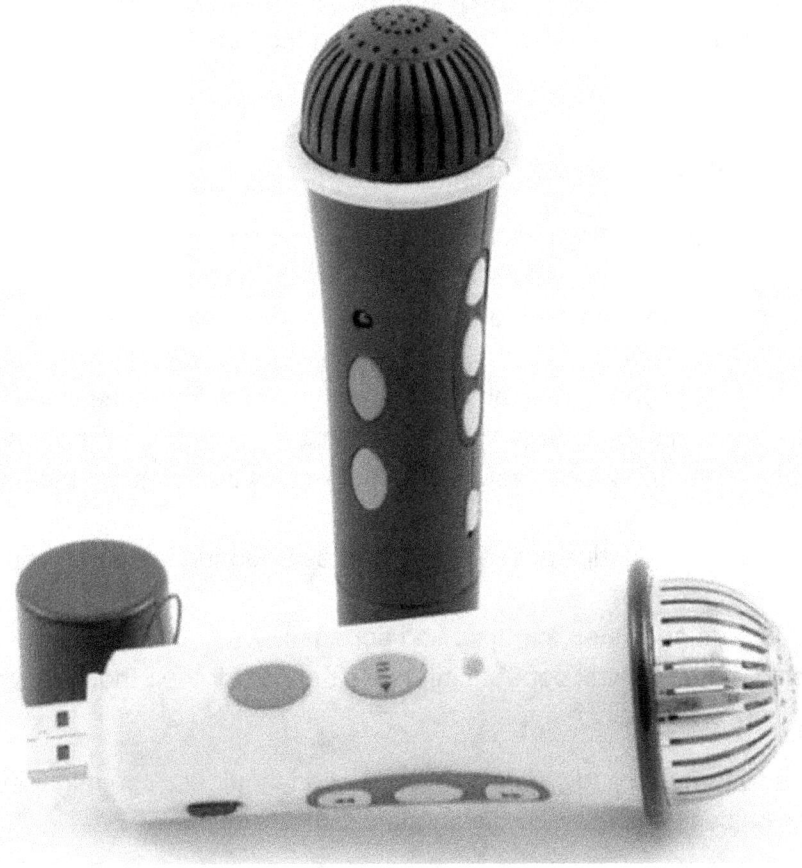

It has a 128MB memory that can record up to 4 hours of sound. It records in WAV or MP3 format so you can take the files and put them directly into Audacity or similar Editing Software.

It has a built-in rechargeable battery which can be charged through USB. You can buy a small charging hub to charge 5 at the same time.

And the best thing about them is the price. They retail at about £30 each but you can get discounts for buying in packs of 5 or 10. Find out more from the TTS Site.

(http://www.tts-group.co.uk/)

The sound quality is pretty good. Visit my original blogpost to hear it.

The EasiSpeak does look a little childish in yellow (I think the black one looks quite good) which may put older children off using it – but TTS are producing Easi-Speak Pro which is £10 more but does look a bit more "adult" and less Fisher Price... It also has dual headphone sockets and an input for an external sound source. This is not yet on the TTS site, but should be available soon.

They are a really neat bit of kit, and can have a wealth of uses in the classroom. They would be ideal for podcasting – either by putting the files into Audacity first, or taking the MP3 files straight off the Easispeak and putting onto your school VLE or uploading to a Podcasting site.

The MP3 files could also be attached to an interactive whiteboard file – would be good for recording short sound effects or words that play when they are clicked.

Here's some other ideas for using them:

- English – Use for role play interviewing, drama-script reading and listening back to recordings.
- Languages – use for role play, oral work – immediate playback to see how they sound.
- Maths – Record in your times table songs and rhymes for all the class to sing to.
- Science – Record sounds from varying distances – how does the sound alter?
- Geography – Interview local residents about issues that concern them with their local environment.
- History – Use on field trips to see how attitudes to popular culture, work and home life have changed.
- Music – Record and listen to music and sounds.
- Citizenship – use for "vox pops" to interview people for their thoughts and opinions on different topics.

They could be used to make audio books, or instructional guides. You might even use them to make revision guides which can be placed onto the school network.

Here's a link to my podcasting presentation I produced last year which may offer additional ideas: http://www.slideshare.net/dannynic/podcasting-presentation-637058

I'm looking forward to playing with these some more. I've bought a set of 5 for my training courses so hopefully I'll soon have some recordings from teachers that we can share!

Podcasting with a Dictaphone

Originally posted October 5 2008

http://www.whiteboardblog.co.uk/2008/10/podcasting-with-a-dictaphone/

I've been getting ready to do a podcasting training day in a few weeks and have been looking into different ways to podcast.

A neat little gadget that I picked up this week is the Olympus Digital Voice Recorder. I bought the WS-311M model, but there's a few different ones out there. I bought mine from Amazon for about £50 but shop around and you might get a better deal.

Basically what you get is a pocket-sized voice recorder that you can take anywhere with you. It runs of a single AAA battery and the 512MB model can record about 8 hours of audio, more if you change the recording quality (up to 130 hours or so).

This would be a very convenient way of getting interviews into a podcast since the students could take this anywhere; they could record "Vox Pops" with people around the school, or even outside the school. The Olympus has an external microphone jack if you wanted to plug a better microphone into it.

The neat bit is getting the files off the device. Basically you slide the battery compartment off, and it reveals a USB stick. Simply plug the Olympus into a USB port (You might need to use the supplied USB extension cable if your port is hard to get to) and then you can just take the files off as you would with any other USB file stick.

To process the files, I had planned on using Audacity, as it seems to be the one that everyone recommends. It's free, which is always a bonus. But this is where I hit a slight issue. The Olympus records as WMA files, and due to licensing issues Audacity cannot open WMA files.

This problem is not a major one, however. A quick look on Google turned up a nice, free, file converter that will convert WMA files to MP3 files with a single right click. It's called Switch, and you can get it here: http://nch.com.au/switch/

It was a very simple job to convert the file (or files) from the Olympus into MP3 to play around with in Audacity.

I've recorded a sample podcast with the Olympus, which I have then uploaded to Podomatic.com. I guess I could host it directly on this blog, but I wanted to see how Podomatic worked.

The direct link to the podcast on Podomatic is here.: http://bit.ly/hDU7hL

Podcasting Slideshare presentation here: http://slidesha.re/gSyelV

NASA DIY Podcast Resources

Originally posted December 2 2010

http://www.whiteboardblog.co.uk/2010/12/nasa-diy-podcast-resources/

If you're looking for some ideas to incorporate podcasting into your science/technology lessons, then take a look at these resources provided by NASA.

http://bit.ly/fdmBk8

NASA's Do-It-Yourself Podcast activity sets the stage for students to create their own video/audio show that features astronauts doing experiments on the International Space Station or NASA experts explaining scientific concepts.

NASA provides a set of audio and video clips along with links to images and information about a STEM-related topic. Students can choose as many items as they want to include in a project and download them to their computer. Students can use the information provided or conduct their own research to write a script for an audio or video production.

Using a camcorder, digital audio recorder, microphone or webcam, students can record additional narration and create other scenes or interviews. Students can then mix and mash their recordings with the NASA clips and edit the production.

To edit audio check out Audacity, or investigate Aviary to do it online. All PC's will have Windows Movie Maker installed, which is basic but does the job of editing video. If you want a commercial product for podcasting try Podium.

Upload the finished file to your school website, blog or VLE and share their good work

http://www.nasa.gov/audience/foreducators/diypodcast/index.html

Vocaroo

Originally posted April 13 2009

http://www.whiteboardblog.co.uk/2009/04/vocaroo/

If you want to try your hand at podcasting, but don't want to be fiddling about with sound editors or suchlike, then take a look at Vocaroo. (http://vocaroo.com/)

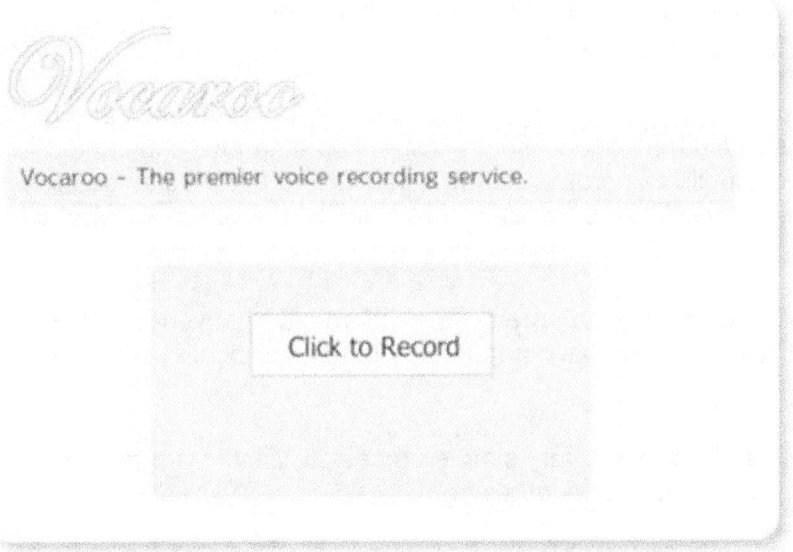

Basically Vocaroo is a website which will let you record a sound file, and then share that file with anyone who wants to listen to it. You can share the link via email, put the link on your blog, embed a simple player into your blog, or download the sound as a .wav file to your computer.

All you need is a microphone, the website does the rest. You get a single button to click to start recording, just start talking and click the stop button when you're done. It's pretty simple.

It will also give you a small flash applet which you can embed into your blog.

You (or your students) could record revision information, step by step tutorials/guides, stories, news reports (real or imagined) and much more.

If you want to make a start in the world of podcasting but want a very no-frills way of getting a recording of your voice onto the Internet, then try Vocaroo out.

Podium for Podcasting

Originally posted September 28 2010

http://www.whiteboardblog.co.uk/2010/09/podium-for-podcasting/

I've had the chance recently to have a little play with Podium from Lightbox. Podium is a PC based podcasting software which enables users to create, edit and publish audio and video podcasts from a simple interface, meaning that pupils do not have to work with a number of different software packages in order to podcast in lessons.
http://www.podiumpodcasting.com/

Podcasting with Podium is very easy, pupils are able to create, edit and publish their audio or video podcasts all during one lesson! Podium has a handy scripting tool which allows for group working as pupils can create scripts together and assign dialogue to different members of the group. When they begin recording, they each know whose turn it is to speak.

The Podium interface should look pretty straightforward to anyone used to software such as MovieMaker or Audacity. There's not too many buttons to confuse and provide too much choice.

Recording audio and video is a very simple process. Click the red record button, and if your webcam or microphone is set up, off you go!

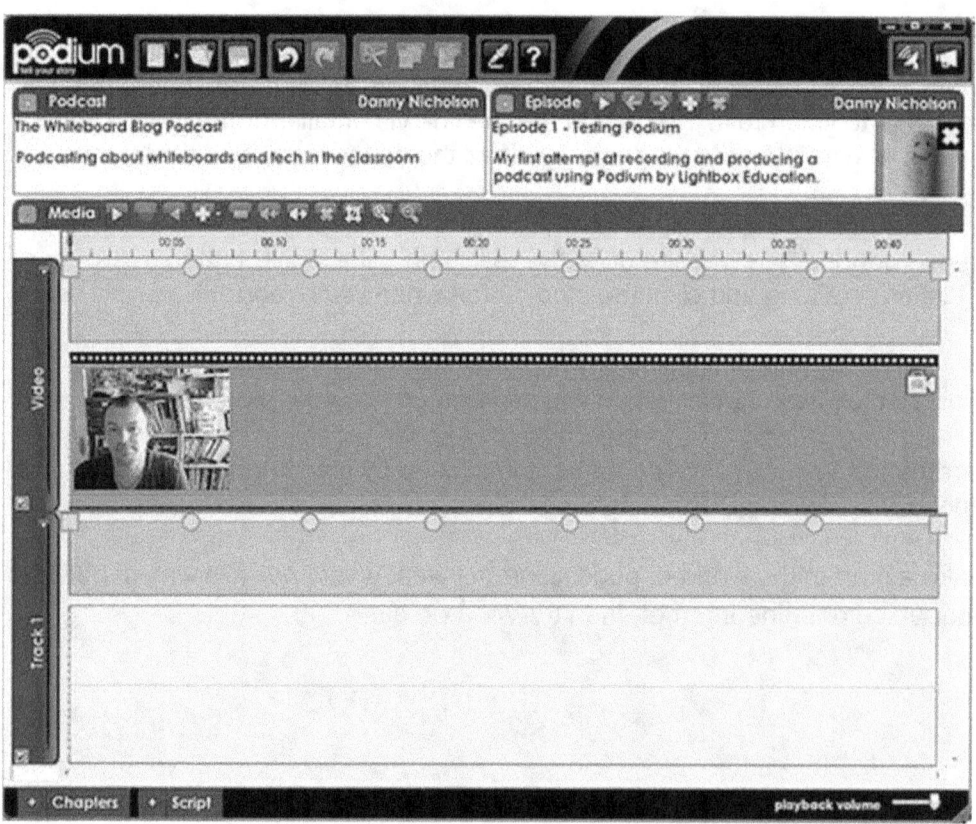

There's no way of changing the settings within the main piece of software. You need to run an additional application called Podium Options that installs at the same time. Make sure you keep the manual nearby as it has initial password to get into this area (You can change the password once in).

I found this a little confusing at first (as someone who rarely reads the manual first and just dives straight in), but I can see why it's done as pupils should not need to ever go near these. If you make changes to the settings, you need to exit Podium and go back in to get them to take effect – as I found when trying to modify ftp information and select which folder to upload into.

I had a little difficulty getting my FTP settings correct, I wanted to put my podcasts into a podcast folder – which causes some confusion. But once it was sorted the software would automatically upload an audio and video podcast to the designated folder. I found that if you add a podcast folder into the settings, you also need to add it to the web address, I assumed it would do that automatically.

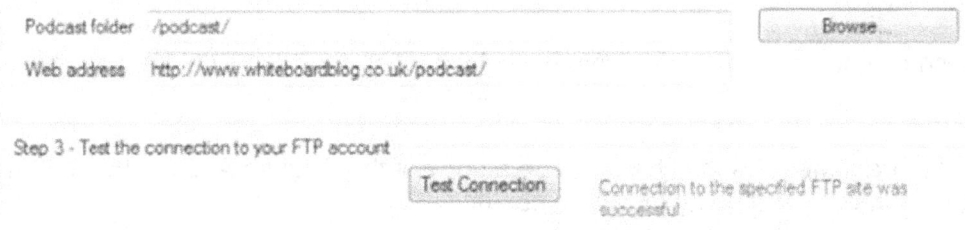

Once recorded, and edited – it only takes one click to upload the podcast to your ftp site. You can if you wish purchase hosting space from Lightbox, or use your own school space. You can set a password for uploading so that pupils can be restricted from uploading before the teacher has had a chance to approve the finished product. Podium will then produce the rss feeds that your visitors can subscribe to:

So.... by of way of testing the whole thing out, here is my quick video podcast feed produced by Podium automatically as an mp4 file:

Whiteboard Blog – Testing Video Podcast : http://bit.ly/h5dXS0

and here's the audio one if you want to hear but not see me : http://bit.ly/hVAYys

In all the process was very simple and once you'd got to grips with the interface for Podium the whole thing was very easy to do. Apologies for the quiet audio, I think that's more down to my own audio settings on my system. I did this in a hurry!

Getting Podium:

If you like the sound of Podium, you can download a trial version from the Podium website. http://www.podiumpodcasting.com/trial/

Also, if you come to TeachMeet Essex, there will be a copy of the Podium Audio version in the charity raffle, so someone will go away with a copy!

Podcasting Links:

For more ideas, Podium have produced a free booklet 'Top tips – 50 podcasting ideas for the classroom' which is well worth downloading, even if you don't use Podium. http://bit.ly/gd5lkV

My presentation on Podcasting can be found on SlideShare here. http://slidesha.re/gSyelV

Mini Wireless Keyboard and Touchpad Gadget

Originally posted December 5 2009

http://www.whiteboardblog.co.uk/2009/12/mini-wireless-keyboard-and-touchpad-gadget/

Here's another option for those times that teachers want to interact with something they are displaying on their whiteboard (or just on a projector) without having to go to the computer.

This mini wireless touchpad and keyboard is an inexpensive way device that could be quite handy for use in the classroom. Want the students to do a drag and drop task? Pass this around the classroom. Want simple text input? this would do that too. I found it slightly easier to use than a tablet. You still have to look at the screen rather than the pad, like you do with a tablet, but I found it much more like using a laptop touchpad.

I found them on Ebay for about £30 inc postage to the UK (shipped from Hong Kong). Or you can get them in Maplins in the UK for £39.99. Mine has just arrived, so I haven't had a chance to test the full range of it yet, but the blurb says it can have a range of 10m. Not brilliant, but should cover a standard classroom?

The device comes with a charging lead (it charges from USB) and a receiver. I plugged it into my Windows 7 laptop and it installed painlessly.

It's definitely an interesting little device which does provide a little more flexibility in how you use your Interactive Whiteboard resources with a class.

Some Tips for Twitter

Originally posted April 1 2009

http://www.whiteboardblog.co.uk/2009/04/some-tips-for-twitter/

I've posted before about how I've become a huge fan of Twitter. I've demonstrated it on my Web 2.0 courses and I get the impression that a lot of people are either unimpressed and can't see the point, or are overwhelmed at the idea of this huge stream of information. And I'd agree that for the uninitiated, looking at someone else's Twitter stream go flooding past can be a little like trying to decipher The Matrix.

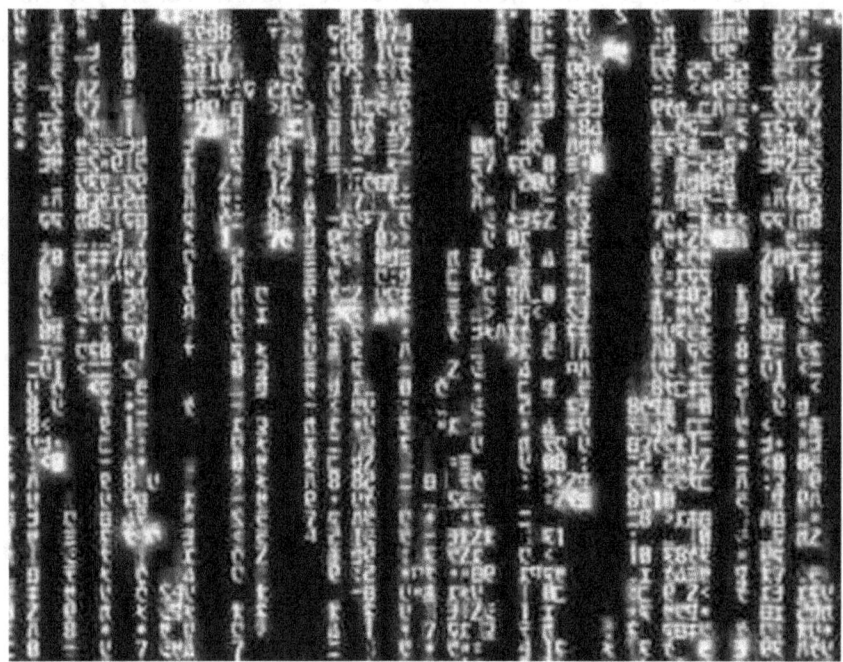

I've found Twitter invaluable as a personal learning network. But there is a critical mass to it. If you only follow a few people it can seem quite dull. For it to be useful, you need to start following a lot of people. And hopefully entice those people to follow you.

Here are some tips to help you make the most of Twitter.

1. Follow a few key people. Lurk for a while and see who they talk to. Click on the names of the people they talk to and read their bios. If they seem like interesting people, follow them too. (Edit – yes this does sound a little like stalking! But it's an effective way of finding new people to follow…)

For IWB's start with: @ChrisBetcher, @ActivEducator, @MySmartSpaces (And me! @dannynic)

For inspiring teachers using technology follow: @Tom Barrett, @Joe Dale, @Jose Picardo, @Mark Warner, @DougBelshaw

2. Use some of the search tools to find people. Try Twitter search to see who's talking about things you are interested in. If you see people using hashtags, eg #uksnow or #teachmeet they are making it easier to follow one particular topic. Search for that phrase on twitter search to see other people talking about the same topic. You can also try some of the

Twitter directories such as WeFollow – don't forget to add yourself to the directory too! (http://wefollow.com/tag/edtech)

3. Make sure you put something in your bio. Mention that you are a teacher or have an interest in web2.0. If you follow people they will look at your profile and make a decision whether to follow you or not. If you don't have many updates you may look a little like a spammer 😃ttin   g them know your interests will let them make a judgement about following you back.

4. Use a Twitter client such as Tweetdeck. It runs in the background and automatically updates itself. Makes it easy to see straight away any @messages or direct messages.

5. Twitter on your mobile with dabr.co.uk. It's a much slicker site to use than the original twitter one when accessing it via a mobile phone.

6. Don't feel you have to keep up with everything that is being said. Dip in and out. You will never absorb every message that's being posted by the people you are following. Check it from time to time and scan through the posts for anything interesting.

7. Message people directly by putting an @ sign in front of their username – eg @dannynic will make sure the message is seen by me. Clicking on the @yourusername link in Twitter will show every message sent directly to you, whatever time of day it was sent.

8. Don't be afraid to lurk for a while – follow people and listen to the conversation. Lurking is not a bad thing. Join in when you feel ready.

9. Have fun! Twitter is all about conversation and networking. Talk to people and share.

10. Learn to love the Fail Whale. It's just a sign that Twitter is too busy and can't yet cope with lots of people. Go do something else and try again later.

Here are some other Twitter posts that you might find useful

How e-learning can contribute to raising achievement : http://bit.ly/eXIUfr

Understanding how Twitter works: http://bit.ly/eRn32E

Twitter is Messy : http://bit.ly/g9Przf

A teacher's guide to Twitter : http://bit.ly/hqdJet

21 Interesting Ways to Use Twitter in the Classroom : http://bit.ly/fh5qmT

Explaining Twitter Presentation : http://bit.ly/gmuodu

Twitter Newbies FAQ : http://bit.ly/hF2uoB

Online Spaces and Codes of Conduct

Originally posted May 26 2009

http://www.whiteboardblog.co.uk/2009/05/online-spaces-and-codes-of-conduct/

Following on from my blog post (http://bit.ly/i3odLj) about the teacher who got in trouble for twittering, I've had a little bit of time to think about some of the implications of this. I was also given this link to the same story as reported in the Daily Telegraph which makes things sound a little worse. (http://bit.ly/dWa1j5)

My first response is that this story would never have hit the media were it not for the mention of Twitter, which seems to be the tech buzzword of the moment. And I do think that there is more than just a hint of overreaction from the local authority.

But the situation is worrying – I'm trying to promote the use of Twitter as a way for teachers to build up a network of experts that they can draw upon when needed, and stories like this are going to discourage teachers from taking it up.

Taking some of the quotes from a "parent" and a "local councillor"

"She is paid a lot of money to do her job and it is unbelievable that she sitting talking about them on a computer rather than teaching."

"I do not pay my council tax so that staff can waste time on these sites."

"People should be spending time with real people rather than with cyber friends."

"It is a drain on public resources. It's shocking."

All of which show a basic lack of understanding about what Twitter is and how it is being used. The one about "cyber friends" is an interesting one. Personally, if I have any question about teaching, I can ask my network on Twitter and get an answer within minutes is an amazing thing, and is one of the reasons why I recommend Twitter to teachers.

The General Teaching Council for England has a code of conduct for teachers. There is new guidance in draft form at present, but for now this is the one that will be applied to us. The code of conduct states that:

Registered teachers may be found to be guilty of unacceptable professional conduct

Where they:

1. Seriously demean or undermine pupils, their parents, carers or colleagues, or act towards them in a manner which is discriminatory in relation to gender, marital status, religion, belief, colour, race, ethnicity, class, sexual orientation, disability or age

and also

Where they:

8. Otherwise bring the reputation and standing of the profession into serious disrepute.

Which is a bit of a "cover-all" statement that seems to cover any manner of behaviours.

So if a teacher is using social networking sites such as Facebook and Twitter then you do need to be aware that these guidelines could apply to your actions.

This is particularly true with Facebook. I have heard of some schools where the Head has banned all members of staff from having a Facebook account. Personally, I don't think that's a fair way to deal with it. Facebook is a very useful way of keeping in touch with friends and family around the world and I don't think the way to react to it is to just ban it outright.

I wrote about this last year, (http://bit.ly/dPGeWR) and this is something I warn my PGCE students about as they make the transition from Student to professional teacher.

When using Facebook, it is probably a good idea to stick to the following rules

1. Make your profile visible to Friends Only, (limited access), Only people you add as a friend can see your status updates.
2. Make your photographs visible to Friends Only.
3. Be careful about who you add as a friend. Do not add students, past or present.
4. Do not use your status updates to complain about particular classes or students.

Be aware that anyone you add as a friend will be able to see your updates. You can still set up groups of friends that have limited access, so you may want to consider that as an option.

I have no problem with a school that blocks Facebook access via their network. But blocking staff from having an account is unreasonable action in my opinion.

With Twitter, the problems are similar. Be aware that anything you say can be taken out of context. We all like to have a moan and a gripe about particular students in the confines of the staffroom, but should these comments be shared in a public space.

The first thing for teachers to consider is to protect their updates. I used to think this defeated the point of twitter, but you might want to consider that as an option. By protecting your updates you have a measure of control over who can read what you say.

This does not mean that what you say cannot be re-tweeted by one of your followers though. It's not going to be completely private.

So what is fair for teachers to say on Twitter, and what might bring them into disrepute? How would your headteacher react if they saw some of the things you said. What about a parent? Or a Student?

Would you want students reading that Set X is full of nutters? Or that you are too hungover to teach well today? Should you be discussing job interviews or arguments/disagreements you have had with other members of staff? Would you be in trouble for putting forward your political or religious views (or lack of them)

I may say that I am mustering the energy to mark a stack of student assignments, but I wouldn't use Twitter to complain about the general quality of them – or to say how many failed etc. That's something I would keep until I saw my students again and told them face to face.

It may well be that what is being said is tongue-in-cheek and not meant in a serious way. But looking back at the way the Twittering Teacher story was reported, tweets were cherry-picked and quoted out of context. If your headteacher did that to you, would you be able to explain them away?

What should you do if a parent followed you on Twitter? Or a student? How would the things you are saying come across to a parent?

Is there mileage in teachers having two accounts. One that's personal and not linked to the school which they can protect. And one which is more for school use?

I'm not giving many answers here. I don't have the answers. And only you will know how your headteacher would respond if a parent made a comment about the content of your twitter stream or your personal blog.

Image by Matt Hamm, http://www.flickr.com/photos/matthamm/

I think the news story last week has been a bit of a wake-up call to teachers. Twitter may well be the buzzword of the moment, and maybe in a year's time we will all have stopped using it for something new. But the principles will remain. How do we, as teachers, exist in these online spaces? How can we teach responsible use to our students if we are less responsible ourselves. How is it fair that a doctor can have a twitter or Facebook account, but not a teacher?

If the headteachers policy is to ban all these tools and pretend they don't exist, how can we teach responsible use? Why do schools even bother with filtering when students can access all this via their mobile phones anyway?

I'd be interested in knowing what you think. Please discuss this in the comments. If you would rather have the comments on her anonymously, then mail me, and I'll copy the text as a comment and leave out any names.

Update: And if you want to explain to your head why you should be using Twitter in the Classroom, use this excellent presentation by Tom Barrett. http://bit.ly/fh5qmT

My Extended Memory

Originally posted April 22 2008

http://www.whiteboardblog.co.uk/2008/04/my-extended-memory/

I have an average memory. I mean, it's OK but it's nothing special. I can remember birthdays and I can quote whole chunks of Eddie Izzard routines but I do tend to forget things. I'm bad at remembering hardware specs and prices. I often forget the web address of that great site I just saw in a teachers magazine.

So my memory needs a little help sometimes. Luckily technology can help me. In the form of my mobile phone.

I don't always have a pen or a piece of paper with me. or if I have written it down I may not have that bit of paper on me when I need it. But I always have my phone with me. Which means I always have a camera with me. And this is where it can really help.

I see a web address in an article or on a poster that looks interesting. Simple, I get out my phone and I take a photograph of it. I see a new digital camera in a store and I want to go home and check out the reviews and price-compare online. Easy, I just take a photo of the shelf label and look it up when I get home. Most modern phone cameras act as pretty good document cameras.

A domestic example; I need to buy some more washing and proofing products for my Ski gear to get it ready for next season. I always get mixed up which products we need. So I took a photo of the bottles. Next time I find myself in a ski store I can just look up the image on my phone and buy the right products. The chances are that any piece of paper will have long been lost by the time I end up in a store.

The camera in my phone acts as a memory enhancer. I'm quite a visual learner and I need visual reminders. I could type things into my phone too, although I find that can be slower than a photo. I do make use of the Notes feature in Outlook (which syncs to my phone) for longer notes and reminders of work-related addresses and passwords.

There are other features in the phone that I could also use – the voice memo feature for example, but I haven't made much use of that yet. And there are many web2.0 sites like Remember the Milk etc. that can help with to-do lists if you want to take it to another level.

I do try and remember these things normally too. I don't see myself as a slave to my phone. But the technology helps to make my life just that little bit easier. And prevents our kitchen filling up with unneeded products!

How could we harness some of this in the classroom? As a science teacher, I can see ways we could use them in the science lesson. Want kids to remember the apparatus set up? Easy, take a photograph of it. Maybe take a video of the trolley going down the ramp or the weights on the spring. Use the voice memo to record the results as they read them out. Get them to add important dates such as coursework deadlines or homework into the calendar of the phone.

Some kids could aid their revision by using their PC to record themselves reading out important facts they need to know for their exams. They can put it onto their phone/iPod as an MP3 file and listen to it on the way to and from school....

An extreme example maybe, but some students could benefit from taking a new look at the computing power they routinely carry in their pockets.

The Internet itself also acts as a way for me to extend (and share) my memory. I use my del.icio.us feed to add websites that I want to remember. Tags help me search for them later. If I have found a good website that I haven't got a lot of time to look at, I can add it to del.ico.us and then access it later on when I have more time. I may not be on the same computer or even in the same location, so a standard bookmark isn't going to help.

On training days, I am often asked for lists of good websites. I used to do this in Word. But you can guarantee that as soon as you print it off you find several more you could have added. Dynamic bookmark lists such as del.ico.us or Diig means I can share the lists with people and know they have the most recent version. Tags mean I can direct trainees on my whiteboard days to http://del.icio.us/dannynic/iwb and my PGCE students to http://del.icio.us/dannynic/pgce.

Similarly I use my blog as a brain dump. Many posts are more for my benefit than for my readers. It's nice to share though, so if others also find the links useful then that's great.

So taking this all into account I actually have a very good memory. But it's not all inside my head!

Iris Connect – lesson observation with video

Originally posted September 27 2010

http://www.whiteboardblog.co.uk/2010/09/iris-connect-lesson-observation-with-video/

As a PGCE tutor, I do a lot of lesson observations. I've also just completed a module for my Masters on Coaching and Mentoring. It often comes up in discussion about the benefits of the teacher themselves being able to observe themselves. Teachers are often surprised when they see their lesson from a different perspective.

The use of video allows teachers to make more specific observations than if they have to rely on memory (see Rosaen et al., 2008). The use of video allows the observer to slow things down and so facilitates specific and detailed observations. Parts of the session can be replayed, which enables the observer to capture what was missed the first time either orally or visually.

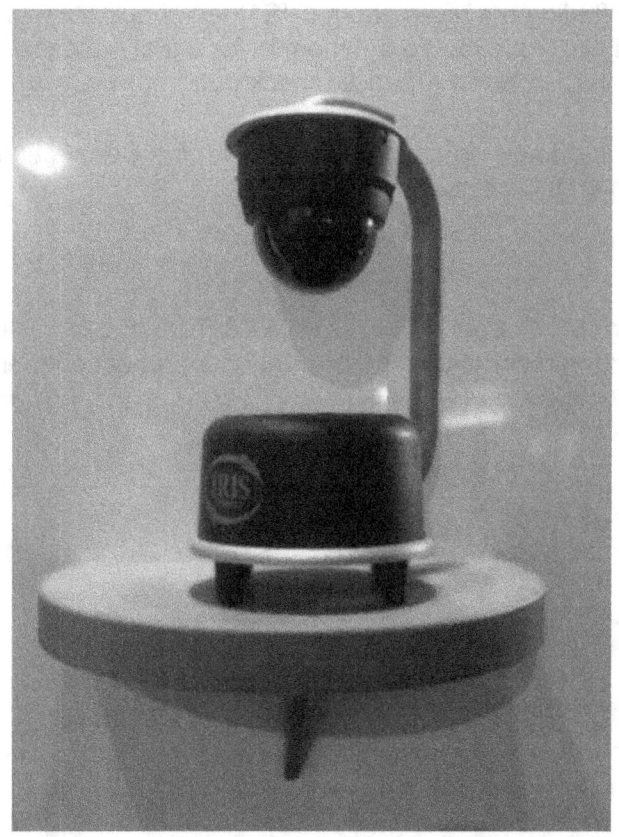

Technology also allows moments to be frozen in time through the isolation of specific clips that can be extracted for further analysis. This would be useful for looking at body language and visual cues – it would be possible to even watch the film with the sound off and look purely at visual cues.

Many schools are implementing peer coaching systems where colleagues observe each other's lessons. I'm also aware of schools that are looking for examples of good practise to share on CPD days etc.

With this in mind, I was very interested to get involved with a product called IRIS Connect. This is essentially a networked video camera which can be positioned at the back of a classroom. A web-based interface allows the teacher to record a lesson themselves, or for an observer to record it for them. With an observer, the camera can be panned and zoomed around as needed. The teacher wears a Bluetooth microphone to make it easy for sound to be recorded.

The video is recorded on the system and can be recalled at any time. It can be shared with colleagues, or kept private.

When watching the video – an observer can add notes which are time stamped alongside the video and can even be overlaid. The teacher can also make notes, or respond to the questions from the observer. Schools can add electronic versions of their lesson observation sheets to allow different criteria to be recorded, which can then be printed as a report.

It's an interesting bit of kit – and I've already been into schools which are using this as part of a CPD programme on improving teaching and learning through observations and peer coaching.

If you are interested in finding out more about IRIS, then check out their website (http://www.irisconnect.co.uk/) If you do get them in for a trial – please tell them where you heard about them! If you're in North America, check out: http://www.therenow.net/

By way of disclosure – I am now an approved trainer for Iris Connect, and so am part of the team providing training on this product in schools.

Research:

Rosaen, C., Lundeberg, M., Cooper, M., Fritzen, A., & Terpstra, M. (2008) Noticing: How does investigation of video records change how teachers reflect on their experiences? *Journal of Teacher Education*. 59 (4), 347-360.

More research on the Iris Connect website.

Prezi

Originally posted February 20 2009

http://www.whiteboardblog.co.uk/2009/02/prezi/

I've spent an hour or so this afternoon playing with a new website called Prezi. I first saw the site mentioned on Mark Warners blog (http://markwarner.me/), and I signed up for the beta. This morning I got my Beta invite. http://prezi.com/

Prezi provides a very different way of producing presentations and maybe can change the way we think about presentations.

Rather than working on separate slides, you add different elements to your page. At the moment you can add text and images and also drop videos and pdf files onto the page. You can surround these elements with a frame or leave them as they are.

It takes a while to get used to the user interface, and it's well worth watching the introductory videos first. But once you get the hang of it, it's quite intuitive to drop items, rotate them, scale them and move them around.

Once the items are on the page you can link them up into a path using the path tool. When you view an item full screen you can then move forwards and backwards along the path to the next item. Alternatively you can just zoom in and out and select different items in any order. Great for non-linear presentations where you just have slides which can be viewed in any order.

I've had a quick play with Prezi just to get my head around how to make it work. You can view my sample presentation here: http://prezi.com/9991/

If you like the look of Prezi, you might be able to get on the Beta test. Contact details are on the site and explain you are in education. Either that or wait until the site goes live, whenever that may be. You might also like to take a look at the Prezi blog which explains more about the site.

Support sites for teaching assistants

Originally posted June 22 2009

http://www.whiteboardblog.co.uk/2009/06/support-sites-for-teaching-assistants/

Today I was delivering some training for Teaching Assistants. We wanted to give them the opportunity to try out some of the resources that are available on the Internet to use with students.

I put together a list of sites that we played with during the day. I've reproduced the list below.

A full list of all these sites (plus others) can be found at: http://www.delicious.com/dannynic/TA

Good SEN Resource Sites

PlasmaScreen and Whiteboard room : http://www.whiteboardroom.org.uk/

SEN Teacher : http://www.senteacher.org/

Help Kids Learn : http://www.helpkidzlearn.com/

ISSEN – SEN and Science : http://www.issen.org.uk/

Create your own characters – Stimulus for creative writing

- http://reasonablyclever.com/mini/flash/minifig.swf
- http://www.simpsonsmovie.com/main.html
- http://www.buildyourwildself.com/
- http://www.mrpicassohead.com/create.html

Interactive Sites for Support / Revision

Northern Grid Mini apps : http://bit.ly/e2blM9

NumberNut : http://www.numbernut.com/

Triptico : http://www.triptico.co.uk/

TeacherLed : http://www.teacherled.com

Wall of Words : http://bit.ly/gvVRMl

Skool.co.uk : http://kent.skoool.co.uk/index.aspx

Quizzes : http://ThatQuiz.org

Oswego Numeracy Games : http://resources.oswego.org/games/

Fun Tools and Things to Try

Wordle : http://www.wordle.net

Word Sift : http://www.wordsift.com

Five Card Flickr : http://web.nmc.org/5cardstory/flickr.php

WallWisher : http://www.wallwisher.com/

PhotoPeach : http://photopeach.com/

Build your own Bayeux Tapestry : http://bit.ly/dKQFiV

Bubbl.us MindMaps : http://bubbl.us

Computer Help

Technology Tutorials : http://www.bltt.org/tutorials/

Online computer tutorials with pictures : http://inpics.net/

Two New Digital Storytelling Tools

Originally posted October 15 2009

http://www.whiteboardblog.co.uk/2009/10/two-new-digital-storytelling-tools/

Here's two digital storytelling tools that you might enjoy, thanks to my amazing Personal Learning Network (PLN) on Twitter.

First, thanks to @NikPeachey for the link to this great comic book creator based on the characters and scenes in Spore. It works similar to Comic Life, and lets you choose characters and vehicles etc. and add speech bubbles. It's great fun.

http://www.mashon.com/spore/creator/

Also, thanks also to @web20classroom for this very cute Story Maker, perfect for a IWB. Aimed at younger students, it again lets you choose characters and scenes but will also update the text of the story depending on characters chosen and their actions. Go check it out!

http://bit.ly/e5A6So

Happy storytelling!

Digital Storytelling with Comic Master

Originally posted September 29 2010

http://www.whiteboardblog.co.uk/2010/09/digital-storytelling-with-comic-master/

Comic Master is another in a long line of online comic creators that would be great for digital storytelling. (http://www.comicmaster.org.uk/)

Supported by Reading for Life, it allows students to create their own graphic novel using pre-designed characters and backgrounds. The end product can be printed A4 size.

The working area is a little small, but you can zoom in and work on individual panels which does make things easier.

If you like this kind of thing you should also check out:

- Doctor Who Comic Creator : http://bbc.in/fcHnCC
- ToonDoo : http://www.toondoo.com/
- Spore Comic Creator : http://bit.ly/eIG5rg
- SuperHero Squad : http://bit.ly/gPjJ7j

You can find more on my delicious feed. : http://www.delicious.com/dannynic/comic

The Great Wordle Crisis

Originally posted March 1 2010

http://www.whiteboardblog.co.uk/2010/03/the-great-wordle-crisis/

I've mentioned before that I am a big fan of Wordle. It's a fantastic tool for making word clouds – and as such can be used for text analysis (try it with some written work and see what words you over-use) or just for fun image creation: http://www.wordle.net/

There was a ripple of outrage yesterday on Twitter when it was discovered that Wordle had been taken down, apparently over a trademark infringement involving the Wordle name.

Luckily, after a brief outage, the site was back up and running yesterday evening, but this does demonstrate the need when planning to use any web tool in the classroom to have a "Plan B". Just because a website was working when you planned the lesson, does not mean it will be working when you actually deliver it. Free web apps can be quite transient and may not always be there when you need them. (I have also had a few issues in schools where the Wordle java code gets blocked, so an alternative is handy that actually works in that school)

I'm really hoping that the chap behind Wordle gets the trademark issue sorted, so that Wordle does not get threatened again. It's good to have some alternatives bookmarked just in case though.

Wordle Alternatives:

By way of an alternative – here are a selection of other Word-cloud generators – none are anywhere near as good as Wordle, but they might fill a gap should the site go down again.:

- http://www.abcya.com/word_clouds.htm
- http://tagul.com/
- http://tagcrowd.com/
- http://worditout.com/
- http://www.imagechef.com/ic/word_mosaic/
- http://wordsift.com/

I've collated a list of these sites on Delicious here: http://delicious.com/dannynic/wordle.

Some are better than others, but most don't quite do what Wordle does so well.

Here are just a few ideas on how you could use Wordle in the classroom:

- Use to introduce a topic – pupils could guess what they will be learning about.
- Comparing different newspapers – look at the same story in a Broadsheet and a tabloid newspaper (website) and compare the wordle clouds produced – how do the words used differ?
- Self-reflection on work – as Wordle makes a word larger the more frequently it is used, pupils will be able to see at a glance which words or phrases they are over-using. Are they using the word Nice or Good too often?
- Use to analyse the content and gist a longer written text, especially with exam or higher level groups
- To introduce new vocabulary or to memorise new vocabulary/vocabulary lists
- Revision of key topics and vocabulary – pupils can create their own wordles or they can be given them to use
- To give presentations without reading from a sheet and just using prompts
- Encouraging creative writing from a selection of key words from a word cloud
- See results of a class survey visually – maybe use an Etherpad to collect the text first, then paste into Wordle

Tagxedo – Another Word Cloud Maker

Originally posted April 6 2010

http://www.whiteboardblog.co.uk/2010/04/tagxedo-another-word-cloud-maker/

Tagxedo is another word cloud maker in the same vein as Wordle and many others.

http://www.tagxedo.com/

It allows you to create a visually interesting word cloud from a chunk of text, a file or a URL.

You can play with the shape, font, colour scheme in much the same way as Wordle, then save the finished image as a png file or add it to the online gallery.

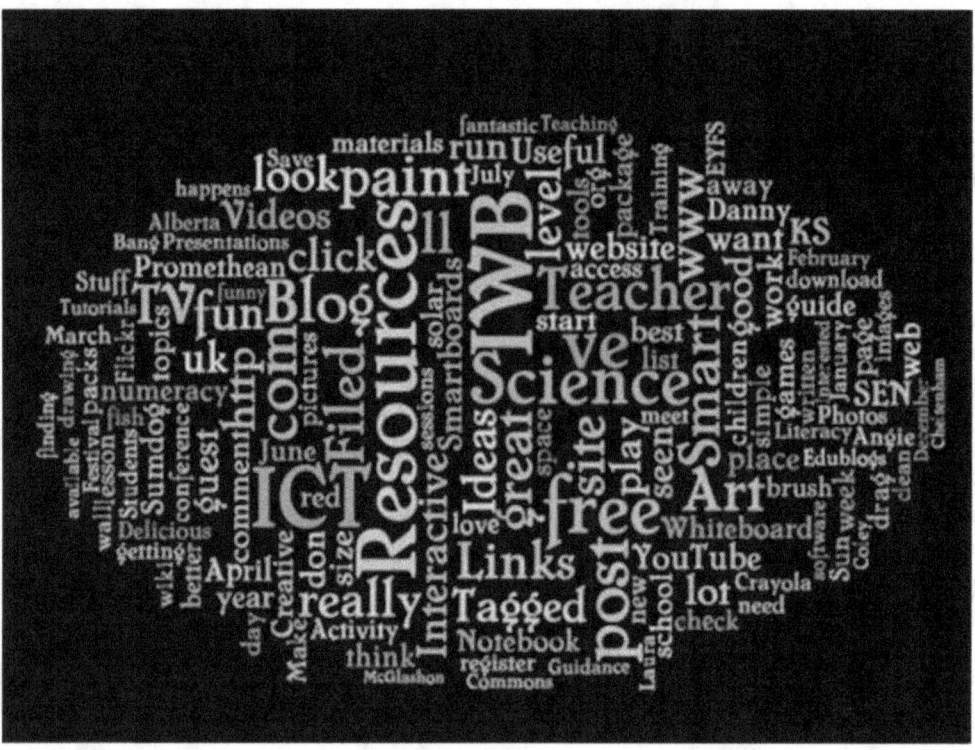

It's well worth exploring. Take a look: http://www.tagxedo.com/

For some ideas on how to use Word Clouds – check out this blog post from last month. (see previous page) There's also some links to other Wordle alternatives.

WallWisher

Originally posted May 4 2009

http://www.whiteboardblog.co.uk/2009/05/wall-wisher/

Wall Wisher is an online notice board maker. It gives you a virtual space where you can post short text notes in the same way that you could put post-it notes onto a notice board in your classroom. But this noticeboard can be shared between people all over the world. As well as text notes you can add images, video and links to other websites.

It's a neat way of getting a shared space to collect ideas from people for a brainstorm. Or to post resources for a topic. Students could ask questions about a topic which you (or each other) can then answer

Doug Belshaw set one up and posted the link on Twitter – very quickly ideas were coming in from lots of people. You can see the wall (now locked) here : http://bit.ly/hRhi7a

You can also see a "what's so great about the smartboard" wall that Jim Hollis posted on his blog the other day : http://bit.ly/i23jLE

As an experiment – I've set a Whiteboard Blog wall up here. Apparently you can embed the walls into your blog.

http://www.wallwisher.com/wall/whiteboardblog

Obviously with any open online space there is a risk of abuse. Wall Wisher only has two mode – one where only you can add stuff to the wall, and one where anyone can add stuff. Obviously it would be nice to have a more controlled protection where you can set people up to access the wall, or need a password to get onto it. You can lock the wall to protect it once you have enough ideas on it.

Wall Wisher is an interesting idea – and I am sure there are lots of ways it could be used in the classroom. I'd be interested to see how it develops, and whether there will be future modifications that allow more control over the space.

If you do use it with your class – leave a note in the comments to say what you've done. I'd love to hear from you!

Stixy Collaborative Noticeboard

Originally posted October 18 2010

http://www.whiteboardblog.co.uk/2010/10/stixy-collaborative-noticeboard-tool/

Stixy is another online noticeboard tool, a rather cool rival to WallWisher.

http://www.stixy.com/

Stixy allows you to create tasks, appointments, files, photos, notes, and bookmarks on their Stixyboards, organized in whatever way makes sense to them. Then they can share their Stixyboards with friends, family, and colleagues.

Like WallWisher you could set up a Stixy board for class projects, for brainstorming or for the collection of notes and resources.

You can control who has access, and whether visitors can read or amend the board.

Add notes by dragging from the toolbar at the bottom of the page

You can add photos and documents too!

TODO
19   8:00 AM

COMMENTS
To Do Notices etc can be added as reminders – maybe project deadlines?

Here's a demo board I've set up: http://www.stixy.com/guest/86940

It's well worth a look: http://www.stixy.com

TV on Your Whiteboard

Originally posted June 18 2008

http://www.whiteboardblog.co.uk/2008/06/tv-on-your-whiteboard/

There are different ways to get multimedia content onto your IWB. YouTube is pretty good, but it can be something of a lottery. Buying professional CD's and DVD's is another option.

One other way that has interested me for a while, is turning your computer into a Television. This is becoming easier and easier.

A few years back I bought a plug in device that was the size of a paperback book. It was quite awkward to use and the picture quality and recording quality was pretty poor.

I have just bought a new device that has really impressed me. It's called the Pinnacle PCTV Nano stick and it is a hybrid Digital/Analogue TV tuner stick.

First thing to impress me was the price, it was only £35 in PC World. Secondly is the size, its tiny. And the third thing to impress me is the picture quality. Plugged into my normal house aerial the quality was pretty good, and we're not a particularly strong area for television reception.

Using the supplied, portable aerial was less impressive. I was not able to get a signal at home. I am going to look into some kind of digital booster and see if that makes things better. I don't want TV on the move as such, but it would be nice to have a system that I could use if no rooftop aerial connection was possible.

The Stick comes with Pinnacle TVCentre Pro software so that the television picture is shown in a window on your computer screen. This software will also let you use your computer as a hard drive/DVD recorder and it is this aspect that interests me for use on an IWB.

You can save TV programmes as straight MPEG files or DivX format. It will also export for devices such as iPods etc. I could take the DivX file and copy it straight onto my Archos to view on the train for example. File sizes can be large, but recording directly onto DVD would avoid filling your hard drive too quickly.

For a teacher who wants to record snippets of a TV programme to show to a class this is ideal. You could record adverts that use really bad science and then get the class to pick the science apart.

It could also connect to the coax output from a video recorder and let you digitise any of the old video tapes that you have hanging around in your department cupboards that haven't yet been put onto DVD.

Obviously copyright is an issue here, and I would check this with your school first.

There are several other PC/TV Sticks out there. Pinnacle are doing a few, and also check out Happauge for other PC/TV devices.

YouTube Edu

Originally posted April 4 2009

http://www.whiteboardblog.co.uk/2009/04/youtube-edu/

YouTube has now launched a new section of its famous video sharing website that organizes the video channels of more than 100 colleges and universities. It's called YouTube Edu : http://www.youtube.com/edu

The idea is to flag up the educational videos to make them easier to find. It's a little similar (and I would guess shares very similar content) to Apple's iTunesU section of the iTunes Store. (http://www.apple.com/uk/education/itunes-u/)

YouTube Edu lets viewers sort clips by school or number of views, and the schools offer content ranging from complete courses to campus events to information for prospective students. There's also a search facility to find clips on the subject you want. The bulk of the content so far seems to be from US colleges and Universities, but I would expect UK (and other) colleges to get involved in the future – I know Oxford and Cambridge are on iTunes U already, as is the Open University.

The content may be too high level for KS3/KS4 but you might find it useful for A Level students.

One of the most popular videos so far is The Science of Watchmen: http://bit.ly/g1Osl5

An alternative site, Academic Earth (http://academicearth.org/) also launched last week, offering lectures from Harvard, Yale, MIT and other schools. And don't forget Teacher Tube as another educational video site which is probably more useful for KS3/KS4.

YouTube XL

Originally posted January 31 2010

http://www.whiteboardblog.co.uk/2010/01/youtube-xl/

YouTube is an excellent resource to use in schools but the biggest problem is quite often some of the offensive comments that invariably get left below popular clips. When showing clips on your interactive whiteboard, you don't really want to be showing those comments to your class.

YouTube XL is one way to get around that. Basically YouTube XL is a skinned version of YouTube designed to use on large-screen televisions. The interface makes it simpler to use by cutting out a lot of the clutter on the page. In fact, it makes YouTube a whole lot easier to use on an IWB. The advantage of losing the clutter means that there are no comments on view – you just have the videos.

Try it out now : http://www.youtube.com/xl

As an alternative – another way to safely view YouTube videos is to use http://www.safeshare.tv/ and also there's http://quietube.com/

View Pure – A YouTube Cleaner

Originally posted August 9 2010

http://www.whiteboardblog.co.uk/2010/08/view-pure-a-youtube-cleaner/

View Pure is another way to watch YouTube without all the on-screen clutter and dodgy comments. Basically you go to View Pure, enter the URL of a YouTube video and it strips out everything but the video. Very simple to use. You can even drag a button to your desktop which does the job.

You can also then take the URL of the page you get, and hyperlink to that page. Like this http://viewpure.com/LTCtfT8KFc4 (video is safe for work and if you haven't watched it, it's quite funny!)

It doesn't moderate the content though, so you still have to use YouTube resources wisely. You will still need a YouTube connection at school though, this is not a way around filtered content. If you can't access YouTube in school, this will not work.

As an alternative – check out YouTube's own YouTube XL. (http://www.youtube.com/xl)

As well as http://www.safeshare.tv/ and also http://quietube.com/

Visualisers

Originally posted March 24 2009

http://www.whiteboardblog.co.uk/2009/03/visualisers/

In advance of a training day I am doing on Friday about Visualisers, I'm putting this short post together to collect together some useful resources to direct teachers towards.

A visualiser, (sometimes called a Document Camera) at its simplest, is a video camera mounted on a stand that connects to a data projector. You can then place objects below the camera and project the image onto your interactive whiteboard.

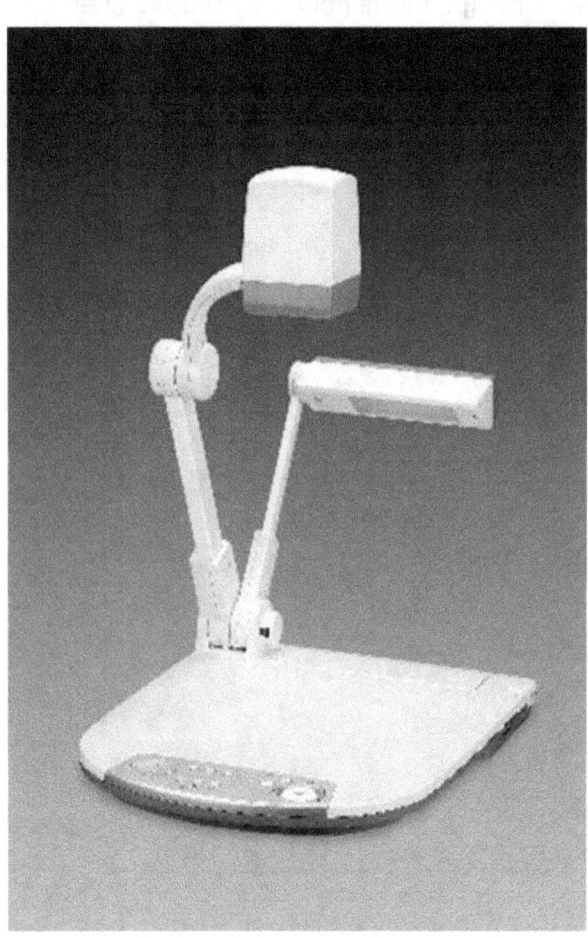

You can pretty much put anything below the camera and display it to the whole class. It is great for showing 3D objects, sharing books, children's work, photographs and even demonstrating drawing techniques. Anything where you would usually have students crowded around a front bench to see something being demonstrated could be displayed on a visualiser.

Usually, the visualiser also allows you to record images or video snapshots of whatever it is you are demonstrating. If you run your visualiser via your PC you could also use your interactive whiteboard tools to capture and annotate over the top of whatever you are showing the class.

The Visualiser Forum (http://www.visualiserforum.org/) is a blog that aims to help promote the effective use of visualiser technology in schools. There are some very useful posts and case studies on there, such as this guide to using them in the Primary classroom.

Here is a good case study from Hertfordshire Grid for Learning. (http://bit.ly/f53N8H)

Also check out this video on Teachers TV with the Visualiser Forum's very own Dave Smith. http://www.teachers.tv/video/24043

Becta have also produced a handy guide to using them. You can read it here (for now, until Becta goes) http://bit.ly/fK1Nm6

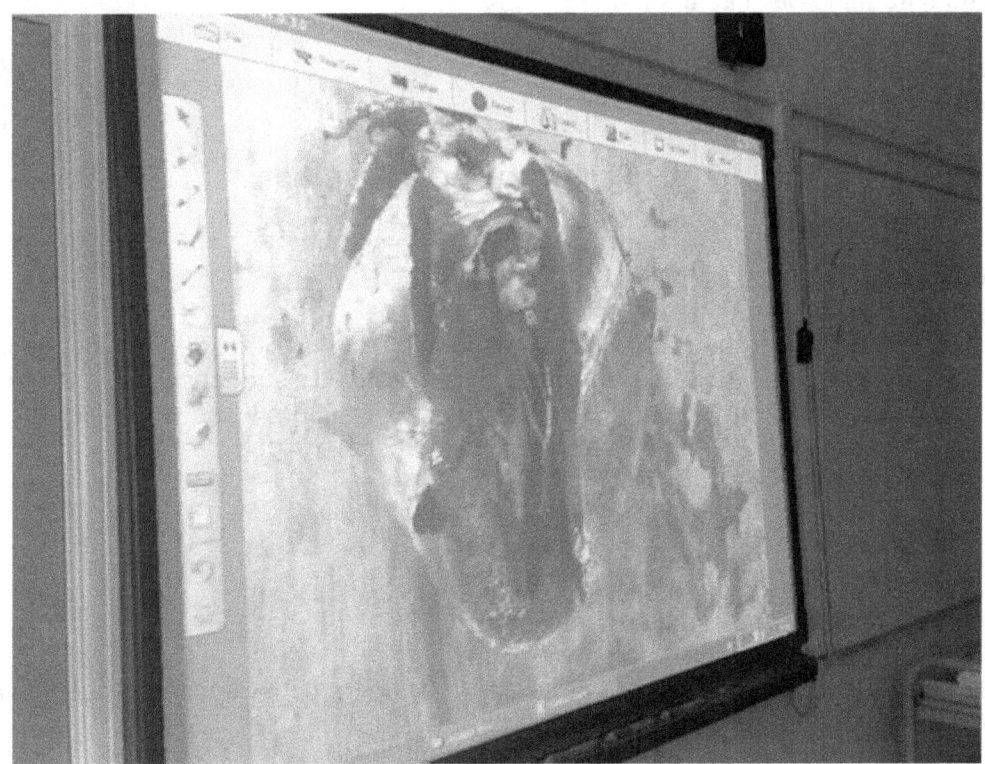

Using a Visualiser

Originally posted March 31 2009

http://www.whiteboardblog.co.uk/2009/03/using-a-visualiser/

I ran a training day last week for a college where we looked at Visualisers (sometimes called Document Cameras). Through the day we tried out some different things that you could do and I took some screen grabs.

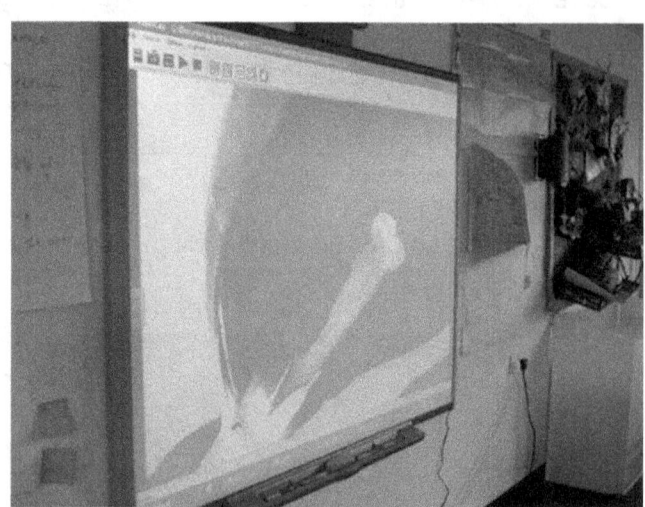

I have put the screengrabs and a few photographs from the day into a short presentation. Hopefully it will help to illustrate some of the ways that you could use your Visualiser in conjunction with your interactive whiteboard. (Warning, if you're squeamish – it does contain close up photos of an animal heart....)

View it here : http://www.slideshare.net/dannynic/visualiser-demo

If you do have a Visualiser then make sure that you have it installed so that is connected to your computer, rather than just connected to your projector. This means you can then use the desktop annotation tools of your interactive whiteboard to draw and write over the top of the images. You can also use the camera tools to snapshot images into your IWB software (e.g. Smart Notebook or ActivStudio)

Here are a few ideas for using your Visualiser

- Display good examples of students work.
- Show pages from books – save photocopying
- Model examination questions – write answers on the paper – work through as a class.
- Dissections – heart, kidney, plants, flowers, fruits etc.
- Display intricate models / objects
- Show parts of a circuit
- demonstrate how to use technical drawing tools – or maths tools such as rulers and protractors
- Use to make collages – assemble objects below the camera. Take snapshots as the image builds up.
- Video experiments – colour changes in chemistry – iodine clock/thiosulphate experiments. Remember visualisers on a flexible arm don't only have to point downwards – they can be angled to look at things side-on too.
- Show how to use small gadgets such as calculators, pda's (or even iPhones/iPad) – no need to use software and cables to mirror/simulate them on a computer.

Also check out the Ideas to Inspire presentation about Visualisers for a few more ideas. (http://bit.ly/dZuwiG). If you own a Lumens visualiser, then I've produced a short guide that tells you a little more about this particular brand of visualiser. You can view it here. (http://scr.bi/hqHWbV)

Of Monkeys and Bananas

Originally posted September 25 2010

http://www.whiteboardblog.co.uk/2010/09/of-monkeys-and-bananas/

Found this online recently (http://bit.ly/engnxB). Apparently it is based on actual research, (http://anse.rs/fVzz3L) and although may not exactly be as described it's still a nice story:

Start with a cage containing five monkeys.

Inside the cage, hang a banana on a string and place a set of stairs under it. Before long, a monkey will go to the stairs and start to climb towards the banana. As soon as he touches the stairs, spray all of the other monkeys with cold water.

After a while, another monkey makes an attempt with the same result – all the other monkeys are sprayed with cold water. Pretty soon, when another monkey tries to climb the stairs, the other monkeys will try to prevent it.

Now, put away the cold water. Remove one monkey from the cage and replace it with a new one. The new monkey sees the banana and wants to climb the stairs. To his surprise and horror, all of the other monkeys attack him.

After another attempt and attack, he knows that if he tries to climb the stairs, he will be assaulted.

Next, remove another of the original five monkeys and replace it with a new one. The newcomer goes to the stairs and is attacked. The previous newcomer takes part in the punishment with enthusiasm! Likewise, replace a third original monkey with a new one, then a fourth, then the fifth. Every time the newest monkey takes to the stairs, he is attacked. Most of the monkeys that are beating him have no idea why they were not permitted to climb the stairs or why they are participating in the beating of the newest monkey.

After replacing all the original monkeys, none of the remaining monkeys have ever been sprayed with cold water. Nevertheless, no monkey ever again approaches the stairs to try for the banana. Why not? Because as far as they know that's the way it's always been done round here.

And that, my friends, is how company policies are made.

Replace company with education. Don't just do something because it's "how we've always done things".

Don't be those monkeys.

Stephenson, G. R. (1967). Cultural acquisition of a specific learned response among rhesus monkeys. In: Starek, D., Schneider, R., and Kuhn, H. J. (eds.), Progress in Primatology, Stuttgart: Fischer, pp. 279-288.

Mentioned in: Galef, B. G., Jr. (1976). Social Transmission of Acquired Behavior: A Discussion of Tradition and Social Learning in Vertebrates. In: Rosenblatt, J.S., Hinde, R.A., Shaw, E. and Beer, C. (eds.), Advances in the study of behaviour, Vol. 6, New York: Academic Press, pp. 87-88: